Herbert Lee Williams

_THE
NEWSPAPERMAN'S
PRESIDENT _____

_____ Harry S Truman _____

NELSON-HALL
nh Chicago

LIBRARY OF CONGRESS CATALOGING IN PUBLICATION DATA

Williams, Herbert Lee.
  The newspaperman's president.

  Bibliography: p.
  Includes index.
  1. Truman, Harry S., 1884-1972—Views on the press.
2. Truman, Harry S., 1884-1972—Relations with
journalists.   3. Press and politics—United States—
History—20th century.   4. United States—Politics
and government—1945-1953.   I. Title.
E814.W54   1984   973.918'092'4   84-1115
ISBN 0-8304-1064-3

Manufactured in the United States of America

10   9   8   7   6   5   4   3   2   1

The paper in this book is pH neutral (acid free).

Contents

To Lee Williams with many thanks for
his help on the next volume; best wishes
for his future success.
Independence,   Harry Truman
Dec. 17, 1954.

Preface

IT SEEMS LIKE YESTERDAY. THE QUICK, STIFF-SHOULDERED man in impeccable attire stepped out of his private office into the small waiting room, rammed his opened hand in my direction, and said, "I'm Harry Truman."

Somehow the atonal voice, the thick-lensed glasses, the jutting lower lip were less real to me than they had been in countless news pictures and broadcasts. But it was the man, all right — the man who had dropped the bomb a few years earlier to spare me the inconvenience of having to participate in what would have been a nasty invasion of Japan.

"I'm Williams. Mr. Hillman and Mr. Noyes told me to check in here today to work on the memoirs."

"Oh, yes. They're on the tenth floor. C'mon, I'm goin' down there now."

It was a brisk dash behind the notorious Truman stride, along the south corridor of the Federal Reserve Bank Building and down the back stairs, with not a word exchanged.

As we entered Room 1002, Hillman and Noyes scrambled out of their chairs and whispered in unison, "Mr. President . . . " They stood at reverent attention while Truman stated his business in a few good-natured sentences and left abruptly. Hillman and Noyes turned to me. My indoctrination into The Job was about to begin.

Simply put, the former president was getting his memoirs written in accordance with a contract he had signed with Time, Inc. He was to be paid approximately three-quarters of a million dollars for one million words of copy. In 1954, that was a lot of money.

To master-mind the project, two of Truman's ablest confidants had been imported to Kansas City not many months after the chief executive left the White House. William Hillman, a veteran reporter who

From Herbert Lee Williams, "I Was Truman's Ghost," *Presidential Studies Quarterly*, Vol. 12, No. 2 (Spring 1982), pp. 256-59. Reprinted by permission of the publisher.

had once served as director of the Hearst bureau in London, eventually ended up on the speech-writing staff of the president. Hillman had already produced his own Truman photo-history, *Mr. President.* David Noyes, successful industrialist and dedicated Democrat, was as likable as he was brilliant. His genuine admiration for Harry Truman approached the dimensions of a passion.

And how did I manage to insinuate my way into this editorial select committee? I, who had voted for Dewey in 1948? Well, I didn't. I was drafted.

It was on the evening of April 6, 1954, that the dean of the School of Journalism at the University of Missouri knocked on my door and introduced me to Hillman and Noyes. Both were beginning to experience early twinges of advancing deadlinitis, and had come to search the hallowed halls for a ghost. They needed a writer who could and would come to Kansas City to help in the production of the memoirs of a president. Dean Earl English felt that I could handle the assignment.

Certainly, no struggling doctoral candidate could refuse such a journalistic windfall. I accepted the offer, cancelled a lease or two, saw the wife and baby safely home to mother, and packed off to Kansas City.

Back in 1002, which was to be my salt mine for the better part of a year, Hillman and Noyes sat me down to read the first 100,000 words they had amassed. Immaculately typed on loose-leafed pages, the final manuscript was the work of the secretaries in the Truman suite up on the eleventh floor (Rose Conway, who had run the private office for almost eight years in the White House, and Frances Myers, a Pentagon employee during the same period).

At the end of a long first day, just as I was coming up bleary-eyed out of this verbal baptism, I was asked to affix my signature to a formal letter of clearance:

Kansas City, Missouri
May 3, 1954

Dear Mr. Truman:

In consideration of your engaging and continuing to engage me to render services in connection with a book that you are writing

under your contract with Time, Incorporated, I hereby agree
that:

1. Any material that I have prepared or shall prepare in the
   course of such services, is and shall be your sole property and
   I shall retain no copy thereof.

2. I shall not at any time publish or disclose to any person the
   contents of, or any description of, any unpublished letters,
   memoranda, reports or other documents, to which I shall
   have gained access in the course of my performance of such
   services, or which shall have been shown to me by you or by
   any person working with you; and I shall make no copy of
   any such document except as required for the performance
   of my services.

Sincerely yours,

Honorable Harry S Truman
1107 Federal Reserve Bank Building
Kansas City, Missouri

This made it official—I was now a ghost writer for a retired president
of the United States. It promised to be a fascinating experience.

Few Americans, perhaps, give any thought to the sheer magni-
tude of national historical resources which their outgoing presidents
are allowed to take with them, to be housed later in library monu-
ments. The Truman papers weighed in at a staggering thirty-nine
tons, not counting crates full of plaques, gifts, models, framed
tributes, and assorted mementoes which were temporarily stashed in
bank vaults and other storage facilities around Kansas City.

The cream of the White House communication mix from 1945 to
1952 had been systematically ladled into fifty large metal file cabinets
which now lined the walls of the eleventh-floor suite. In these were all
of the personal and official correspondence of the president:
transcripts of 2,003 public speeches and 324 press conferences; a
multitude of inter-office memoranda and directives; minutes of

countless executive sessions; copies of more than 31,000 dictated letters, plus handwritten notes to Mamma or sister Mary; in short, records of just about anything and everything that crossed Truman's mind during his tenure in office.

A volume of memoirs, it should be noted, does not constitute per se a history book. Rather, it is a narrative of the writer's recollections of experiences through which he or she has lived, of events and impressions which made their mark on the memory. The historian, who must begin where the memoirs leave off, faces the more tedious and more demanding task of filling in the chinks, verifying and amplifying the data. Memoirs can be quite legitimately what the author chooses to remember.

It didn't take me long to become fairly familiar with the documents, serialized and chronologized as they were for easy access to researchers. However, there was one forbidden tree in the garden—a file safe whose combination was kept secret. Here were stored communiques awaiting final declassification, intended "For The Eyes Of The President Only" (or the ex-president). Included were reports, I was told, on persons considered to be security risks. Here also were items which would prove of value to collectors—messages bearing the signatures of Tito, Churchill, Hitler, Hirohito, Stalin—and even an occasional souvenir like the $40,000 jewel-encrusted baton sported by the late Field Marshal Herrmann Goering.

The first bundle of files I was given, to take down to 1002 where I was to digest the contents and regurgitate them in memoirs form, covered the entire lend-lease story, from the time that Truman inherited the program from FDR through to its conclusion a few years later. After this came, week by week in relentless and seemingly endless phalanxes, assorted substantive chunks like the financial arrangements with Great Britain after the war; Truman's reorganization of the executive branch; demobilization and the issue of universal military training; the total budget and fiscal policy of the first administration; the so-called 21-point program; the climactic Potsdam Conference; back to an out-of-sequence tilt with the prepresidential period, from haberdasher to veep with the Senate record sandwiched in between; the 1948 whistle-stop campaign; and so on ad infinitum. Yes, there was also a section on the pressing problem of inflation.

Confessedly, under the sheer volume of the work, I often found the procedure of producing the memoirs to be more interesting than the subject matter itself. More often than not, writers find that the most gratifying part of the story is the telling of it; at least that has been my experience as a journalist.

And this was essentially a reporting job. It called, not for expertise in the ramifications of political science, but for the instincts of a newsman, the simple ability to study the available record and report what it said in terms interesting and understandable to the average reader. I found, however, that I did have to psych myself up for each assignment. To write in the first person singular as though Truman's experiences had been my own, without allowing a trace of my personality to invade his thought or manner of expression, was a discipline not always easy to follow. Even a ghost has feelings.

To assure the "authorship" of the author, an elaborate rewrite method was employed. As I completed my narrative version of each assignment, Hillman and Noyes would set up a conference with the former president, and we would gather — along with stenographer armed with stenotype machine — in Truman's spacious office, where the decor was admirably suited to reminiscence.

Truman presided at his handsome walnut desk from Blair House days, flanked by the furled presidential flag and the oversized globe of the earth, which was a present from General Eisenhower. Under foot was the conspicuously large Persian carpet, a gift of the Shah of Iran in happier days. Lining one wall was a splendid collection of histories, biographies and reference works, most of them inscribed gift copies from the authors. An office bar and expensive leather-sheathed chairs completed the furnishings, along with original portraits of Democratic Party heroes and enlarged snapshots of daughter Margaret. In such surroundings, under the piercing gaze of Jefferson and Jackson, I often had the feeling that I was in a microcosm of the national capital.

But it was in these get-togethers that the memoirs got on true course. As my manuscript was read aloud, usually by Hillman, the ex-president would listen intently. His approval or criticism was solicited almost paragraph by paragraph. The whole idea was to jog the memory of the man who had been there, to add the auto to the biography. For this reason, past luminaries from the Fair Deal administration were lured to Kansas City from time to time to participate in the conferences. Secretary Brannan (Agriculture) came to one of the sessions; Snyder (Treasury) to one on fiscal matters; Acheson (State) to another on foreign policy. Former special assistants Steelman and Lloyd chipped in. These knowledgeable counselors were able to induce Truman to recall particular details of events or almost-forgotten impressions of specific persons with whom he had dealt.

Through it all, I was free to ask for clarification on any statement I may not have fully understood even as I was writing it down. I was probably more representative of the general audience to whom the book would be addressed than were the highly informed Washington veterans. Be that as it may, the conferences elicited much of the conversational and anecdotal material from Truman which otherwise would have been missing from the record.

As each session was concluded (one might run two or three hours) I was provided with a verbatim transcript of the discussion. With my edited original plus the fresh fodder, I would retreat to 1002 and weave the two together into a new document. This was the creative process: putting flesh on the bones of the narrative, stitching on an appendage here, skin-grafting an impression there, injecting color and vitality into dormant sentences passim. It was the most rewarding phase of the writing operation, not only because of the challenge it presented, but also because it produced the final manuscript — which, after all, is what I was being paid to do.

The last stretch in the procedure was delivery of my completed version to Truman, who would take his copy home with him and read it to Bess. This chore sometimes kept him up past midnight, especially if the chapter was a long one, but he never failed to return the manuscript the following morning. To Truman, who was an insatiable reader (he perused three to five newspapers right down to the editorials each day), proofing a hundred or more pages of copy was no great problem. He seldom penciled in a suggestion or an emendation, except perhaps to question a date or to change a bit of profanity to innocuous slang, or to cross out a reference to "whisky" and substitute "refreshments." It was my job to put it down the way I found it; his prerogative, of course, was to put it the way he wanted it left.

Naturally, others were working on the memoirs at intervals. No retiring head of state could undertake alone such a research and editorial project and hope to finish it satisfactorily in a decade or so. Additional help was brought in toward the end of the year as *Life's* editors arrived to begin processing the accumulated 800,000 words (about half of the total volume was to appear in weekly installments before Doubleday published the dual edition of the text in full).

That's all there was to it. It was time for me to return, phantom-like, to the shades of academe. The ghost writer has little solid evidence to show beyond his W-2 form—no mention, no credits, no recognition—just money. (Well, all right: $6,500.) Being no more enamored of anonymity than most writers, I have since found it more fun to publish books over my own name. Lord Byron said it for us: "Tis pleasant to see one's name in print, for a book's a book though there's nothing in't."

Oh yes—about the man himself. What could be written of Truman that hasn't already been published? His trigger temper? His healthy patriotism? His foot-wriggling energy? His dogged singledmindedness? What I remember is:

- His boyishness. Unashamed of his cursing, drinking and poker playing habits, he nevertheless was not above apology. As I walked into his office one morning for a reference book, he was mixing himself a highball. In consideration of my tender years, perhaps, he instinctively dropped both hands below the level of his desk top. "I fix one of these every morning to settle my nerves," he gratuitously explained, then hastened to add, "but don't you follow my example on this."

- His folksiness. Going out to his old-fashioned home at 219 North Delaware Street in Independence for dinner, or just to deliver copy when he was recuperating from his gall bladder surgery that summer, was not unlike dropping in to visit my own dad. He resisted air conditioning until his doctor ordered it installed.

- His humor. When a visiting rabbi from Israel came into his office and, like others before him, pronounced a Hebrew blessing on the man who was the first to recognize the new state, Truman the Baptist walked out to Rose Conway's desk and whispered with a grin, "If these Jews keep on blessing me I'm gonna get to heaven in spite of you Catholics."

- His naturalness. Showing me a scar on his wrist from boyhood days, he told me how his mother had filled the open wound with black pepper. "It burned like hell, but it sure killed the infection."

- His politics. He preached it, believed it, lived it, worshipped it. "It's the greatest game in the world."

- His humility. When I asked him to autograph a color print of himself sitting at his desk with an open Bible he replied, "Aw, my signature's not worth anything," and then he wrote:

"To Lee Williams with many thanks for his help on the next volume; best wishes for his future success. Harry S Truman, Independence, Dec. 17, 1954."

Dec. 17, 1954? It seems like yesterday.

The history of Harry S Truman's relations with the American press as president of the United States began on April 12, 1945, and ended on January 20, 1953, the dates of his assumption and relinquishment of the high office. This book does not propose to retell the general history of the Truman years, but it nevertheless sheds new light on certain approaches to the unfolding events of this vibrant period of postwar change. Neither is the present work intended to be biographical. But, as it follows Truman through the mature years of his public life in an effort to discover the true character of his always lively associations with the press of the country, it presents some new information as to what manner of man he was.

If the narrative has a claim to uniqueness, it is that the recorded testimony is almost entirely from the mind and the mouth of the president himself. This provides a "homespun" quality to the text plus valuable insights into little-publicized facets of his character, his background, his tastes, and his personality — all of which, in turn, bear directly on his relations with the press.

Like all public figures, the thirty-third president was a product of his time. His dynamic predecessor, Franklin D. Roosevelt, exploited radio as a remarkably effective medium of public communication; Truman's nasal, atonal voice simply could not approach the stentorian mastery of the airwaves by which FDR had held his audiences spellbound. Nor was television, which was just aborning, the instrument for Truman (or for Eisenhower either, despite some expert coaching from Robert Montgomery) that it was to become for the photogenic John F. Kennedy. It was primarily the newspapers that served as the platform — whether for information or misinformation — upon which Truman acted out his career of public service. He interacted with all of the mass media, of course, but his peculiar affinity for the public prints made him predominantly the newspaperman's president.

When this writer first consulted Mr. Truman on his feeling with regard to the feasibility and significance of an analytical study of his relations with the press, his reaction was one of enthusiasm. "Few presidents," he remarked, "have been as misunderstood or as misrepresented in the press as I have. It is a story that needs to be truthfully told."

So let the story be told — as much in the words of Harry S Truman as possible. The reader will find it to be a story as full of earnestness, of gusto, and of humor as was the man himself.

Chapter 1

APPETITE FOR NEWS

"I have an idea that I read more daily papers than any other person in the nation."

THE EARLIEST OF TRUMAN'S BIOGRAPHERS ATTEST TO TRU-
man's unusual proclivity for reading. McNaughton and Heymeyer
state that "he read faithfully the Congressional Record and the newspapers, and spent long hours in the reading room of the Library of
Congress."[1] Another ventured the assumption that "Truman's
reading tastes in a sense define his character."[2] Be that as it may, his
reading of current events was an established part of his White House
routine, as observed by Allen and Shannon: "Every morning he reads
the Washington papers and the *New York Times* and the [*New York*]
Herald Tribune."[3]

The president himself hinted of his reading practices to a group
of editors and publishers of the Gannett Newspapers at a special press
conference early in his first administration: "I get a resume of all the
press comment in the country nearly every day, a complete setup of
the sentiments of the various sections of the press in the country, on
all questions that are pending—like the Pearl Harbor investigations,
the Attlee-Mackenzie King conference, and things of that sort."[4]

His first director of the Bureau of the Budget, Harold Smith,
recorded his personal surprise at the president's apparent range of
reading despite the pressure of his executive duties. Smith posted this
entry in his diary following one of his regular conferences with the
president: "I was reminded of George Soule's article in the *New
Republic*, but decided not to mention that periodical and simply commented that one line we didn't follow often enough was the comparison with the post-World War I period. He turned to his table,
picked up the *New Republic* open at Soule's article."[5]

An article in the *New York Post* observed in 1946 that "nowadays
he reads about 30,000 words a day—not including political speeches
prepared for delivery by members of the Cabinet. . . . The president's daily reading starts with the New York, Baltimore, and
Washington papers."[6]

If Truman's reading of newspapers was extensive, it appeared
also to be intensive. Clemens states that "Truman would read the
newspapers voraciously, even down to the want ads and comic
strips."[7] The following paragraph that the president wrote in a letter
to a friend supports Clemens' contention that Truman was a meticu-
lous reader: "You don't know how very much I appreciated your
sending me Jim Cox's book. I have read the reviews in the New York
papers and in the *Washington Star* and was hoping somebody would
send me the book."[8] On at least one other occasion the record suggests that he read newspapers even down to the book review section:

"I can't tell you how very much I appreciated your book. I've read reviews in the *New York Times* and the *Herald Tribune*, and I was very anxious to have a chance to read the book itself."[9]

Further evidence of his practice of reading discerningly appears in the following excerpts from two different letters in which he makes mention of letters to the editor which he had read in the New York newspapers and reveals an alertness to the positioning of the first and to the source of the second: "The *Times* evidently thought very well of it since they put it at the top of the column and published it immediately."[10] "I read with a lot of interest your letter of March twenty-third and also read a letter signed A.A.B. in the *New York Herald Tribune* dated March twenty-fifth. I am sure that letter was written by you too."[11]

Truman was an inveterate reader of newspaper cartoons, comic as well as political.[12] In a letter to George Lichtenstein, creator of "Grin and Bear It," he remarked: "I notice you are starting the Senators series again. I got more chuckles and kicks out of them than any series of cartoons that came out while I was in the Senate."[13]

The president frequently called attention to cartoons in the course of his comments at press conferences, and once he used this favorite medium to answer a question as shown in the following excerpt:

Q: Do you approve the method of the five and ten economy resolution?

The President: I can answer that question very well as I did the other day. Remember the cartoon that was in the Washington Star last night, with the dear old Congress hitting itself on the head with a hammer and asking me please to have him stop that? (*laughter*) That cartoon answers that.[14]

The president's liking for cartoons made of him an avid collector as well as a faithful reader.[15] In a speech at Little Rock, Arkansas, in June 1949, when Truman was presented with a cartoon on wood, he revealed this little-known information about his private collection: "I appreciate this very much. You are very kind to me. I have got, I think, as great a collection of cartoons as any man in public life. I have cartoons from the beginning of my political career down to the present time. I must have three or four hundred of them."[16] And again at a breakfast of the National Cartoonists association in 1951, Truman referred to his hobby as follows: "I have, I think, as large a collection of cartoons on myself as any other president ever had, and I am very proud of them. There isn't wall space enough in my present cramped quarters in the White House Office to hang them all up, so I hang as many as I can for awhile then take them down and hang some others. And these will go with that collection. I shall probably take them out of the book and have each one of them framed, and when I get my archives building constructed, I will put these in a special room."[17]

A more detailed account of his newspaper reading habits was elicited from the president at one of his press conferences which was held especially for members of the American Society of Newspaper Editors, as demonstrated in the following dialogue from the transcript of the conference:

Q: Mr. President, this may seem trivial but I think it would interest us. You say you read a great many editorials. Could you tell us a little about how they are screened, whether they come to you, what method . . .
The President: (*interposing*) No sir, I take the papers themselves, and I read at least a dozen daily papers every day. Then there are a great many instances where editorials are mailed to me from out of town. But I spend — you see, I get up before daylight every morning — I have the reveille habit — and I spend a good part of that time going over all the Washington papers — *Baltimore Sun* — *Philadelphia Bulletin*, and many others that I have time to read. But I read them myself because I like to read them. And I find out lots of things about myself that I never heard of. (*laughter*)
Q: Ever read any from beyond the Alleghenies regularly?
The President: Yes, I get the *St. Louis Post-Dispatch*, sometimes the Pittsburgh papers, and the *Kansas City Star*. On occasion I get some West Coast papers. That is, editorially they — of course, by the time they get here the news is stale, but I usually read the editorial pages of these papers. The *Morning Register* I read sometimes, and Chicago papers — always very fond of the little afternoon Chicago daily [*Chicago Times*] consolidated with the Chicago *Sun*. I never thought much of the rest of the Chicago papers. (*laughter*).[18]

One of the little-publicized burdens of the office of president is to be deluged with clippings of newspaper articles from supporters and opponents alike. Truman exhibited some impatience with persons who sent him clippings of articles he had already come across in the course of his regular reading, as illustrated in this routine letter of acknowledgement: "I had already seen the editorial, and several more like it in various other New England papers. I don't know why in the world people seem to think that it is impossible for me to get facts. I have an idea that I read more daily papers than any other person in the nation."[19]

In a letter to Governor Smith of Missouri in 1950, the president said: "I don't read the *Star-Times,* or the *Post-Dispatch*, or the *Globe-Democrat*, or the *Kansas City Star*, unless somebody sends me a special clipping from them for my perusal."[20] Whether this signifies a change in his earlier professed habit of reading the *St. Louis Post-Dispatch* and the *Kansas City Star* or is a contradiction of the earlier statement[21] is a matter of conjecture. The record shows clearly, however, that Truman maintained his impressive program of daily newspaper reading through to the end of his presidency. His impromptu answer to a question at a press conference in 1952 bears this out:

Q: Mr. President, I was just wondering if you are aware now of General Eisenhower's availability for the Republican presidential nomination?
The President: Tony, I read five or six papers every morning, and I am."[22]

Perhaps a more convincing illustration than any other that Truman's regular appetite for newspaper copy was one manifestation of a deep-seated consciousness of the importance of the press is that which appears in the first article he wrote after leaving the White House in 1953.[23] He begins the first article of the series with a description of what he must have considered one of his most typical patterns of behavior—reading the morning paper. In the opening paragraph, he recites the narrative of events of his first morning at home as follows: "The morning paper[24] was in the front yard. I picked it up and took it into the living room where I sat down to read. A headline on the first page said . . . that I was always going to be Mr. President."[25]

The theme of the newspaper's role in his personal destiny lingers throughout the first installment of "Mr. Citizen," as Truman continues: "The newspaper in my lap had started me thinking about these things but it wasn't the first time. I had come to a decision months ago while still in the White House. . . . Were the people going to let me become a private citizen? Or was I going to have to live up to the 'Mr. President' the newspaper suggested?"[26]

In the second installment, the former president recounts once more the pattern and the reasons for his lifelong newspaper reading habit: "Back home now, in Independence, I run on the same schedule I've followed for years, up at 5:30, dress, then downstairs to read the paper the boy has flipped over the fence. This is the first paper of the day; later come four or five others from different parts of the country. You do not get all the facts from just one paper, and unless you have the facts, you can't think properly."[27]

While Truman may not have opted for "newspapers without government" rather than for "government without newspapers" in accord with Jefferson's advice, it is certain that his consumption of newspaper information exceeded that of the average American reader by a considerable margin.

Chapter 2

OF PRECEDENTS AND PRESIDENTS

"It is a most difficult thing these days to find reporters and editors who know anything about . . . history."

IF TRUMAN'S NEWSPAPER READING HABITS GIVE SOME IN-
dication of his "press consciousness," his degree of familiarity with
the historical development of American journalism should provide
another clue to the measure of his general awareness of the importance of the Fourth Estate. The record contains a number of allusions
by the president to press history. Truman's first reference, which
reflects a rather uncharitable partisan viewpoint toward one of the
outstanding characters of journalism history, appears in a letter written in 1947 to the postmaster-general of the United States:

April 15, 1947

Dear Bob:

I appreciate very much your thoughtfulness in sending me the
first day cover of the Pulitzer stamp.

I'll give you credit for being a very broad-minded person in putting out a postage stamp for that old bird. If he ever did anything for the Democratic party it was by accident and not
intentional.

Sincerely yours,

[signed] HARRY S TRUMAN

Twenty-six days later, in an address to the Gridiron Club of
Washington, Truman demonstrated a more kindly regard for
Pulitzer: "This year there was a memorial stamp honoring the
memory of a great publisher — an immigrant, incidentally. One of his
sayings is printed on that stamp. I am glad it is there so it will be read
by everyone in our country. It expresses a profound truth: 'Our
republic and its press will rise or fall together.'"[2]
During one of the exchanges of light banter which characterized
many of his press conferences, the president dropped a hint of his

familiarity with one famous event in the period of New York's penny paper development:

Q: Mr. President, have you seen any flying saucers?
The President: Only in the newspapers. (*laughter*)
Q: Any explanation of them from over here?
The President: Only the explanations I have seen in the newspapers. Did you ever hear of the moon hoax?[3]

A reputed lover of ancient history, the president seemed to be particularly intrigued with a famous demagogue of the Grecian era. On more than one occasion he drew an analogy between Alcibiades and the responsibilities of modern journalism. Here he constructs a moral for radio journalists: "And I don't believe in government by propaganda, but the thing that you have to be careful of is that some day a fine-voiced, goodlooking demagogue doesn't get control of the air and do what Alcibiades did to Greece. He can do that now to the whole of the United States. I think I have myself, according to the Hooper survey, talked to as many as 40 million people at one sitting. Now that's a responsibility, a very grave responsibility—to see that ability and power is used for the welfare of the greatest republic I think the sun has ever shone on."[4]

In a talk to members of a fraternal society, he made the comparison again to emphasize the importance of freedom of information: "Then they [the Greeks] had the greatest demagogue of all times, Alcibiades. There never was one like him. He had the voice of a siren. He had the looks of a god. He had the voice that took the Greeks around any way he wanted them to go. Now we have that same danger to contend with in this country, and if we are not careful some demagogue is going to come along and get us. (*laughter*) We won't do that—we certainly won't do that if all of you are informed and keep yourselves informed on just exactly where we are going and why."[5]

The classical allusion becomes somewhat involved later when a *Buffalo Courier Express* editorial mentioning Alcibiades draws the following observations from the president: "They are tangled up . . . on the demagogue business I did not compare Henry Wallace to Alcibiades. Dean Alfange compared him to Aeschines, and Aeschines is the person Henry most resembles. Of course, when Alcibiades went over to the enemy, that is Sparta, he followed a line that Henry is now following. It is a most difficult thing these days to find reporters and editors who know anything about ancient history."[6]

A further suggestion of Truman's general knowledge from press history is illustrated in the following comments during a press conference:

> *The President:* That's the front of the White House. The Chesapeake and Potomac canal used to run along down there—and John Quincy Adams used to go down there and swim every morning. Some lady reporter had been trying to get an interview with him for a long time.
> *Q:* (*interjecting*) Ann Royal.
> *The President:* (*continuing*) She went down and sat on his clothes and let him talk to her. (*laughter*) I thought you would be interested in that."[7]

To answer a question on an issue that was highly controversial and inflammatory in 1949, Truman once again turned to a period in history of vital interest to the American press:

> *Q:* (*interposing*) Mr. President, an awful lot of fine people are apparently being branded as reds, unemployables, subversives and whatnot, these days; and there are any number of trials, hearings, employment situations in the army, and whatnot. Is there any word of counsel that you could give on this rash of . . .
> *The President:* (*interposing*) Yes . . .
> *Q:* (*continuing*) . . . branding of people . . .
> *The President:* (*continuing*) . . . I gave it to you once before. I am going to suggest that you read the history of the Alien and Sedition Laws in 1790 under almost exactly the same circumstances, and you will be surprised at the parallel; and then also read how they came out.[8]

Toward the end of the same press conference, a reporter brought the President back to the same topic:

> *Q:* Mr. President, to go back to the Alien and Sedition Laws, how can we apply the lessons of that time to the solution today?
> *The President:* Well, continue to read your history through Jefferson's Administration, and you will find what the remedy was. Hysteria finally died down, and things straightened out, and the country didn't go to hell, and it isn't now.

Q: Mr. President, the first thing Jefferson did was to release eleven newspaper publishers from prison. (*laughter*)

The President: Yes. I think he made a mistake on that. (*more laughter*)[9]

These obviously innocent references to the Alien and Sedition Laws were seized upon by a personal critic of the president, who made a rather weak attempt to use the statements against him.[10] But Truman's interest in the history of public hysteria as one of the phenomena in the development of mass communications in America led him to have a study made of the subject and later to deliver a complete address on "What Hysteria Does to Us."[11] Commenting on the role of the press in this respect, he made the following remark in a personal interview: "The antiadministration press made a glamor boy out of McCarthy; then they found they'd made a Frankenstein out of him. Read that little piece of history of mine and you'll find out that the Whigs and the Republicans have always profited by hysteria eras."[12]

Near the end of his first term, Truman became acquainted with Pollard's *Presidents and the Press,*[13] and from then on his expressions manifest an increasing interest in that aspect of journalism history. He told members of the National Conference of Business Paper Editors early in 1948: "I have been reading a book by a fellow named Pollard, *Presidents and the Press.* When you read what the press had to say about Washington, Jefferson, and Lincoln, and the other presidents, you would think that we never had a decent man in office since the country began. (*laughter*)"[14]

Two years later he attested to the impression which had been made on him by Pollard's book in a letter to a special assistant to a district attorney. "If you will read Mr. Pollard's book — *The Presidents and the Press* — you will find that comparatively speaking I've been very kindly treated by most of the press. George Washington, Thomas Jefferson, Andrew Jackson, Abraham Lincoln, and Grover Cleveland were the most abused presidents, and I think Cleveland topped them all — he hated the press and let them know it, and they took it out on him."[15]

The president revised his opinion from time to time as to which chief executive had been accorded the worst treatment by the press, as the following comments reveal:

"Cleveland, I think, was the most misrepresented of any president who ever sat in the president's chair."[16]

"Lincoln was, I think, about the most thoroughly abused man that ever was in the presidential office."[17]

"If you really want to find the man who was about the most abused man in the history of the country in the press, go down to the Library of Congress and read some of the newspaper comments on George Washington."[18]

"Nobody was as roundly abused as Cleveland in his first term."[19]

"There never was a more thoroughly misrepresented man than Thomas Jefferson."[20]

Other references indicate that Truman was genuinely fascinated by the historical details of the press relations of his predecessors. Furthermore, his offhand manner of recalling the facts suggests more than a passing interest in and familiarity with this particular phase of press history, as illustrated in the following remarks: "Well, you know what Lincoln said, He said, when he was asked if he read all the mean things that were written about him by Horace Greeley and the editor of the *New York Herald*, he said no, that if he did, he wouldn't have time to take care of the business of government. That's not verbatim of course."[21]

"But do you know that when he [George Washington] went out of office, the principal paper in the great city of Philadelphia said that they were getting rid of the worst dictator the country ever had, it was a good thing he was going to retire, and they hoped they would never see him again. They attacked him so bitterly over the Jay Treaty and over Citizen Genet, and one or two other things, that is the reason he retired instead of running for a third term."[22]

"When Lincoln made his [Gettysburg] speech, which lasted about three and a half minutes, the editor of the *New York Tribune* and the editor of the *Chicago Tribune* said 'the President of the United States also spoke, and made the usual ass out of himself.' You didn't know that, but that is a fact."[23]

Of course, the above observations by the president are not entirely accurate.[24] The looseness with which he recited such instances raises a legitimate doubt as to the thoroughness of his understanding of journalism history. But what is being shown here is that he had a more than ordinary interest in and familiarity with a broad range of history, of which newspaper history constituted a noticeable portion.

The president's reputation for consulting precedents and parallels in history in arriving at many of the decisions that he had to make while in office has been well publicized. His decision in 1951 to take an unprecedented step in releasing for publication many of his private papers while still president of the United States stemmed partly from his knowledge and appreciation of a remote parallel in journalism history. This is recounted by Hillman: "Conscious deeply of the spontaneous world opinion that makes its own history today, President Truman, thumbing through some history books like the professor he hopes to be someday, told me: 'You know, if Andrew Johnson, for example, had not given special interviews to a number of different newspaper correspondents, voicing his views on problems confronting him, a good deal of important historical material of the presidency of Andrew Johnson might not have been unearthed or even known.'"[25]

Truman's supposed aspiration to teach history is not supported by any declaration of the president himself. In answer to a newsman's question at a press conference in 1952 regarding a rumor that Truman was going to become a history professor at the University of North Carolina, the president replied: "Well sir, I will tell you something about that. I am no historian. I have no college degrees except honorary ones that they have given me since I have been in the Senate and president of the United States, and I don't believe there is any college in the country that would consider me qualified to teach history —or anything else. (*laughter*)"[26]

Chapter 3

CREDIT WHERE DUE

"Now you gentlemen—you editors—
you have as great an influence on the
welfare of this country as any other
set of men in the country."

THE PRESIDENT'S ATTITUDE TOWARD THE AMOUNT AND kind of influence wielded by the American press embraced some interesting contradictions, judging from his public comments on the subject. Despite frequent and repeated expressions—particularly after his election in 1948—of disregard for and disbelief in newspaper influence upon public opinion, Truman also left some convincing testimony that suggests a genuine and continued respect for the very attribute of the mass media that he occasionally belittled or denied existed. For example, in a reference to the newly organized Food and Agricultural Organization of the United Nations, he said to newsmen: "Of course it [FAO] could not operate by itself very well, but I think it is one of the fundamental things of the United Nations set-up, and there is no set of people who can put that over in this country and round the world like you people can. In fact, we can't operate unless you give us the necessary publicity and sell the matter to the people as a whole and to the world."[1]

Three months later, speaking in a vein reminiscent of the philosophy of Jefferson, he professed: "I think you people can contribute very materially to the solution of the problem, if the facts are continually brought home to the people as a whole. I have found that when the people of the United States understand a problem and the facts are honestly placed before them, we have no trouble getting along in the right direction to get the job done. I have always said that if reasonable men know all the facts, the conclusions will take care of themselves. I am pleased to have you all here, and glad to meet every one of you, and you can make a contribution to the reconversion program. It is *your* program. I am merely the umpire at the top of the heap, trying to get the job done by every means at my command."[2]

Beginning on January 16, 1946, Truman initiated at the White House a new procedure known as the "budget seminar" to aid newsmen in understanding the federal budget. He conducted eight of these annual seminars, many of which lasted between two and three hours, in the movie projection room in the east wing of the White House. For the benefit of reporters, he called into the seminars the secretary of the treasury and the director of the Bureau of the Budget to assist in explaining the fiscal details of the government and in answering questions. According to one witness, the president went to great lengths to procure specially drawn charts and graphs, which he used for easel presentation in the seminars.[3]

This effort to give the White House correspondents a clear and complete picture of his financial program was consistent with his often-expressed belief that if the people could get the facts through the newspapers, they would understand and support the policies of his administration. That the budget seminars were an innovation in White House press relations is attested to by a confidant of the president, who pointed out that, by contrast, "President Roosevelt would never discuss the budget with newsmen; he had a strong distaste for going into the grocery bill in public."[4]

The following instance, in which he gives permission to reporters to quote him verbatim, reflects Truman's desire to use the power of the press in an effective way as an aid in combatting the threat of inflation:

Q: Mr. President, are you still calling this a hold-the-line policy?
The President: Yes.
Q: On the . . .
The President: (*interposing*) I beg your pardon?
Q: Is it a new line you are holding?
The President: No, it isn't. It's a bulge in the old line. (*much laughter*) You have heard of bulges in military lines, haven't you? (*more laughter*)
Q: You don't expect a breakthrough, do you, Mr. President?
The President: I do not. If you will all cooperate with me, there will be no breakthrough.
Q: Mr. President, may we quote that word "bulge"?
The President: Yes.
Q: May we quote those two sentences?[5]

The president gave permission to quote the two sentences when the question was repeated about fifteen lines later.

Truman gave evidence of his faith in newspapers as the major medium of information when he told a radio audience of his veto of the price control extension bill: "I returned it with a long message stating my reasons. I hope that you will all read that message in your newspapers."[6]

A letter written late in 1946 provides a novel picture of the president speculating on the possibility of establishing a newspaper in Missouri to serve as a Democratic party organ. The idea had been suggested to him earlier in a letter from Senator Frank P. Briggs of Macon, Missouri. Briggs had outlined some of the problems of news coverage, business management, and party acceptance in setting up a newspaper "in which the Republican mistakes would be given to the public in no uncertain terms."[7]

Truman's reaction to the idea of a party newspaper in the home state is couched in circumspect language, but his reply leaves no doubt as to his appreciation of the potential value of the political influence of such a newspaper:

December 28, 1946

Dear Frank:

I read your letter of the eighteenth with a lot of interest and there has been much talk in times past about a Democratic newspaper in Missouri.

Of course, a successful paper which would give the Democrats a fair deal would certainly be helpful, but the task seems to me to be a tremendous one, and it is a task for an experienced news-paperman. You know more about these things than I do because I have never had any experience in the newspaper business. I think it would be well to discuss the matter with Roy Harper and with Hannegan on the theory that, if such a project would be undertaken, they would be exceedingly helpful in obtaining subscriptions, advertising, and meeting the preliminary expenses.

I don't want to say whether the project should be started or not, although in my opinion, it would be a fine thing for the Demo-crats to have a paper which would tell the truth about their plans and aspirations. There is no such paper in Missouri at the present time with a statewide circulation.

Sincerely yours,

[signed] HARRY S TRUMAN[8]

In an outspoken appeal for newspaper support during the infla-tionary crisis of 1947, Truman strongly emphasized the need for cooperation from the press; speaking at a news conference, he said: "I am trying to give you all the facts that I can. I want you to know just what I know, to know the helplessness of the executive branch of the government through the present situation. There is nothing we can do."[9]

Repeatedly, in 1947,[10] the president demonstrated a concern for widespread readership of the public prints. He made this observation in a speech regarding an amended executive order that laid down the guiding policies of the government during the postwar reconversion period: "To guide labor and management in their interpretation of this executive order, I have today issued an amendment—which I hope every one of you will read carefully in your newspapers tomorrow—amplifying the order and setting forth three classes in which wage increases may be granted even though price ceiling increases may result."[11]

Early in the election year of 1948, Truman expressed real concern over the territorial influence exerted by the antiadministration *Chicago Tribune* in a letter to Senator Wheeler: "Naturally people who are in the area of the *Chicago Tribune's* influence never receive the facts in regard to the situation as it actually is, and the *Chicago Tribune* circulates all over Montana and influences the Montana press to a very great extent."[12] And a second letter a few weeks later answering one in which Wheeler had discounted the *Tribune's* influence in his section shows that Truman would not be easily dissuaded: "I still think that the *Chicago Tribune* has a tremendous influence in that part of the world, although I may be mistaken."[13]

Truman told members of the newly organized National Conference of Editorial Writers in 1947 that "you have a tremendous influence on the welfare of this country. You can either make it or break it. I say that advisedly."[14] In a formal address before the American Society of Newspaper Editors, the president made no effort to veil his recognition of press influence: "You editors make a distinct and important contribution to the operation of government in the United States. Your frank expression of views on current affairs has great value to our people in helping them to form their judgments. It is because of the influence you have upon the course of our democracy that I am glad to have this opportunity to discuss with you one of the major problems confronting our country."[15]

Following these remarks, which he read from his prepared manuscript, Truman launched into an unrehearsed, off-the-record talk that, according to the critics, delighted his audience for half an hour.[16] During the course of this informal talk, he said: "Now you gentlemen — you editors — you have as great an influence on the welfare of this country as any other set of men in the country. I am not proposing to tell you how to run your business. I have been told that when a fellow fails at everything else, he either starts a hotel or a newspaper. (*laughter*) But I know I am not competent to run either a hotel or a newspaper, but I do know what I am talking about in this instance."[17]

Once again, while engaged in a whistle-stop campaign during the summer of 1948, the president seemed to have in mind the 54 million newspaper readers in America when he remarked: "I brought a lot of reporters with me on this trip, and I venture to say there isn't half of them ever saw anything west of the Appalachian Mountains, and I hope they will tell their eastern readers and constituents just exactly what they have seen in the last three or four days. If they do, we will have a united country for the development of our resources, and the things that make us great."[18]

An interesting observation appears in a letter to the editor of the *Mexico* (Missouri) *Ledger* with regard to the influence of news-papers: "I myself am strongly in favor of the rural papers. I think they do more good and have more influence than all the metropolitan papers put together. I tried my best to prove that conclusively last year, and I think that it was successfully done."[19]

The president enumerated the agencies that helped to "shape those attitudes of mind" that the National Conference of Christians and Jews apparently was promoting in 1949 and was careful to include the press, as the following comment reveals: "In looking over your record of performance for the last year, I have been impressed by your comprehensive day-to-day program of education. . . . You have reached not only the schools and the colleges, not only the churches and synagogues, but factories and shops, the press, the radio, and the movies. . . . You will, I am sure, go on to every agency that helps shape those attitudes of mind which are important to good citizenship."[20]

After five years of dealing with the press, the president continued to profess a genuine respect for the unchallenged influence of news-papers despite the fact that he had been elected in 1948 with much of the press in opposition. "You and I," he told the leading editors of the country, "have a great many important problems in common, and one of the most important of these is the responsibility we share in helping to make the foreign policy of the United States of America."[21]

Then, in language that was as explicit and as positive as he could make it, he said: "No group of men in this country is of greater importance to our foreign policy than the group your society represents."[22]

"In many countries today," the president continued, "the papers print about foreign affairs only what their governments tell them to print. They can't add anything or cut anything. In the democracies, the papers have a free hand. Only in a democracy is there such mutual trust and confidence among citizens that a private group is given such an all-important role in determining what the nation as a whole shall do. There is too much nonsense about striped trousers in foreign affairs. Far more influence is exerted by the baggy pants of the managing editor."[23]

During his western campaign in the off-year electioneering of 1950, Truman attacked newspapers frequently but continued to demonstrate his basic faith in their influence upon readers, as such comments as the following reveal: "I have just come from Lincoln, where I made a speech on the major farm problems which we face. . . . I hope you will all have a chance to read about it in tomorrow's papers."[24] "And now, we have good prospects for continued prosperity. Almost every newspaper you pick up gives new evidence of increasing business activity."[25]

The reaction of the voter to candidates and issues was, of course, a subject close to Truman's heart. Toward the beginning of his last year in office, he received a discourse on voting behavior from a professor of political science at the University of Wisconsin, and replied to the professor's letter in part as follows: "I certainly did appreciate your good letter of the fourth regarding the average voter — how he thinks and what makes him act. I always put myself in the place of the voter when I am thinking about his reaction. . . . The average voter in our great republic reads his local newspaper and sometimes listens to speeches and arguments by candidates. . . ."[26]

It might be deemed presumptuous to point out that Truman placed local newspaper reading ahead of listening to the candidates themselves in the above comment, but this may have been deliberate and not accidental. Speaking before a press conference later in the year on the same topic of influencing the behavior of the nation's voters, he again placed newspapers first: "Newspapers, magazines, radio and TV, and other media can do much to enlist interest in this subject."[27]

Less than three months before leaving office, while making his last political campaign tour, the president betrayed his abiding respect for press influence when he used an opposition publication to prove his point to his audience: "You don't have to take my word for it. Let me read you something from a magazine, a magazine that is no friend of mine—and very few of the slick magazines are friends of mine or the Democratic party, either—this is from the October eighteenth issue of *Business Week,* a magazine that is read mostly by Republicans. [Here he reads two paragraphs on progress made in the distribution of wealth under the Democratic administrations.] Now there you have it. There you have it—in the words of an opposition magazine. That is what the Democratic party means to you."[28]

Such references from the primary sources of information, as well as some observations from the outside,[29] indicate a genuine understanding and healthy appreciation of the general influence of the press on public opinion. It may be no exaggeration to say that Truman exhibited a stronger "press consciousness" than most men who have occupied the office of president.

Chapter 4

Bouquets Before Brickbats

"I am not here just to butter up the press. I do not think it is perfect. But, it is the best press in the world and it is doing a fine job."

It is apparent that Truman's attitude toward the press often went beyond mere awareness of its existence and respect for its influence. On occasion he went out of his way to laud either the profession in general or one of its representatives in particular. For example, he complimented Jonathan Daniels in these sincere statements written a few months after he became president: "I read your article on President Roosevelt in the last *Liberty* last night and I certainly did enjoy it. I wish that you and all his friends would continue to see that these friendly articles are published. . . . It is a fine article, and I don't know when I have read one I enjoyed more."[1]

When Russell Stewart became general manager of the *Chicago Times* late in 1945, he received the following note from the president:

November 27, 1945

Dear Russ:

Just learned that you have been made the "big boss" of the *Times*.

Congratulations to the *Times*. Best of luck and I know you will make a good paper a better one.

Hope to see you sometime in the near future.

[signed] HARRY S TRUMAN

When asked at a press conference how he felt about the manner in which newspapers were supporting the country, the president replied: "I think they are doing it. I think they have done it. . . . I think the general idea of the press is to support the foreign policy as it is outlined now, and I think that the vast majority of the press is anxious to see this reconversion thing a success. I don't think it's a political football in the press. I can't say as much for the Congress. (*laughter*)"[3]

Truman was lavish in his praise of the *Shelby News* in Kentucky for that newspaper's journalistic treatment of his daughter, Margaret, in connection with her visit to Shelbyville — which was the native city of the president's four grandparents — in the spring of 1946: "The news story was beautifully done; the editorial was highly appreciated; and the columns — 'Who'd 'a' Thought It' and 'Home Town Chatter' were as nicely done as anything of the sort I have ever seen."[4]

Truman paid tribute to the newspaper world during its special week in the fall of 1946.[5] In February of the following year, he made these highly complimentary remarks about the press: "Our press in general has outgrown the provincialism, the narrow isolationism, of another era. It has accepted as its province Wendell Willkie's 'One World.' It is doing a valiant service in educating us to understand that we must live in that 'one world.' As they did during the war, reporters go to distant and perilous parts of the earth to bring us the news. The news-gathering apparatus of our press is far-flung and highly efficient. More and more we are learning, and in no small measure through the medium of the press, how closely our democracy is under observation."[6]

On the same occasion, he had this compliment for the black press: "These newspapers show an understandable concern with the problems of relationship between the races. From the columns of the Negro press, example after example can be cited of reporting and editorial writing which deal with these problems in the courageous and constructive manner which we expect of the best of our journalism."[7]

Truman's third year in office left the columns of journalism publications well sprinkled with generous tributes to the press.[8, 9, 10] One of these occurred in the president's remarks to the Washington Gridiron Club, a group noted for anything but compliments: "This is the greatest governmental system in the world. Our press has helped to make it so. As I have said before, our press has done a particularly fine job in making clear to the people the full meaning of our policy of aid to Greece and Turkey. Our press can take some share of the credit for the resounding majority which the Greek and Turkish aid bill has just won in the House of Representatives. I am not here just to butter up the press. I do not think it is perfect. But, it is the best press in the world, and it is doing a fine job. It is an integral part of our democracy."[11]

Again Truman praised the press for its cooperation in connection with the Greek-Turkish bill, this time in a talk at the Muehlebach

Hotel in Kansas City: "I want to say also that the press is to be commended — complimented — on the manner in which the program was explained to the country. I think the press made a great contribution toward informing the people of the United States — toward showing just exactly what the intention of the legislation is."[12]

In the hometown of a famous journalist in 1948, the president remembered to pay tribute to both the living and the dead: "William Allen White was one of the country's great men. He was a great editor, he was a humanitarian, and he has always worked for the right, in my opinion. And he has a son who is following in his footsteps, and who is doing a very magnificent job in the newspaper field."[13]

Journalism was again commended by the chief executive in a speech on highway safety: "Newspapers, magazines, and radio broadcasts are giving more constructive attention to highway safety than ever before. A thorough public understanding of the problem is essential, and these agencies are giving splendid assistance."[14] Shortly before the president turned over his personal papers to William Hillman for publication in 1951, he paid the noted journalist this compliment: "It gives a fellow a lift to have somebody in your business who is really on the beam."[15]

Truman wrote the following commendatory letter in acknowledging an invitation to attend a testimonial dinner in honor of William Southern and Frank Rucker, publishers of his hometown paper:

April 5, 1951

Dear Mr. Mayor:

I was most happy to receive your letter of the third informing me of the dinner to honor Mr. Southern and Mr. Rucker. I certainly wish I could be present.

I've known Mr. Southern ever since I was a very small boy and I've known Mr. Rucker ever since he came to Independence. I think these two men have made a great contribution to the County Seat of Jackson County. I've always been very fond of both of them and I hope they will have a happy career, although I was exceedingly sorry to see them leave the *Examiner.*

Sincerely yours,

[signed] HARRY S TRUMAN[16]

William T. Evjue, Wisconsin publisher, came in for a word of warm praise from the president as a result of sending him a copy of an editorial he had written about Senator Joseph McCarthy. Truman wrote: "I wish we had more people in the Senate who are as interested in the truth and welfare of the country as you are."[17] Another implied tribute to the *Independence Examiner* appears in this excerpt referring to the *Richmond* (Missouri) *News*: "You tell Mrs. Harl that I am glad she still sticks to her hometown paper—I do too."[18]

Surprisingly enough, the most extravagant applause accorded any journalistic effort, as far as the record shows, went not to a newspaper man or an experienced writer in the field of public affairs—but to an actress. When Tallulah Bankhead, daughter of the renowned Senator, published her autobiography in 1952,[19] she submitted an advance copy to the president. His appraisal was most enthusiastic, as the following comments reveal: "The proof copy of your book arrived a day or two ago and I haven't been able to put it down. It is undoubtedly the most interesting book I've had in my hands since I have been president of the United States. You say in that book that you are a professional actress and have no idea of becoming anything else. It is my opinion that the demand on you for more books in the same vein as this one will undoubtedly be your profession from now on. Thanks again for your thoughtfulness in sending me an advance copy of your wonderful book. . . ."[20]

Undoubtedly some of the president's more felicitous remarks concerning the press stemmed from personal or political relationships. But many of his tributes appear to be predicated on a genuine esteem and appreciation of the press or its representatives. The following statements from a letter written to Adlai Stevenson during the heat of the 1952 campaign—and at the end of Truman's long public career—are illustrative of the ultimate tribute to the press by the chief executive. In this short comment, which is spontaneous and unsolicited, he pays the highest compliment to the *Baltimore Sun* and its reporters that can be offered a newspaper or a journalist—that of objective, truthful reporting: "I am enclosing you a couple of articles out of the *Baltimore Sun* of yesterday. The *Sun* supports Ike, but I'll say this for the *Sun,* it has objective reporters, and Joe Short informs me that the two men who wrote these articles which I have marked are among the ablest of the *Sun*'s staff and are truthful gentlemen."[21]

Chapter 5

SEEING DOUBLE

"Boys, when I take out after the one-party press, that doesn't include you. It only includes your publishers. . . ."

PRESIDENT TRUMAN OBVIOUSLY DID NOT TAKE THE MASS communicators for granted. On the contrary, he consciously recognized the press as a factor to be dealt with in the public affairs of the nation, in the fortunes of the Democratic party that his administration represented, and in matters concerning his own political career and personal life. How did he deal with this recognized element in his capacity as chief executive? Was he able to channel it to serve his administration's purposes, or was he to be victimized by the power of the nation's free press?

The answers to such questions would seem to provide us with both positives and negatives. It is necessary to understand that Truman maintained from the beginning a bifocal view of the press, seeing it as two separate and distinct images and not as a single entity. To him, the press was as divided a creature as Stevenson's Hyde and Jekyll. He felt that the two segments that he detected in American journalism often had entirely different methods, attitudes, motives, and resources. It all depended on which classification one had in mind.

Truman consistently labeled one section of the press as the "working press." He included in this category the reporters, correspondents, photographers, and other hired personnel in the lower echelons of the newsgathering and newswriting organization. These were the men and women with whom the president regularly came into direct, personal contact and with whom he developed a remarkable familiarity. In the other side of the dichotomy Truman placed the owners, publishers, managers, editorial writers, columnists, headline writers, and any others who seemed to him to be connected with policy-making with regard to the presentation of news and editorial comment. He applied various appellations from time to time to this segment of the press.[1]

Observers of White House press relations have agreed that Truman's contacts with the working press were, as a rule, good.[2] Pollard points out the distinction that existed in favor of the working press, as far as Truman's total relations were concerned, and indicates that it was a situation which he inherited from his predecessor: "It was greatly to his credit that he steadily maintained good relations with the working press. As with Franklin Roosevelt, his quarrels with the newspapers for the most part were with the publishers."[3]

The president made a number of allusions to the dual nature of the press. When the chairman of the Federal Communications Commission complained, in a memorandum to the president, of having been misquoted in the press, Truman replied: "You know when the newsboys' 'bosses' are against you there isn't much use in making statements about them, although I can see your viewpoint very readily in the matter about which you sent the memorandum."[4]

The emphasis that Truman placed upon the difference between the reportorial journalists and all others became even more apparent during his second term.[5] On December 1, 1948, he wrote a letter to the United States ambassador to Chile in which he said: "I've never cared a great deal about what the editorial writers and columnists say about me on the editorial page if I can get a fair break on the front page in the news columns."[6]

On the occasion of his two hundredth press conference, a reporter asked the president a point-blank question and got a revealing answer:

Q: Do you become a little annoyed with us at times?
The President: Well, I never get annoyed with you. I get annoyed with your bosses, sometimes. (*much laughter*)
Q: (*interposing*) Mr. President, . . .
The President: (*continuing*) I think most of you try your best to be entirely fair. I have never had any reason to quarrel with you.[7]

When Truman complained to the correspondents that his ideas about congressional consultation with the executive branch of the government had received no publicity, he made it clear that he was not blaming the working press and showed that he considered copyreaders a part of the "other side":

The President: . . . and I am not scolding you, I am just stating a fact."
Q: Mr. President, what *was* that statement that was not used last week?
The President: Oh, I will have somebody read it to you. I didn't bring it with me, Bob [Nixon], but I made a clear and complete statement about consulting the legislative branches, and it wasn't quoted anywhere. I will send it to you . . .
Q: I would sure like to see it.
The President: I will give it to you.
Q: I know that *I* reported it fully out of here.
The President: Well, you probably did, I say, but sometimes your rewrite man doesn't do exactly what you want.[8]

Later, in the same session, the president reiterated, "I like all of you, and I think you are making a sincere effort to report things as they are. I am not blaming you at all for things that don't come out in the papers"[9]

The delineation was most sharply drawn in Truman's final whistle-stop speech of the 1952 campaign in St. Louis, which was also his last public address as president outside the capital. Speaking in terms of political preference, he nevertheless provided evidence of the same two-sided opinion of the press that he had held on the day he had taken office almost eight years before: "But this campaign has brought out another fact about the press. The publishers may be mostly Republicans, but the working newspaper men — like most working people throughout the country — are for Stevenson. That is true of the newspaper men on the Stevenson train, and most true especially on the train of the Republican candidate for president.

"I want to say a word to these newspaper men, especially the ones who have been going around the country with me. Boys, when I take out after the one-party press, that doesn't include you. It only includes your publishers — and you and I can agree that they are not too bright, anyway. You fellows are all right in my book. And I mean it."[10]

Writing with regard to Truman's overall attitude toward the working press, Pollard suggests that a marked change was apparent with the beginning of his second term. Pollard states: "The election of 1948 was a tremendous turning point in the public career of Harry S Truman. Not only did it make him president in his own right for a full four-year term, but it gave him a degree of self-assurance and downright self-confidence that amounted to cocksureness and approached the aplomb of Franklin D. Roosevelt himself."[11] When asked about this specific observation, during a personal interview, Truman emphatically denied any inconsistency and said: "That's not true, and I think my press conference transcriptions will show that that's not true. My attitude has not changed. I always treated them as fairly as I knew how, but I didn't let them run over me. If they tried to pull a smart-aleck stunt, they got it right back. The working press was always just as friendly as could be."[12]

This raises a question regarding the nature of the president's relations with the working press. Whether Truman's attitude was an unchanging one, as he states, or one that was considerably altered by his triumph in 1948, as Pollard suggests, is best determined by an examination of the data.

On April 15, 1945, while Truman was still overwhelmed with the great responsibility that fate had suddenly thrust upon him, he penned in his diary: "On visit down to Senate I saw all the senators who were present that day; in addition saw Senate pages, employees of the Senate, all members of Senate press gallery, told newspapermen if they ever prayed, which I very much doubted, that they had better pray for me now."[13]

Further indication of an easy, intimate relationship with newspapermen is contained in the following conversation at the beginning of his seventh press conference:

The President: Hello, Tony [Vaccaro], how are you this morning?

Q: Fine.

Q: Good morning. How are you?

The President: Oh, I'm all right—I'm all right.

Merriman Smith: [who broke his arm VE-Day] Mr. President, I want to thank you for that letter.

The President: Well, I was going to come out to see you, but you moved home too quickly. What I am particularly interested in is, are you going to sue the president for damages for falling out of that door? (*laughter*)

Merriman Smith: If you are willing.

The President: Well, I would have to let you in the court. (*more laughter*)

Merriman Smith: I promise not to put in a relief bill.

The President: All right. I don't think you need one. (*then to other newsmen*) Good morning, how are you? Looks like you had a good day. Hello, Pete. Thanks for that article.

Pete Brandt: Yes.

The President: (*laughing*) I am handicapped in writing letters to each one of you fellows, because I'm afraid I'll skip somebody. (*then to Jim Wright, sitting down*) How are you feeling this morning?

Jim Wright: Thank you—fine.

Voice: All in.[14]

At the spring 1945 meeting of the Washington Gridiron Club, whose proceedings are never recorded, the president as guest speaker made some kind remarks about two correspondents that resulted in the following friendly exchange at the press conference:

Pete Brandt: Thank you very much for those remarks last Saturday night, Mr. President.
The President: That was from the heart, Pete.
Bert Andrews: I thank you, too.
The President: All right. Same to you.[15]

Truman was a frequent caller at such newsmen's institutions in the capital city as the National Press Club, the Gridiron Club, the White House Photographers Association, and the White House Correspondents Association.[16] In 1947, he remarked in a letter to the president of the National Press Club: "Don't get the idea into your head that I am ever bored by any of the dinners that it is my privilege to attend. I always have a good time wherever I go, and I particularly enjoy the press and photographers dinners. Sometimes they are rather nerve-racking when I have to sit through a lot of speeches and then make one myself, but most of them are worth all the trouble that is put into them."[17]

Tony Vaccaro, correspondent for the Associated Press, was one of the members of the working press for whom the president evidenced real fondness. This memorandum in 1948 was typical of the jovial communications exchanged frequently between the two:

January 23, 1948

Memorandum for: Tony Vaccaro
                 Press Room
                 The White House

From: The President

Tony you have the reputation of asking terrible questions in the most innocent and unusual manner and I don't mind telling you that I like it.

I also like your new "specs" and I hope you'll get a new hearing apparatus so that you can hear as well as you can see.

HST[18]

There is no evidence in the first year following his election of any abatement in Truman's pleasant relationship with the working press. A more wholesome atmosphere of informality and good humor could hardly be imagined between the president of the United States and representatives of the press than that which is pictured in the following excerpt from the transcript of a press conference held at an early hour in the press room of the B.O.Q. in Key West where the White House correspondents and photographers were quartered. The official recorder begins the transcript as the president walks in on the unsuspecting newsmen:

Q: My God! — this is *on* the record!
The President: What's that, Joe [Fox]?
Joe Fox: This is on the record.
The President: Yes.
Q: Everybody here?
The President: We'll have to wait a few minutes, I guess, to see that everybody is protected. (*Merriman Smith appeared in blue pajamas with burgundy spots*)
Q: Have you ever seen anything like the dead still walking! (*much laughter*)
Merriman Smith: I stayed up all night working on official papers. (*more laughter*)
Q: Nixon will never forgive me as long as he lives.
The President: Is Bob up?
Q: Where's Nixon?
Q: He's shaving.
Q: He's up — he's down! (*more laughter*)
The President: How are you all this morning?
Mr. Ross: This reminds me of the time I held up the president's plane in the jungles.
The President: At three o'clock in the morning.
Q: Where's Nixon? (*Mr. Nixon appeared*)
Q: Okay, we can go now.
The President: We can go now. (*conference gets underway*)[19]

In March of the following year, again at Key West, the president invited the newspapermen to a picnic on the lawn of the Little White House, serving hamburgers, hot dogs, lemonade, pretzels, and beer. Then as the press conference that followed the picnic got underway, he intimated that he would have a scoop for them later and warned that he didn't want the new fence around the lawn broken down in the rush to get the news on the wires. The "scoop" came midway during the conference:

> *The President:* I think the greatest asset that the Kremlin has is Senator McCarthy.
> *Q:* That will make the papers tomorrow morning on page one!
> *Q:* Would you care to elaborate on that?
> *The President:* I don't think it needs any elaboration.
> *Q:* Brother, will that hit page one tomorrow!
> *Q:* If you think we are going to bust down the fence on what you have got later, that's a pretty good starter. (*laughter*)[20]

The transcript of the conference closes with the following lines:

> *Q:* Mr. President, we have had a wonderful time at your lawn party, and thank you very much. (*much laughter*)
> (*there was a mad scramble for that fence*)[21]

The president's attention at about this time was called to the criticism of his postelection attitude that was coming from sources other than Pollard, and he took pains to exonerate himself of the charge as follows: "I do have a comment that I want to make to you, that I want to have an understanding with you on. Some of my good friends who write columns, and whom I read with pleasure, have been saying lately that I had a 'cocky' attitude. Now, I don't like that word, because I think it is 'confident' that they want to say. And if you remember, after the election in 1948, I was exceedingly careful not to appear cocky, or as if I wanted to press somebody down. I am not in that mood now. . . . And I don't want to assume any cocky attitude toward anybody, no matter who he is. I just want to make that plain—because I don't feel that way, and never have."[22]

Consistent with the good-natured relations of his early years, Truman in 1951 presented to the thirty-three press and radio correspondents and photographers who went on the Wake Island trip with him a beautifully embossed citation that said: "This subject did fly the Pacific skies over the International Dateline to report the historic conference of President Harry S Truman and General Douglas MacArthur on Wake Island, October 15, 1950. . . . That by so crossing this divider of days, today's news at once becomes tomorrow's and all is editorial confusion.[23] Later, in the same year, the president again indulged in a bit of whimsy with the newsmen:

> *The President:* Please be seated. I have a communication here from one of your members that is right interesting. It says:
> "From day to day I show up neat,
> Even in the worst of heat,
> I'm not the one to shed my coat,
> And open my shirt, or bare my throat.
> I yield to none in my scorn of pain,
> Smiling at sun and laughing at rain.
> I appeal for other sons of toil
> Who pant, perspire, and even boil.
> A coatless conference would do a lot
> To ease the distress of those who get hot."
> (*laughter*)
> Now, I think I told you once before that anybody who wants to take his coat off could do it. (*more laughter, some newsmen took off their coats*)
> *Q:* Who is the author of this masterpiece, Mr. President?
> *The President:* The boy with the pink tie [Tony Vaccaro].
> *Q:* Oh — I don't know him!
> *Q:* Now we can stay a long time! (*more laughter*)
> *The President:* I may make you put them back on, if you do.[24]

There is no indication during Truman's final year in office of any decline in the rapport that he enjoyed with the working press. To the contrary, the data show that he consistently maintained a good relationship with the representatives of all the media. He wrote the following note to Frank Bourgholtzer of NBC: "I enjoyed the trip around the White House with the television contingent very much, and it seems to have made quite an impression on the country. At first I thought maybe we were not doing the right thing, but I believe we did. I hope you have a grand time on the coming whistle-stop campaign with Eisenhower and Taft. When you come back I'll be glad to talk with you about it."[25]

Truman received a warm letter of appreciation from William S. White of the *New York Times* bureau during the last week of 1952 expressing gratitude for the pleasant conditions under which newsmen had been permitted to work while covering the White House. In his reply, Truman acknowledged his personal esteem for the working press: "Thank you for your good letter of December twenty-fourth. Those of the news staff of the great newspapers who have been close to the operations here are almost unanimously of your frame of mind, and I appreciate it more than I can tell you. I'll treasure your letter as long as I live."[26]

Chapter 6

WINDOW TO THE WHITE HOUSE

"The two high points in the whole (first) nine days were the appearance before Congress on Monday and the press conference on Tuesday."

THE WHITE HOUSE PRESS CONFERENCE HAS BEEN CALLED the president's "front-page pulpit."[1] Since 1932, at least, the institution has undoubtedly proved itself as an unmatched news outlet for the chief executive as well as a valuable news source for correspondents. Whether Truman made as much use of the press conference as his predecessor has been debated in a number of studies,[2] but that question is not pertinent here. What is relevant is the record of Truman's manner of conducting his conferences with the working press.

Truman held his first press and radio conference five days after he took the oath of office. He held his last one just five days before leaving the White House in January 1953. In the intervening period of nearly eight years, he met the newsmen in a total of 324 conferences at fairly regular weekly intervals. While most of these were general conferences open to authorized press representatives, approximately a dozen were held for restricted groups, such as the executive committee of the Negro Newspaper Publishers Association[3] or the editors of monthly magazines of the Standard Railroad Labor Organization.[4]

In addition to the special conferences, there were eight budget seminars devoted entirely to a study of the annual budget coincident with its submission to the Congress each January. These sessions were disproportionately long as compared with the ordinary press conferences. The longest on record, number 164 (January 8, 1949), contained approximately 12,440 words. The average length of the press conference was three thousand to four thousand words. The shortest of all filled less than a page in the official transcript:

> *Voice:* Welcome home!
> *The President:* I am glad to be here. The finest place in the world, the United States is! Ed [Ed Lockett, *Time* magazine] How are you?
> *Mr. Lockett:* Fine, sir.
> (*two pictures were taken at this point*)
> *The President:* Is everybody here?
> *Mr. Ross:* I think they're all in, Mr. President; yes, they're all in.
> *The President:* I have only a simple announcement to make. I can't hold a regular press conference today; but this announcement is so important I thought I would call you in. *Russia has declared war on Japan!* That is *all!*
> (*Much applause and laughter, as the reporters rushed out.*)[5]

The president's first press conference was, in most ways, typical of the 323 that were to follow.[6] The notable exception was that it broke all records for attendance, exceeding the number present at any conference held by Roosevelt and packing 348 newsmen into the executive office and adjacent corridors.[7] Pollard quotes *Editor & Publisher* as saying that Truman began his presidency with "a larger acquaintance among newspapermen than Hoover or Coolidge ever enjoyed or than Roosevelt had" in 1933.[8] According to Admiral Leahy, who was present at the president's first meeting with the press on April 17, 1945, Truman acquitted himself well. Leahy later wrote: "His direct, positive way of handling the news gatherers was very pleasing to me."[9]

Truman apparently did not feel some of the confidence himself that Leahy observed in him, judging from a paragraph in a letter to his mother and sister the day after the press conference: "Tuesday morning all the reporters in town and a lot more came to cross question me. They gave me a pretty hefty fifteen minutes, but even that ordeal seemed to click."[10] And in a second letter to his mother and sister three days later, the new president again referred pointedly to that first press conference. The first part of the letter reads as follows:

Blair House
1651 Pennsylvania Avenue

April 21, 1945

Dear Mamma & Mary:

Well, I've been the President for nine days. And such nine days no one ever went through before I don't believe. The job started at 5:30 on the afternoon of the 12th. It was necessary for me to begin making decisions an hour and a half before I was sworn in and I've been making them ever since.

The two high points in the whole nine days were the appearance before Congress on Monday and the Press Conference on Tuesday. Evidently from the comments in all the papers and magazines both appearances are successful.[11]

Because of the extraordinary attention that was focused on Truman's first press conference and in view of the fact that he placed it in his own thinking on a level of importance with his appearance before the joint session of Congress, the record of that conference is included here. The transcript itself provides one of the best pictures of Truman's beginning relations as president with the representatives of the working press and reveals more clearly than abbreviated excerpts can the short, direct answers that were to become typical of Truman's method of dealing with the questions that were fired at him.

The transcript of White House Press and Radio Conference number 1 follows:

The President: Good morning—good morning.

Q: Will you take it sort of slow for us today, please, sir?

The President: Surely—surely. Anything I can do to accommodate you.

Mr. Daniels: (*to the president*) The boys say, will you speak fairly slowly?

The President: Yes, I will do that. (*then standing up*) Is everybody here?

Voices: No, sir! (*laughter*)

Q: They will let you know, sir.

The President: All right.

Q: We have a quorum this morning, sir.

Q: He will yell . . .

The President: (*interposing*) I judge we have—I judge we have.

Q: He will yell "all in," when they are all in.

The President: (*sitting down*) All right.

(*a pause here, as great numbers of newspapermen and women continued to come into the room. Still photographers began taking pictures*)

The President: It looks like they are all here.

Q: Have you had any official complaints from the boys yet, about the early hours you keep? (*laughter*)

Q: We are going to write you a formal note, sir.

The President: (*laughing*) Oh, yes?

Q: Probably do some of us good to get up early. (*more laughter*) It will get us to bed earlier at night.

The President: You just wait. I haven't started yet. Wait until I really get busy. Wait until I *really* start to work.

Q: I heard you were later than usual. Is eight-thirty late for you, sir?

The President: Yes. I left home at eight-thirty. I usually leave home at eight.

Mr. Daniels: (*to the president*) They will give us the signal when they are all in.

The President: All right.

Q: Got a full house today, sir.

Q: This looks like an all-time high. (*newspapermen and women overflowing into the corridors and on the porch*)

Q: (*indicating*) Who is he?

The President: His name is Reinsch—Leonard Reinsch. Let me see, how do you spell it? R-E-I-N-(s)-C-H. He is going to help—I will tell you about it, so that everybody can hear.

(*another pause here, as newspapermen continue to come in*)

The President: I am waiting for the "starter gun." I wish I was in a "high chair" where I could see everybody.

Q: You ought to use the National Theatre for this.

The President: I should.

Q: I have never seen it this crowded.

Mr. Donaldson: All in.

Mr. Daniels: (*to the president*) All in, Mr. President.

(cries of "Sh-sh-sh")

The President (standing up): The first thing I want to do to you is to read the rules: "News emanating from the president's [press and radio] conferences with the press will continue to be divided in categories already known to you, and in keeping with the practice of President Roosevelt's news meetings with the press. These categories are: first, off the record, confidential announcements which are to be kept secret by the newspapermen attending the conferences and not passed on by them to outsiders. Background—or not for attribution—information which may be given to the press for its guidance and used, the source of which cannot be published nor disclosed. In other words, it cannot be attributed to the president. News information which may be attributed to the president, when it is given to the press by the president at his conferences, but which cannot be directly quoted. Statements by the president cannot be directly quoted unless he gives special permission."

Now, I have asked Mr. Early and Mr. Hassett, Mr. Daniels, and Judge Rosenman, and they have offered to stay and help me get things organized, for which I am very grateful. And my staff will stand the training with those gentlemen.

I have asked Mr. Connelly to be my confidential secretary. Mr. Reinsch is going to help me with . . .

Voices: (aside) What? Reinsch? Reinsch?

The President: (continuing) —press and radio affairs.

Q: Mr. President, can you give us that full name?

The President: Matthew J. Connelly.

Q: How do you spell it?

The President: Leonard Reinsch. Connelly spells it the Irish way. *(laughter)*

Q: How does Mr. Reinsch spell his name?

The President: How is that?

Q: Reinsch—how does he spell his name?

The President: R-E-I-N-C-H—S-C-H—S—there's an S in there. I forgot the S.

Q: Can we have something about where he is from?

The President: He has been a radio executive for Governor Cox. Mr. Connelly has been with me all the time. Mr. Reinsch was connected with the National Committee during the last campaign as the radio expert for the National Committee. So I got acquainted with him. And he is efficient, I will tell you that. And so is Mr. Connelly. So are all these other gentlemen. That is no reflection on anybody, you understand? *(laughter)*

I received a communication from Mrs. Roosevelt which I want to read to you. You will be given a mimeographed copy of it as you go out. This is dated April 16, 1945.

(reading): "My dear Mr. President: There have been many thousands of letters, telegrams and cards sent to me and my children, which have brought great comfort and consolation to all of us. This outpouring of affection and thought has touched us all deeply, and we wish it were possible to thank each and every one individually. My children and I feel, in view of the fact that we are faced with the paper shortage and are asked not to use paper when it can be avoided, that all we can do is express our appreciation collectively. We would therefore consider it a great favor if you would be kind enough to express our gratitude for us. Sincerely, Eleanor Roosevelt."

Now, there has been some question as to where I stand on various things, particularly Bretton Woods. And I am for it. We need an international monetary setup. And I would have supported that proposition had I stayed in the Senate, and I would have done everything I possibly could as vice president to help the president get it through the Senate. I am for it all the way. I hope that is plain enough.

Q: Does that include also the monetary fund—stabilization . . .

The President: (interposing) It includes the program as sent to the Congress by the president. That is as plain as I can make it. And I believe that's all. If you want to ask me anything, I will try to answer; and if I don't know, I will tell you.

Q: Mr. President, . . .

Q: (interposing) Mr. President, in that same connection, would you say, just for the record, on reciprocal trade, has the president requested . . .

The President: (interposing) Yes. That was the other thing I wanted to mention.

Q: (continuing) . . . about the Export-Import Bank.

The President: *(continuing)* I am for the Reciprocal Trade Agreements program. Always have been for it. I think you will find in the record where I stood before, when it was up in the Senate before, and I haven't changed.

Q: What about the Johnson Act repeal?

The President: You mean the Johnson Act now pending for repeal?

Q: No, the Johnson Act which prohibits loans by private individuals to the defaulted governments.

The President: Well, that is a matter I will have to look into and study. I haven't given it any thought. I can't answer that question at this time. I will answer it for you later.

Q: Mr. President . . .

Q: (interposing) Mr. President, are you going ahead with the public power ambitions of your predecessor?

The President: Wherever it is possible and necessary, I am.

Q: Mr. President, in that connection the term of T.V.A. Chairman—(*cries of "Sh-sh-sh"*)—Lilienthal will be expiring in a few months . . .

The President: (interposing) I am not discussing appointments this morning of any sort.

Q: Yes, sir.

The President: I am—when it comes to me to meet that situation, I will meet it; and you will know about it.

Q: Mr. President, could you tell us how you feel about the Missouri Valley Authority?

The President: I think I made a speech in New Orleans endorsing the Missouri Valley Authority. I advise you to read that speech.

Q: Mr. President, probably as much as any group the passing of President Roosevelt is very keenly felt by the Negroes in America, as they looked upon him as sort of a symbol of justice and equal opportunity. I wonder if you would comment on the things that they were so specifically interested in and felt they knew where the president stood: on the Fair Employment Practice, the right to vote without being hampered by poll taxes, and all that?

The President: I will give you some advice. All you need to do is to read the Senate record of one Harry S Truman.

Q: Mr. President, do you mind discussing a companion piece to the Missouri Valley Authority, about the St. Lawrence? Can you tell us anything about that.

The President: I don't want to discuss that this morning.

Q: Thank you.

Q: Mr. President . . .

Q: (*interposing*) Mr. President, do you have any . . .

Q: (*interposing*) Mr. President, is there any possibility that you will go to the United Nations Conference at San Francisco near the end?

The President: There is not.

Q: Will you send a message, Mr. President, to the San Francisco conference?

The President: I shall probably welcome the delegates by an opening statement, when they arrive for their first meeting.

Q: Thank you.

Q: Over the radio?

The President: Yes.

Q: Could you tell us, Mr. President, some of the considerations that led to your decision not to go to San Francisco?

The President: I have a competent delegation going to San Francisco to negotiate and represent the interest of the United States. I shall back them up from this desk right here—(*knocking on it*)—where I belong.

Q: Do you expect to see Mr. Molotov before he goes across . . .

The President: (*interposing*) Yes, I do.

Q: *(continuing)* . . . before he goes to San Francisco?

The President: Yes. He is going to stop by and pay his respects to the president of the United States. He should.

Q: When do you expect him to arrive? *(laughter and applause interrupting)*

Q: Can you tell us something about your visit with the American delegation this morning?

Q: Mr. President, will Mr. [Secretary of State James F.] Byrnes go to San Francisco in any capacity?

The President: He will not. Mr. Byrnes is going back to South Carolina, and when I need his advice I shall send for him.

Q: Have you any plans for Mr. Byrnes to take any public office?

The President: I have not.

Q: Mr. President, do you have a desire, as soon as possible, to meet the other Allied leaders—Marshal Stalin and Prime Minister Churchill?

The President: I should be very happy to meet them, and General Chiang Kai-shek also. And General De Gaulle; if he wants to meet me I will be glad to see him. I would like to meet all of the Allied heads of governments.

Q: Have you initiated any move towards that end, Mr. President?

The President: I have not.

Q: Mr. President, do you approve of the work of the Truman Committee? *(much laughter)*

The President: There was another announcement I wanted to make. It was about these press conferences. Due to the fact that I have such a terrific burden to assume, I am going to have only one press conference a week. I shall have one in the morning and one in the afternoon—turnabout—week about. And I shall have that press conference on the days in the middle of the week as soon as I think I have something to say, or news to give out; and you will be notified in plenty of time so that you can come right down here Tuesday, Wednesday, or Thursday of each week; but I am not setting any specific day nor any specific hour, but to say that one will be in the morning and the next one will be in the afternoon.

Q: Mr. President, will Mrs. Truman have a press conference?

The President: Beg your pardon?

Q: Will Mrs. Truman have a regular press conference?

The President: I would rather not answer that question at this time. Mrs. Roosevelt is having her last meeting with the ladies of the press on Thursday, and that question will be answered at a later date.

Q: Mr. President, there are published reports that your administration plans to lift the ban on horseracing. Can you comment on that?

Voices: (*interposing*) Louder—louder.

The President: Say it again, so that they can hear it. (*laughter*)

Q: Mr. President, there are published reports that your administration plans to lift the ban on horseracing. Can you comment on that?

The President: I do not intend to lift the ban.

Q: Mr. President, . . .

Q: (*interposing*) Mr. President, can you give us your views on the disposal of synthetic rubber plants?

The President: No, I cannot. That is not a matter for discussion here. It will be discussed at the proper time.

Q: Mr. President, can you say anything about cabinet?

The President: No. Of course, I asked the cabinet to remain. That is as much as I want to say.

Q: Mr. President, . . .

Q: (*interposing*) Mr. President, what is your feeling . . .

The President: (*interposing*) Let this fellow have a chance back here. *You're* in the front row. (*laughter*)

Q: Does that statement of yours on horseracing apply to the ban on the brownout and the curfew too?

The President: I think they have done a lot of good for the morale all over the country, and I have no intention of pushing Mr. Byrnes' office. Somebody over here? (*indicating another questioner*)

Q: Started to ask you if that applied after VE-Day?

The President: Let's wait for VE-Day to come, and I will take care of the situation at that time. Now, what was your question? I beg your pardon, the lady wants to ask a question. (*laughter*)

Q: Mr. President, there is a story out that Stalin had reached an agreement with the new Polish government approved by the United States and Britain. Can you comment?

The President: I don't want to discuss that at this conference. Now, what was your question?

Q: It has been asked, sir. (*much laughter*)

Q: Thank you, Mr. President.

The President: Well! Thank you!
(*applause for the president*)
Mr. Daniels: (*to the president*) That was good.
The President: That was all right?
Mr. Daniels: Yes, sir. Good!
Q: Goodbye, Mr. President.
The President: Goodbye! (*laughter*)
(*The president then shook hands with many of the newspaper-men and women, who all lined up, taking many minutes*)[12]

Chapter 7

THE NO-COMMENT COMMENT

"I used to answer those all the time, and I confused them all the time."

IT CAN BE SURMISED FROM THE RECORD OF THE FIRST
press conference in the preceding chapter that the president was
given to answers that were likely to be abrupt and final. As a
result, his press conferences were generally far shorter than those
of his predecessor, sometimes lasting not more than ten or twenty
minutes.[1] On one occasion, John S. Knight, speaking for
members of the American Society of Newspaper Editors at a
special conference with the president, drew attention to this factor in apologizing for a rather unrewarding session. Knight said:
"Mr. President, I think I should say by way of explanation for the
fact that this may have been a duller news conference than the
ones to which you are accustomed, that in another administration one or two questions were usually good for an entire evening, and your short direct answers—(*laughter*)—direct answers
have rather exhausted the 'well' more rapidly."[2]

Allen observes a trend away from the quickness noticeable in
the early conferences: "Sometimes he answered questions too
quickly and certainly at press conferences; later he learned to be
more cautious, as any president must. The surprising thing is that
he made so few mistakes in those first weeks."[3]

McNaughton and Nehmeyer draw attention to the same
tendency: "Harry Truman had always been frank with reporters.
Sometimes his language was cockleburr rough. He never minced
words. He carried this policy over into the White House, never
realizing its implications. The president's predilection caused him
untold embarrassment. It took him two years to learn that 'no
comment' saves a world of distressful reaction."[4]

The record indicated that Truman did learn the value of circumspection in his answers to the questions that were fired at him
from every angle, but his critics have undoubtedly overplayed the
"embarrassment" that he suffered as a result of his straight-from-the-
shoulder type of answers. After his retirement from office, he made
this observation in connection with his manner of coping with controversial or leading questions: "They're legitimate, but you have to be
on the lookout for them. They are loaded questions. Their objective is
to get a quick answer on something that required further thought,
something that would have to be amended or explained. I used to
answer those all the time, and I confused them all the time. The president always reserved the right to answer those questions he
wanted to."[5]

While Truman's answers to questions began to reflect more circumspection, as pointed out above, they seldom suggested a resort to circumlocution. For example, the following refusal to comment is nevertheless direct:

Q: (Tom Reynolds, *Chicago Sun*) In that connection, sir, do you want to run in 1948? (*much laughter*)
The President: Don't you think you are a little previous on that? When 1948 comes along, I will have to make a decision, which I will make. I am not thinking of 1948 now. I am trying to get through 1946. (*much laughter*)[6]

Usually he declined without equivocation to answer questions that he thought should remain unanswered, as in the following instance:

Q: Mr. President, can you say how soon American divisions will be moving . . .
The President: (*interposing*) No, I can't—No, I can't. As I say, if I could I wouldn't tell you. You fellows ought to have some idea of security the same as I have.
Q: Well, perhaps this question doesn't violate security?
The President: All right.
Q: Will it be a National Guard division?
The President: I can't answer that.[7]

When reporters occasionally badgered the president for some particularly newsworthy piece of information that he was unwilling to release, he would sometimes bring the questioning to an impasse. In July 1949, after a secret conference behind locked doors at Blair House on the subject of international policy regarding atomic power, newsmen tried repeatedly in a press conference to pry some statement regarding the conference from the president. The quizzing concluded in this manner:

Q: Was what Tydings said about it later erroneous?
The President: I have no comment to make on it.
Q: Mr. President, . . .
The President: (*interposing*) That is as far as I am going. I just won't answer any questions about it at all.

Q: Mr. President, when you say relatively . . .
The President: (*continuing*) I'll just "no comment" them all.[8]

The most fruitless, perhaps, of all the president's press conferences, as far as the correspondents were concerned, was number 256. After racking up fifteen straight "no comments," Truman remarked, "I hate to treat you this way. I would like to give you a lot of headlines."[9] Then followed five more "no comment" answers. The session closed on a slightly ironic note:

Q: I think we might as well give up, Mr. President . . .
Q: (*interposing*) Have we—have we overlooked anything? (*laughter*)
The President: Tony says we ought to give up. No, I have no further comments, Smitty.
Q: Thank you.
The President: I will answer any questions you have got on your mind. (*more laughter*)[10]

This was a regular press conference on a number of varied topics, but the president had objections to most of the questions that were put to him. In addition to the twenty expressed "no comments," he quashed other questions with such favorite expressions as "I'd advise you to read history" or "I'll cross that bridge when I come to it."[11]

Evasiveness, however, did not seem to be a basic characteristic of Truman's answers, even though it did appear from time to time. The sheer number of flat refusals to make an answer to objectionable questions is indication that he was not afraid to exercise the presidential prerogative to decline to commit himself. Very often, the evasiveness was in the questioning itself. Truman often answered indirect questions with indirect comments, but his replies to direct questions were likewise straightforward. The following illustrates that evasiveness could often be attributed to the questioner rather than to the president himself:

Q: We have information in St. Louis that General Vaughn has telephoned Missouri Democratic leaders, asking them what they think about your running for the Senate. Did you know he was doing that?
The President: General Vaughn didn't do that.
Q: What did he do?

The President: He didn't do anything.

Q: Our information . . .

The President: (*interposing*) He didn't do anything, Pete [Brandt].

Q: He didn't make calls from the White House . . .

The President: (*interposing*) No.

Q: (*continuing*) . . . to the Missouri Democrats?

The President: That is — some of them may have called him — first called.

Q: (*interjecting*) No. . . .

The President: (*continuing*) You are talking about the [*St. Louis*] *Post-Dispatch*'s attitude toward General Vaughn — and it isn't the right one.

Q: (*continuing*) . . . what we are primarily interested in is whether you are going to run for the Senate?

The President: Well now, I'll help the situation. I am not.

Q: You are not going to run for the Senate?

The President: I shall not be a candidate for the United States senator from Missouri. (*much laughter*) That satisfies you, doesn't it?

Q: It does.[12]

The president demonstrated a liking for direct questions through to the end of his press conferences. In December 1952, he made a joke out of a reporter's roundabout query as follows:

Q: Richard Balch, Democratic state chairman in New York, was asked whether he thought Jim Farley was a real democratic [sic]. He paused for a while, and the reporter said "No answer?" and Mr. Balch answered "No answer." I wonder if you think Jim Farley . . .

The President: (*interposing*) I have no comment on any comment by anybody else on somebody else. (*laughter*)[13]

One final example is sufficient to demonstrate the president's habit of demanding direct questions from newsmen before he was willing to give direct answers. It was not his inclination to volunteer information, but he seemed ready to provide yes or no replies whenever the question was specifically put to him, as illustrated in the following excerpt:

Q: There has been some speculation that he [J. Edgar Hoover] may replace Mr. McGrath. Is that unfounded?

The President: You mean that he would be attorney general?
Q: Yes sir.
The President: No, that is unfounded.
Q: Mr. President, some young congressman—I have forgotten his name, I think he is from Wisconsin—Republican from Wisconsin—has demanded that you fire Attorney General McGrath.
The President: Well, Eddie, I don't think there's a single member of the cabinet that some congressman hasn't demanded to be fired. They haven't been very successful at that sort of an approach.
Q: Could I put it more pointedly?
The President: Sure.
Q: There were reports—there are reports that you are going to drop Mr. McGrath from the cabinet?
The President: I hadn't heard any of those reports. They haven't reached the White House yet, Eddie.
Q: Is there any—(*laughter*). Are you considering any change, Mr. President, in the post of attorney general? (*more laughter*)
The President: No.
Q: Thank you.
The President: If you had asked it that way in the first place, I would have answered it that way.
Q: I'm sorry—I'm sorry.
The President: It's all right, we have a little fun as we go along.[14]

It is understandable that the president could not always be expected to have at his command information that might be needed to answer certain questions. His advisers, therefore, occasionally suggested in advance answers to expected questions, as revealed in the following document from the director of the Office of War Mobilization and Reconversion:

May 1, 1945

MEMORANDUM FOR THE PRESIDENT
FROM: Fred M. Vinson

If a surrender should be announced, and if you should hold a press conference, you will doubtless be asked many questions about developments on the war mobilization front. Particularly, there will be inquiries about the curfew, the brownout, the horseracing ban and other similar conservation measures.

My staff has prepared an over-all document, in question-and-answer form, relating to developments on the home front in the reconversion, war production, conservation and all similar matters. It represents the considered and harmonized views of all interested government agencies. It has been cleared with all of them, and is being kept up to date on an hourly basis. Prior to the time of its release, I shall submit it to you for your perusal.

It is my plan to release this document at a press conference two days after the announcement of a surrender. Until that time, I have requested the heads of home front agencies to make no statements or comments regarding these matters.

Therefore, if any questions are asked regarding these matters, I think it would be advisable for you to state that I shall hold the press conference on V-E plus-2 (that is, two days after your announcement) and at that time will answer all questions which can be answered. Any premature announcement on these matters would have a disruptive effect on the administrative agencies, who must have a day or so to prepare the orders and announcements necessary to effectuate whatever changes or relaxations will go into effect.[15]

There is no indication in the transcripts of the press conferences subsequent to the above memorandum that Truman made any use of Vinson's suggestion. On February 4, 1946, the president received a similar type of communication from the secretary of the treasury in regard to the pending full employment legislation, two paragraphs of which read as follows:

If the President is asked at a press conference what he thinks of the Bill, I would recommend that he merely say he has already stated his position, is not familiar with the details of the Bill and will make his comments when it is sent to him for signature.

If, however, the President wishes to say more, I would suggest an approach along these lines: While the Bill does not mention full employment and full production, he considers the substance of the Bill to amount to the same things. He is not so much concerned with the words used as with what is done, and will administer the Bill as a full employment and full production Bill which he understands it to be. He should also stress the setting up of a Joint Congressional Committee, which is probably the most important single feature of the Bill.[16]

Oddly enough, no question was asked concerning this bill until the day after it was signed on February 20—that is, at press conference number 49, February 21, 1946.

On only one occasion does the record show that Truman made direct use of a premeditated answer submitted to him by one of the federal agencies. The secretary of agriculture sent him the following technical information in a memorandum dated February 6, 1946:

Two questions which may be asked at your press conference tomorrow and the answers are as follows:

Question: How much wheat is the United States going to ship to starving peoples?
Answer: The need for food is so great that we should like to export from this country, if at all possible, as much as 6,000,000 tons of wheat in the first half of 1946. The measures I have ordered put into effect should make it possible to come closer to what we would like to do by 500,000 to 1,000,000 tons.
Question: How much food are we sending to liberated countries?
Answer: The food—wheat, fats, and oils, meats, rice, dairy products, canned fish, dried fruits, and other products—which

we plan to export during the first six months of 1946 will provide about fifty million people with a diet of 2,000 calories a day
for the same period. Actually many more than one hundred
million people will get some portion of this food as we will
endeavor to make distribution where it is most urgently
needed.[17]

How the president adapted this information to his own use appears in these remarks which he made at his press conference on the
next day: "It is proposed under this program which we have inaugurated, that we hope to be able to ship 6 million tons of wheat in
the first half of 1946. Now, if anybody needs a lesson in arithmetic,
that is about 200 million bushels. The measures ordered should make
it possible for us to come closer to what we want to do by about five
hundred thousand or a million tons. Wheat and other food products
which we plan to export during the first six months of this year will
provide 50 million people with a diet of two thousand calories a day
for a six month period."[18]

So far as the transcripts of the press conferences disclose, this was
about as heavily as Truman ever cared to rely on prepared answers.
He seemed to prefer to formulate his own answers on the basis of
whatever information and advice he could gather on technical as well
as general subjects. When he felt unsure of his ability to give an
answer to a specific question, his practice was to decline altogether or
to qualify his answer as, for instance, in the following illustration
from the same press conference:

> *Q:* Mr. President, does this 6 million tons represent an increase
> in our commitments, or a decrease in our commitments?
> *The President:* No. There is, I think, a slight decrease in our first
> commitments. You will have to get those figures categorically
> from the secretary of agriculture, who has been the conferee with
> our Allies in this setup.[19]

An examination of the evidence indicates an almost complete
absence of "planted" or "fixed" answers given by the president in the
guise of spontaneous or offhand replies to questions. He occasionally
read prepared statements, but these were identified as such and were
usually made available to reporters in mimeographed form at the

close of the conference. The "planted" question, on the other hand, appears to have been an active factor commonly employed by government officials who desired presidential publicity concerning their projects. This is demonstrated in the following excerpt from a memorandum sent to Press Secretary Charles Ross by a state department publicity officer who was interested in getting a favorable statement from the president regarding the work of the American Committee on United Europe: "I have discussed the matter with the Office of European Affairs here in the department. It would be my recommendation that the president not issue a special statement on the subject, but that if a correspondent at the president's press conference should ask him a question (which you might arrange for) as to whether he had seen the reports of statements by the European statesmen, the president might reply that he had been very much encouraged to note the wide interest and support on the part of leading Europeans for European integration and unity."[20]

This practice on the part of government publicity men was one of which the correspondents were well aware. At a meeting that Secretary Ross held with a committee of the White House correspondents for the purpose of discussing proposed changes in procedure of the conferences, Ross asked a question that stimulated some revealing comments on the role of the publicity director of his departments and agencies. The discussion follows:

Ross: Would you be willing to cut down on the number of your people so we could cut down on the attendance some? How many have we been having at the conferences?

Ayers: Running from 125 to 138.

Q: I think you have a point here. There are a lot of free-loaders. It is quite a responsibility saying who should and should not attend a conference. The U.P. usually runs about three people.

Nixon: The I.N.S. has one other person.

Q: One reason for such crowds, I think, is that the government publicity people all come in there. Not only that, but they are pushing up front all the time, and they are in the front row now.

Q: It is quite common now for some of the government personnel to ask reporters to throw questions. The government representatives come in here and try to plant questions with the reporters.

Ross: We don't have more than four or five, do we?

Q: I have seen two or three from the State Department alone. I can give you two from State, one Budget, one Post Office, Agriculture Department, army, navy, at least fifteen or twenty. You could reduce the personnel involved in the press conferences without touching a reporter.

Collingwood: I don't think you should want to cut down on visitors.

Q: I would rather cut out visitors than working reporters.

Ross: What is the function of those others here?

Q: They were interested primarily in the off-the-record remarks that Roosevelt used to make. President Truman doesn't use that. The understanding at that time was that the government people stayed in the back of the room.

Ross: They stay in the back of the room and make notes; they don't ask questions now, do they?

Q: No, but they ask us to ask questions. A public relations man for a government department's prime function is to hurry to inform the agency head how the humor of the president appeared, etc., and also to tell them of any questions pertaining to that department.

Ross: They could get the report on the press conference a lot faster on the ticker. How many people bring stenographers in?

Q: I have noticed recently there were four stenographers. The State Department has two stenographers in there.

Ayers: The State Department uses one and the Voice of America uses one.

Q: Then there is another stenographer always in there. The State Department has four or five people in there.[21]

Chapter 8

SLIPS AND QUIPS

"So I don't let these things bother me for the simple reason I know that I am trying to do the right thing and eventually the facts will come out."

TRUMAN'S METHOD OF ANSWERING QUESTIONS RAPIDLY
and unequivocally produced several embarrassing incidents for which
he was roundly scored by his critics. While the charges ranged from
mere ineptness at handling questions to deliberate misrepresentation
or concealment of the truth, the record indicates that the president's
method, rather than his motive, was chiefly at fault in such instances.
At the beginning of the transcript of Truman's twentieth press conference, this brief exchange with Secretary Ross is recorded:

> *Mr. Ross (sitting at the president's desk):* I don't think of
> anything else.
> *The President:* Well, you watch me, and if I get off on the wrong
> line — I made one harmless little statement about the politics
> situation; it didn't mean a thing — I was just kidding with them.
> But there was an editorial on that. I'll answer them the best I can
> and if I can't answer them I'll tell them so.[1]

From the beginning of his administration, critics found the president's frankness and naivete difficult to believe. When McNaughton
and Hehmeyer wrote about the special press conference which
Truman held at Reelfoot Lake, Tennessee, in October 1945 — at which
he stated that the United States would retain its monopoly of the
atomic bomb — they dramatized the incident as follows: "There was a
wild scramble as reporters jostled from the lodge a few minutes later,
to rush out bulletins quoting the president to the effect that the atom
secret would be withheld by the United States. A cold shiver went up
and down the world's spine. It jolted the man who had not yet formed
any fixed atomic policy. He had not yet learned that when he spoke,
he spoke not as a plain citizen, but as a leader of the foremost nation
of the world.[2]

Official clarifications of disputable answers were sometimes
prepared by the press secretary's office in mimeographed form for
distribution to correspondents at the close of the same press conference in which the questionable statement has originated. The first
of these was issued on December 12, 1945, and read:

At the press conference the President was asked the following
question and made the following answer:

Q: Mr. President, no legislation will be necessary [on price ceilings]?
The President: No, because this is under the War Powers Act.

The President made this reply under a misapprehension. Legislation *is* necessary to fix price ceilings. The memorandum issued today points that out on Page 3, Section 3.

Legislation is not necessary for the establishment of priorities on building materials; and, as indicated in Section 2, on page 3 of the memorandum, priorities are being set up under the War Powers Act without legislation.

The President in answering the question was under the impression that the question referred to priorities rather than price ceilings.[3]

The need for corrections such as the one above and the possibility of the occurrence of errors of this nature can be easily understood and accepted as inevitable from time to time. But a clarification that was considered "the most painful and costly incident in Mr. Truman's early public relations after he entered the White House"[4] was required in connection with Truman's handling of the Wallace-Byrnes issue, in which two important members of his cabinet were at odds on United States foreign policy at a critical moment. The embarrassment began with the president's confirmation of the fact that he had approved Wallace's antiadministration Madison Square Garden address in advance:

Q: Mr. President, in a speech for delivery tonight, Secretary of State—I mean Commerce—Wallace (*laughter*) has this to say about the middle of it, When president . . .
The President: (*interposing*) Well now, you say the speech is to be delivered?
Q: It is, sir.
The President: Well, I—can't answer questions on a speech that is to be delivered.
Q: It mentions you, which is the reason I ask, sir.
The President: Well, that's fine. I'm glad it does. What was the question? Go ahead. Maybe I can answer it. (*much laughter*)

Q: In the middle of the speech are these words, When President Truman read these words, he said that they represented the policy of this administration.
The President: That is correct.
Q: My question is, does that apply just to that paragraph, or to the whole speech?
The President: I approved the whole speech.
Q: The whole speech. Thank you sir.[5]

Later in the conference, a reporter probed the president once more on his unanticipated endorsement of a man who was publicly opposing Truman's own foreign policy:

Q: Mr. President, do you regard Wallace's speech a departure from Byrnes' policy . . .
The President: (*interjecting*) I do not.
Q: (*continuing*) . . . toward Russia?
The President: (*continuing*) They are exactly in line.[6]

Truman was not long in realizing the seriousness of the error he had committed. Within forty-eight hours, he called a special press conference at which no questions were entertained, and the following statement was read by the president: "There has been a natural misunderstanding regarding the answer I made to a question at the press conference on Thursday, September 12th, with reference to the speech of the secretary of commerce delivered in New York later that day. The question was answered extemporaneously and my answer did not convey the thought I intended it to convey. It was my intention to express the thought that I approved the right of the secretary of commerce to deliver the speech. I did not intend to indicate that I approved the speech as constituting a statement of the foreign policy of this country. There has been no change in the established foreign policy of our government. There will be no significant change in the policy without discussion and conference among the president, the secretary of state, and congressional leaders."[7]

The bitterest criticism of this attempt to rectify the mistake appeared in the next issue of *Time,* which said: "By this clumsy lie, the president of the United States got himself out of the impossible situation in which his clumsiness had landed him."[8]

Truman's motives are not up for examination here; the methods that he employed in his relations with the working press are. It would appear that the above incident resulted from his tendency toward trigger-quick, candid answers—a hazard that has to be included in any consideration or appraisal of the method itself. A question that Truman answered extemporaneously with respect to the atomic bomb resulted once again in a hasty clarification. While the Korean conflict was in progress, the following exchange took place at a press conference:

> *Q:* In other words, if the United Nations resolution should authorize General MacArthur to go further than he has, he will . . .
> *The President:* (*interposing*) We will take whatever steps are necessary to meet the military situation, just as we always have.
> *Q:* Will that include the atomic bomb?
> *The President:* That includes every weapon that we have.
> *Q:* Mr. President, you said "every weapon that we have." Does that mean that there is active consideration of the use of the atomic bomb?
> *The President:* There has always been active consideration of its use. I don't want to see it used. It is a terrible weapon, and it should not be [used] on innocent men, women, and children who have nothing whatever to do with this military aggression. That happens when it is used.[9]

Toward the close of the conference, a United Press correspondent checked the president on his earlier statement to be sure he had heard it correctly:

> *Q:* Mr. President, I wonder if we could retrace that reference to the atom bomb? Did we understand you clearly that the use of the atomic bomb is under active consideration?
> *The President:* Always has been, Smitty [Merriman Smith]. It is one of our weapons.[10]

Immediately after this conference, the press secretary issued the following explanatory note:

November 30, 1950

IMMEDIATE RELEASE

The President wants to make it certain that there is no misinterpretation of his answers to questions at his press conference today about the use of the atom bomb. Naturally, there has been consideration of this subject since the outbreak of hostilities in Korea, just as there is consideration of the use of all military weapons whenever our forces are in combat.

Consideration of the use of any weapon is always implicit in the very possession of that weapon.

However, it should be emphasized, that, by law, only the President can authorize the use of the atom bomb, and no such authorization has been given. If and when such authorization should be given, the military commander in the field would have charge of the tactical delivery of the weapon.

In brief, the replies to the questions at today's press conference do not represent any changes in this situation.[11]

The above incident draws attention to the fact that Truman had a tendency to take newsmen into his confidence without retreating to off-the-record territory as his predecessor, Franklin D. Roosevelt, was wont to do. Truman seemed to cherish an unexpressed faith that those in whom he confided would exercise careful judgment and restraint in interpreting his statements to "outsiders," and quite naturally he felt that this trust was broken by reporters trained to deal with the president as a news source. For example, the above incident resulted in a sensational article in the subsequent issue of *New Yorker*, in which John Hersey announced that Truman would use the atom bomb in Korea.[12]

There is an implication in the transcripts of the press conferences of Truman's last two years in office that he made some effort to avoid such incidents as these. A reporter asked if Truman intended to have any private conversations with President-elect Eisenhower during the conferences to which the latter had been invited at the White House. Truman replied: "None whatever. Anything I say to him he is at liberty to quote. He has quoted a great many things already, some of it kind of garbled, but it's all right. (*laughter*)"[13]

A week later, the president seemed to sense that he was being maneuvered into another front-page performance, and he good-naturedly reneged on his earlier statement:

Q: Well, last week you said that General Eisenhower had sometimes garbled some of the things you said. I wonder if you would tell us just what . . .

The President: (*interposing*) Did I say that, Tony?

Q: Yes.

Q: We asked you about him in connection with that invitation, and you said that he had always spoken pretty freely — some words to that effect — and you said sometimes he had garbled what you said.

The President: Maybe I said he got mixed up. I don't think I said he garbled that at all. All of us do that, including reporters.[14]

Truman's inclination to speak his mind honestly, regardless of the consequences, persisted to the end, although there is again evidence that he had learned the value of clarifying his statements before any damage could be done. This is demonstrated in the following excerpt from one of his last press conferences, in which he gets an assist from his press secretary:

Q: I want to get it straight — you said that you thought that it [Eisenhower's trip to Korea] would serve no good purpose, it's just a piece of demagoguery, and that is what it turned out to be?

The President: That's correct. What's the matter?

Q: The current trip that is now a piece of demagoguery?

The President: Yes. The announcement of that trip was a piece of demagoguery, then of course he had to make it. He made the statement. What's the matter, Tony [Vaccaro]? (*Here Roger Tubby spoke to the president*) Well, Roger suggested that maybe some good might come out of the trip. If it does, I will be the happiest man in the world. I hope some good can come out of it.[15]

At the next press conference, the president wisely refused to enlarge on his original statement:

Q: Mr. President, to make sure I understand that earlier remark, what you said last week about General Eisenhower's trip to Korea being . . .

The President: (*interposing*) I said I had nothing to add to it and nothing to take away from it. That's all the statement I made.

Q: Acting a demagogue?

The President: I said — I didn't mention — I didn't mention that at all. I said I had said what I had to say last week, and had nothing to add to it and nothing to take away from it. That's all I said.

Q: Mr. President, your opinion is still the same then?

The President: Oh yes. My opinion hasn't changed.[16]

In summary, it is obvious that Truman was entirely consistent in his method of dealing with questions. He was reluctant to alter his method even after it precipitated some painful experiences in his relations with the press. He wanted to be understood and preferred to speak his thoughts in unadorned language before the press as before his intimate acquaintances. Consequently, the conviction grew with him that even members of the working press that he favored were not above taking unfair advantage of him on occasion.

But he did not allow this feeling to affect substantially his pleasant relations with the working press or to daunt his spirits in dealing with them. With a cheerful philosophy born of his thorough grounding in the history of the experiences of past presidents, Truman reflected that one of his predecessors "was thoroughly misrepresented, and it took fifty years to get at the truth. So I don't let these things bother me for the simple reason I know that I am trying to do the right thing, and eventually the facts will come out. I'll probably be holding a conference with Saint Peter when that happens."[17]

Chapter 9

TEMPER TANTRUMS?

"I am getting tired of all this foolishness, and I'm going to 'bust loose' on you one of these days."

IN THE GIVE AND TAKE BETWEEN PRESIDENT AND NEWSMEN during the course of 324 conferences, there is ample evidence that Truman more than held his own. The brusqueness with which he characteristically answered questions may have created some embarrassment for him occasionally, but it much more regularly created embarrassment for the reporters to whom such answers were directed.

In almost every tart exchange between Truman and one of the correspondents — there were probably not more than twenty-five during his ninety-three months in office — some flavor of the president's particular brand of humor is discernible. Some examples from the record demonstrate nothing more than good-natured teasing, while others give evidence that his sarcastic humor sometimes got out of hand. The following instances illustrate the joshing attitude that was typical of Truman's frame of mind toward the working press.

> *Q:* That is one point that I think a great many people are going to be interested in, about this balanced budget. I am wondering if you might boil it down to a few words of one syllable that the public can understand?
> *The President:* Well, that's your job . . .[1]
> *Q:* The papers had quite a few stories over there [London], and I was wondering why they couldn't get them the ships, what with the surplus of Liberty ships that we built during the war . . .
> *The President:* (*interposing*) You see a lot of things in the papers, sometimes, that you are not right sure about. (*laughter*)[2]

One of his earliest tiffs with reporters came at a press conference held almost a year after he first took office, but it still was not devoid of humor:

> *The President:* Yes, the cabinet met yesterday, but we didn't discuss the situation.
> *Q:* Where did they meet yesterday, Mr. President? I didn't know about it.
> *The President:* There are lots of things you don't know about. (*laughter*)
> *Q:* I thought we usually have it posted when the full cabinet meets?
> *The President:* Well, sometimes it isn't. (*laughter*)
> *Q:* Mr. President, did you say they did not discuss that situation [French loan]?

The President: Yes, they did not, . . .

Q: (*interposing*) What did they discuss?

The President: (*continuing*) . . . they did not.

Q: What did they discuss?

The President: It's none of your business. (*laughter*)

Q: Mr. President, could you tell us the occasion for holding a sort of cabinet meeting without announcing it?

The President: Well, I can hold a cabinet meeting whenever I choose. I don't have to tell you about the cabinet meeting.[3]

Truman's first biting reprimand at a press conference occurred in October 1947, when he objected to a question that seemed to him somewhat insolent:

Q: Mr. President, is it correct, sir, that General Spaatz is being considered for chief of staff to succeed General Eisenhower?

The President: I have no comment to make on that. I never comment on people I am considering for a job. I will let you know when I make the appointment.

Q: Does that mean you are considering it? (*laughter*)

The President: I have no comment.

Q: (*interposing*) Mr. President . . .

The President: (*continuing*) I don't like questions like that, either.

Q: I'm sorry.[4]

During 1948, the president took two more characteristic digs at the press:

Q: Mr. President, could you name some of the specific recommendations of Mr. Baruch which you endorse?

The President: Just read it and compare it with my program which I took down, in the message on the State of the Union. You can do it yourself.

Q: (*interposing*) Mr. President, are you reappointing . . .

The President: (*continuing*) I am not working for newspapers.[5]

Q: Mr. President, outside of your own efforts, what do you think did most to win the election?

The President: Oh—everybody in the Democratic setup did everything he possibly could to help win the election; and soon as the people got the facts, they voted right. They couldn't get the facts from your columns and things, so I had to go out and tell them.

Q: (*loudly*) Well! (*much laughter*)[6]

In a mild exchange of words concerning the president's decision to produce the hydrogen bomb, Truman showed his willingness to toe the line with reporters:

Q: Mr. President, I am not trying to heckle you on this, . . .
The President: (*interjecting*) That's all right. (*laughter*) Try your best, you can't heckle me.
Q: (*continuing*) Senator McMahon has indicated that he is about to make a speech asking for a nationwide public discussion of the issues raised by the superbomb. To do that, facts about it are necessary. Can we look forward to having some disclosures further than . . .
The President: (*interposing*) No, you cannot look forward to anything except what was stated.[7]

The president fired another sharp reprimand at a reporter in a discussion of the same subject the following week:

Q: Can they [atomic policy and general disarmament policy] be considered together, Mr. President?
The President: No, they cannot.
Q: Are you intending to say that you think public discussion does no good?
The President: No I am not. You needn't put words of that kind into my mouth. I will answer your questions . . .
Q: (*interposing*) I thought I was asking one . . .
The President: (*interposing*) All right, proceed. You don't put any words in my mouth.[8]

More than any other incident recorded in the press conferences, this instance and one other previously mentioned[9] seemed to bring forth the president's genuine ire. He apparently resented more than anything else what he considered attempts to read into his answers sentiments which he had not expressed. Truman repeatedly assured the newsmen that he would answer their questions if he could and would tell them if he could not, and it obviously angered him when they appeared to be putting their own interpretation into his answers.

The memory of the above incident rankled in his mind for two weeks, and his temper flared again when he felt the same approach was being tried by a reporter on February 23, as revealed in the following:

> *Q:* Mr. President, in answering that question about the McCarthy investigation, you said you told the Foreign Relations Committee that you would cooperate in any way to disprove the false charges. You mean by that any way short of delivering these records . . .
> *The President:* (*interposing*) I will answer that question when it comes up. You needn't put words in my mouth, . . .
> *Q:* I didn't mean that at all.
> *The President:* (*continuing*) . . . as I told someone else the other day.[10]

Perhaps the most disturbing action by the president, as far as the White House correspondents were concerned, was his sudden departure from custom in granting a private interview to one member of the group. The story of the famous Krock interview is well told in a few paragraphs by Meyer Berger, a colleague of Arthur Krock on the *New York Times*: "On February 13, 1950, Krock was a guest at a dinner party in F Street arranged by Senator Brien McMahon. President Truman was there and Supreme Court Justice Vinson. Krock mentioned to Justice Vinson that he had conceived the idea of doing a study of the president to show that Truman was neither what his enemies nor what his friends pictured. Krock had just sent a formal request to the White House for an interview with the president. Up to that time, the chief executive had never given a one-man press audience.

"The president, aglow with the good dinner, strolled up to the Justice and the *Times* correspondent. He insisted that they remain seated while he stood. He said, with a nod at Krock, 'I want to talk to the Brain Trust.' Justice Vinson said, 'He has a few questions, Mr. President, that he would like to ask you.' The president said to Krock, 'Just come and see me, and ask 'em.' Krock said, 'I already have a request in the works, Mr. President.' The chief executive told him to forget the formal interview application. He said, 'Just tell Charlie Ross I want to see you.'

"During the interview at the White House next day, Krock took no notes — he rarely ever does, except an occasional date or a direct quotation — then hurried back to the *Times* Bureau in the Albee

Building to get the story on paper while the details were warm. The writing took several hours, and on the way home at 3 A.M., Krock left a copy at the White House. It was returned to him that afternoon, with a few slight word changes, and ran in the [*New York*] *Times* of February 15, 1950:

An Interview with Truman:
He Sees Man's Better Nature
Bringing Peace to Ill World

"Krock had carefully avoided the use of the word 'interview' in his story, but the headline betrayed the story's origin. Other Washington correspondents stormed into Charlie Ross' office to protest against the president's granting audience to one newspaperman instead of to representatives of all newspapers, but the president ignored the protests."[11]

This unexpected action by the president was apparently an impulsive decision that he felt was his to make at any time. His violation of the longstanding White House custom was all the more remarkable when viewed in the light of an earlier statement that Truman made in a letter to the editor of the *Texas City Sun*: "It is not possible to give special interviews to individual reporters, to special writers, or other people who have an interest in selling their wares. People who furnish the country with news must all be treated alike, and that is what we endeavor to do."[12]

In an atmosphere charged with resentment, the reporters assembled for the first press conference following publication of the exclusive interview. The usual preliminary exchange of pleasantries was noticeably missing, and the opening question introduced the touchy subject which was developed in the following manner:

Q: Mr. President, was that interview authorized in that form?
The President: It was.
Q: Mr. President, does that represent a softening of your attitude toward columnists, and vice versa?
The President: No, it does not.
Q: Mr. President . . .

The President: (*interposing*) May I say to you gentlemen right now—you seem to be in a kind of disgruntled mood this morning (*laughter*) that the president is his own free agent. He will see whom he pleases, when he pleases, and say what he pleases to anybody that he pleases. And he is not censored by you or by anybody else. I have tried my best to be as courteous to you gentlemen as I possibly can be, and I expect to continue that. But I don't like your attitude this morning, so just cool off. (*more laughter*)

Q: Mr. President, inasmuch as I am not disgruntled . . .

The President: (*interjecting*) Of course you are not—of course you are not.

Q: (*continuing*) . . . I might say to you, sir, as I used to work in the newspaper game (*laughter*) that that particular type of thing is a—these fellows feel, I think, that it is a reflection on every bureau chief and reporter in the White House . . .

The President: (*interposing*) It is nothing of the kind.

Q: I beg your pardon?

The President: It is nothing of the kind.

Q: That is their attitude, and I hope that you will pardon me if I bring it to your attention?

The President: That's all right, but it's nothing of the kind. But I don't stand for anybody to edit my actions. I am a free agent, even if I am the president of the United States.

Q: Mr. President, did you intentionally omit "damn"?

The President: Yes, I intentionally omitted it. I could put it in, if you would like to have it? (*laughter*)

Q: Where should it go in, Mr. President—the "damn"? (*more laughter*)

The President: What?

Q: Where does it go in?

The President: Put your question in, and I will edit it for you. (*more laughter*)

Q: Mr. President, . . .

The President: (*interposing*) Now then, have you got any questions that . . .

Q: (*interposing*) Yes, sir.

The President: (*continuing*) I can answer sensibly? If you have, I will listen to them.

Q: I'm sorry—I think this is not a criticism of your right to do as you please, but of our understanding as to whether others may also obtain exclusive and private interviews?

The President: That will—remains to be seen. I will attend to that bridge—I will cross that bridge when I get to it.

Q: Mr. President, could I return with the feeling only of wanting information, . . .

The President: (*interposing*) Sure, I will give you any information I can—that I am capable of.

Q: (*continuing*) that your giving of interviews goes by favor, and there is no longer a rule? We were under the impression that there was a rule which had—custom at least, which had the binding force of a rule?

The President: It is a custom. I will continue that custom, . . .

Q: (*interposing*) But you will . . .

The President: (*continuing*) . . . but I will do as I please with regard to breaking it. (*laughter*)

Q: Yes sir. That is the information that I want.

The President: That is the answer. You have the information. And I am not disgruntled in the slightest. (*more laughter*)

Q: Why should you be?

The President: I am in as good a humor as I can possibly be, but I would like to answer some questions that have a bearing on the present situation.

Q: I will give you one, Mr. President.

Q: (*interposing*) You think our business is quite important, do you?

The President: Sometimes I am not so sure.[13]

Although the president subsequently gave five other personal interviews,[14] none ruffled the feelings of the correspondents as the Krock exclusive had.[15] One indication of the strained relations that existed in the days following the Krock interview is revealed by the complete absence of preconference banter between Truman and the newsmen in the seven sessions which followed number 217. Not until press conference number 225 does the easy, friendly conversation reappear on the transcripts, to remain virtually uninterrupted throughout the remainder of the press conferences.

In 1951, the president firmly restated his policy of exercising his own choice in the matter of private interviews:

Q: A number of reporters have asked for the record on that Wake Island meeting and had been told that they could not get it as the record was with you and could only be given out with your comment. And then Mr. [Anthony] Leviero, who is a very fine reporter, asked for it and got it. I was hoping that in the future if there was anything to be given out — scoops like that — we could all have a chance at it. (*laughter*)

The President: I remember a certain turmoil that was created by an interview I had with Arthur Krock. And some of your people wept and cried, and finally I made a statement that I would talk to anybody I pleased any time I pleased.[16]

The president was not unaware of the effect that his calculated needling sometimes had on members of the working press. At least once he felt called upon to dull the edge of a sharp retort with which he had addressed one of the correspondents. When John Steel, a member of the Senate press gallery, visited the president's news conference one day, he asked the following question and got the following biting answer:

Q: Mr. President, where do you expect the sincere efforts to block the defense effort to come from?

The President: Where it usually comes from. Haven't you been here when the Congress has been in session? How long have you been in this town? (*laughter*)[17]

Truman apparently felt a tinge of guilt, for he sent an apologetic note to Steel a few days later which read:

October 11, 1950

Personal

Memorandum for John L. Steel
                   USS
                   Press Gallery

From: The President

I didn't mean to embarrass you at the Press Conference the other day, but I couldn't forgo the opportunity to make the remark I did. It wasn't possible for me to mention names because some of the names I would have to include in the list would be members of my own Party. Therefore, I thought maybe you could work the thing out to your own satisfaction.

I appreciated your note very much.

HST[18]

Pollard observes that the president displayed "anger or other signs of temper" at his November 16, 1950, press conference, in which he quotes Truman as saying that he was "going to bust loose on the reporters some one of these days."[19] In this instance, Pollard does not have the facts quite accurate; the date of the conference was November 30, 1950, and Truman's statement was, "I am getting tired of all this foolishness, and I'm going to 'bust loose' on you one of these days."[20] It is believed that Pollard is incorrect in his interpretation of the facts as well. Following the president's remark in the transcript is the parenthetical information, "much laughter." It is not likely that an angry mood would have produced much laughter. Also to be considered is the fact that it was the distressing duty of the president at that particular press conference to announce the invasion of Korea by the hordes of Communist troops from across the Chinese border. Such a remark, if a manifestation of tension, is an indulgence for which a head of state confronted by a possible third world war, could surely be pardoned.

There are other signs that Truman was understandably sensitive to reporters' inquiries during the height of the Korean conflict.[21] This is indicated in the following example:

> *May Craig:* Sir, do you consider that my question was confusing?
> *The President:* Yes. Intended for that purpose, May, I think.
> *May Craig:* No sir, it is a — being discussed at the capitol a good deal, that we are at war and that Congress has not declared war.
> *The President:* I have no comment to make on that, May.
> *May Craig:* Yes sir.[22]

Truman's tendency to dress down the reporters with a gruffness that they could not always be sure was merely feigned, continued to the close of his relations with the working press. In January in 1951, when a reporter asked if the president intended to do any more about establishing a Fair Employment Practices Commission as outlined in his State of the Union message, he replied, "Of course I am. I wouldn't put it in there if I wasn't going to do something about it. I don't talk through my hat."[23]

In the last month of the same year, a curious correspondent once more caught the full force of Truman's periodic chiding:

> *Q:* Do you expect to have Mr. McGrath as attorney general as long as you are president?
> *The President:* Mr. McGrath has made no motion to me that he expects to resign, and I haven't asked him to resign.
> *Q:* Mr. President, I would like to pursue that, if I may. That has been one thing that puzzled so many of us.
> *The President:* Well, you are easily puzzled.
> *Q:* What?
> *The President:* I say you are easily puzzled. Always speculating about something that you don't know anything about, but go ahead.[24]

During his final year in office, Truman was badgered almost to the point of exasperation by questions regarding his future intentions. As demonstrated in the excerpt that follows, he exercised considerable patience and restraint in holding at bay the questions on the subject which bombarded him for months before he was prepared to give an answer:

> *Q:* Mr. President, if you thought that running would help the cause of world peace, would you run?
> *The President:* I will answer that question when I make my announcement.
> *Q:* Mr. President, do you think the cause of world peace would be helped if you ran?
> *The President:* I couldn't hear you.
> *Q:* Just the reverse of that question . . .
> *The President:* (*interposing*) Well, I can't answer it, Ed [Harris]. You needn't try to reverse your questions because I am not under cross-examination. I want to say to you that I know you are very

much interested in this situation. I am interested too. But we don't want to make this thing ridiculous. I have carefully and conscientiously tried to answer all your questions. I always try to do that. But it seems to me that it is about time now for you to wait until I get ready to make the necessary announcement, and then you will have all the information. I don't want to confuse you. I have told you that it is a difficult decision for me to make, and that as soon as it is time for the announcement to be made, you will have the information promptly. So let's go to some other subject that the country is interested in, and discuss that, because I have said all to you that I am going to say on this subject, and I am being kindly to you, and friendly to you. It is not in any spirit of not wanting to cooperate with you. But I am not ready to make the announcement. And when I get ready, you shall have it.[25]

One of Truman's last severe reprimands was leveled at a woman correspondent at a conference held in the National Museum auditorium at which members of the American Society of Newspaper Editors were also present:

Q: Mr. President, Ruth Montgomery, *New York Daily News.* You made a very fine speech last week against colonialism, and then our United States delegate at the United Nations refused to vote to hear the Tunisian case . . .
The President: (*interposing*) Now you—you can't bring up a question like that at this press conference. It has no place here, and I'm sorry. You have to know all the facts, and all the details, before you can come to a sane conclusion on this thing. And you don't know all the facts, and I do—and I can't comment on it.[26]

It is readily apparent from the evidence presented in the foregoing examples that the president's language could in many instances be made to look as though serious rifts existed from time to time between him and the working press. Numerous exaggerated accounts, in fact, were published as evidence of a rocky career with correspondents.[27] Yet, it has been agreed by reliable critics, as pointed out earlier in the study, that Truman's relations with the working press remained good throughout his tenure as president. The excuses might be offered that the correspondents were charitable and indulgent, or that Truman's press secretaries were extraordinarily skillful in smoothing over the breaches created by the president's unfortunate comments, but these would be purely speculative. The only logical explanation that can be drawn from the data is that the newsmen understood and appreciated the genuine good humor that was imbedded in virtually all of the digs that Truman made at them.

Chapter 10

SOFT ON SHUTTERBUGS

"I want one of you expert photographers to come up here and take a picture of this crowd, because this picture ought to go in all the newspapers of the country."

ANY TREATMENT OF THE PRESIDENT'S ASSOCIATION WITH the working press would have to take into consideration his relation with the news cameramen. Coffin, who is perhaps the bitterest of Truman's early biographers, criticizes the president in the following terms: "At the end of his first year in office, Mr. Truman had done several things. He had lost whatever influence he once had over Congress. He had split organized labor and confused the liberals. And he had had his picture taken doing more things than any other man in the White House."[1] Others agree that a new era for photographers had been ushered in with Truman's accession to the high office.[2] His brisk activity was a noted contrast to the sedentary poses of President Roosevelt to which newsmen had been accustomed for fifteen years.[3]

In his relations with the photographers, Truman demonstrated the same good-natured fussiness that has been illustrated in his contacts with the reporters. For instance, he made this remark as an aside during one of his Washington speeches: "That [being photographed] is an ordeal that is necessary for some reason or other. It seems that as many pictures as are taken of the president of the United States, it is always necessary to take just one more. (*laughter*) I have a club over at the White House known as the 'One More Club.' I am the president of the 'One More Club,' and these fellows all belong to it. (*more laughter*)"[4] On three other occasions during the next six years, the president referred to the White House news photographers as members of his "One More Club."

A typical picture of Truman's dealing with the cameramen is recorded in the following episode:

> *The President:* I don't understand all this picture-taking at this news conference.
> *Bill Simmons:* Okay. Cameras outside! (*laughter*)
> *The President:* Somebody's after you! Two more shots and I won't be able to see my notes.
> *Photographer:* Will you say something, Mr. President?
> *The President:* What do you want me to say? (*laughter*)
> *Photographer:* Will you do that again?
> *The President:* All right, I knew if I made a motion, every one of you would have to get the shot. Go ahead — go right ahead. Now let's quit, boys, I can't see. I'm going to have to throw you out bodily if you don't quit that shooting.[5]

In September 1952, the president's quip at photographers is recorded in the transcript of a talk to a group of actors and officials of the Indian motion picture industry: "We are anxious, as you are, for a friendly and peaceful world all the way around. [*a flash bulb exploded at this point*] There must be a communist in the bunch. [*meaning photographers*] Interrupted me at the psychological point. At any rate . . ."[6]

Despite the constant banter with photographers, Truman had a genuine appreciation of photojournalism. This is illustrated in two excerpts from speeches made during his 1948 whistle-stop campaign: "You know, these eastern newspapers just won't believe it when they are told that past eleven o'clock there are ten or twelve thousand people out to listen to me in Ogden. They just think it is not possible. But here you are! Somebody I hope will take a picture of it and send it to all the eastern newspapers."[7]

"I never expected to see a crowd like this at this time of night. I'll tell you what I want. I want one of you expert photographers to come up here and take a picture of this crowd, because this picture ought to go in all the newspapers of the country."[8]

Further indication of his liking for good news pictures is seen in a letter to the editor of the *Battle Creek* (Michigan) *Enquirer and News,* from whom he had received photographs of his daughter, Margaret. He wrote: "Please say to your staff photographer that he is an expert and I know what I am talking about. . . ."[9] He revealed in another letter that he was a collector of specimens of press photography: "I certainly did appreciate yours of the third enclosing me pictures taken on my visit to San Antonio. I am most happy to have them because I keep an album of pictures taken on various trips and I didn't have these that you sent me."[10] He boasted, in fact, that "I have, I guess, about as great a collection as anybody of pictures . . . particularly the pictures that win these prizes."[11]

In all the record, there is nothing to negate the statement of Press Secretary Ross that "there are very friendly relations between the photographers and President Truman."[12]

Chapter 11

A Fight for Facts

"I don't give a 'hoot' what they say on the editorial pages if they will just give me a fair deal in the news."

AFTER LESS THAN A YEAR IN OFFICE, TRUMAN WROTE TO A friend, "I appreciate your trying to get the facts to the people but, of course, they will never know the facts until years afterwards. We have a most unfriendly press and we simply have to take it for what it is worth. . . ."[1] This expression of attitude would appear to contradict the testimony of the foregoing pages with respect to Truman's relations with the press—it would, that is, unless a clear understanding of his concept of the dual role of the press, as explained in the beginning of chapter 5 is maintained.

Attention is now given to the president's thoughts of—and contacts with—that segment of the press that he identified as apart and separate from the "working press" and to which he applied various labels from time to time. The "opposition press," to Truman, was made up not of the newsgatherers and newswriters—the reporters, correspondents, and photographers—but of the publishers and owners, who, he felt, dictated news policies. Along with these, he included editors and columnists, who expressed ideas and opinions of their own or their employers' making that he considered inimical to his own. Very often, Truman sweepingly referred to the press in general as an "opposition press."

A study of the journalistic record of the period is sufficient to show that Truman had grounds for regarding as opponents certain sections of the American press, and—at times—a major portion of that press. *Editor & Publisher* states unequivocally that "the figures show conclusively that the American press did oppose Truman."[2] Havemann observes that "practically all of the critics—the editorial writers, the commentators, and the political scientists—have been highly disdainful, if not of everything he has done, at least a great part of it."[3]

If the American press was strongly critical of the thirty-third president, it may also be stated that the thirty-third president was critical of the American press. The record of Truman's retaliations to press opposition is both voluminous and denunciatory. His criticisms are often couched in language reminiscent of the early recriminations of Wilmer.[4] The charges include "lying press," "irresponsible press," "kept press," "sabotage press," and "one-party press." He referred to "fake editorial writers" and "editorial spasms," and he had much to say about "guttersnipe" and "ivory-tower columnists."

From the beginning to the end of his occupancy of the office of president, Truman expressed a distrust of the general reliability of the information purveyed by the communication media of the country.

At times, he was careful to be specific in his charges of untruthful reporting, but on many occasions he was content to generalize in broad statements about the press or portions of it. In December of 1946 he wrote a friend: "The misrepresentation of the facts by a prejudiced press has caused most of our troubles, foreign and domestic, but truth eventually triumphs."[5]

When John Snyder, secretary of the treasury, sent Truman a copy of a press conference that had taken place in the Treasury Department to prove to the president that he had not been quoted accurately in the newspapers, Truman replied: "I was sure it was a misquotation, done with malice and forethought. . . ."[6]

The indictment of falsification and distortion of the news was spread across the western part of the country in 1948 when the president made his "give 'em hell" tours of the whistle-stops, as his campaign was dubbed by newsmen. To crowds assembled in Kansas, Oregon, and California, for example, he made the following comments from the rear platform of his special train:

"It is almost impossible to get definitely the facts before the people, for the simple reason that there are certain people in the newspaper business and certain people in the radio business who have a distorted view of what the people ought to know and ought to think."[7]

"I came out here so you might see and understand the things for which I stand, and so that you might get the truth and the facts, which you haven't been getting through the press."[8]

"I'm speaking plainly these days. I am telling you facts. Nobody else will tell 'em to you."[9]

The month after his election, Truman asserted once more his conviction that the press in general was given to lying — this time in a letter to the mayor of New Orleans: " . . . of course, having been here for the last fourteen or fifteen years I understand what contortions newspapermen go through to misrepresent the fact."[10] In another blanket accusation, the president stated in 1950: "I came out here to tell you what the facts are. Nobody else will tell you what the facts are, because those people who control the methods of communication want to see the farm program ruined and put out of business. And I am out here to tell you what the facts are."[11]

Truman's crusade for incredulity and discernment on the part of the readers of the American press was relentless. He issued this caution to members of the board of trustees of the American Dental Association in 1951: "And all I want you to do is get the facts, and don't believe what you see in certain magazines and newspapers."[12] Although Truman repeatedly told the men and women at his press conferences that he thought they were doing a competent and honest job of reporting him accurately, he likewise maintained that he was not being given fair treatment in either the news columns or the editorial pages. At a press conference in 1952, when asked if he believed that more readers read the news columns than the editorials, he commented as follows:

> *The President:* Oh yes. I have already said that. I don't give a "hoot" what they say on the editorial pages if they will just give me a fair deal in the news.
> *Q:* Well, Mr. President, when you say that you don't give a "hoot" about the editorial pages, isn't that what your statement was aimed at, sir?
> *The President:* No it was not. It was principally aimed at garbling the news, and there are papers in this country that do garble the news. There are a lot of firstclass newspapers that do not, but there are a great many that do. I could specifically name them if it were necessary, but I won't. And you know who they are as well as I do.[13]

Taking his complaint to the people once again, during the 1952 campaign, Truman remarked in addressing a crowd at Spokane, Washington: "We have produced a budget surplus of nearly $4 billion, and we have reduced the public debt. Now, a lot of you may be surprised. But that's the truth. You'd never guess it by reading the papers."[14]

A specific instance arose in March 1946, when the president was in Fulton, Missouri, with Winston Churchill for the latter's "iron curtain" speech at Westminster College. Secretary of State James F. Byrnes sent the following telegram to Truman:

The *Evening Star* carries story by Constantine Brown that I have advised you I wish to resign and that you have decided to appoint Marshall. I have issued statement as follows quote in answer to a question as to the report appearing in today's *Evening Star* that the Secretary of State had told the President he wished to resign, the Secretary stated that the story was absolutely false and that there had been no discussion whatever between the President and himself on this subject end quote. I think you should also issue statement.[15]

No record of an answer by the president appears in the log of the Fulton trip, but the following message from the presidential press secretary to his assistant in Washington was undoubtedly cleared by Truman:

---

4 March 1946

From: Charles G. Ross
To : Eben Ayers, The White House
NR   White 7

Please tell press that story by Brown about Byrnes and Marshall is absolutely false and unfounded.

[signed] ROSS[16]

When the president returned to Washington, he was queried on the rumored plan for General Marshall to replace Secretary Byrnes. He replied that he knew nothing about it, and added: "That's another matter I saw in the paper the other day . . . it's news to me."[17] The accuracy of Brown's report was proved the following month, however, when Byrnes submitted his letter of resignation on April 16, 1946.[18]

Another member of the presidential family, Secretary of Commerce Henry Wallace, stated in a letter of June 3, 1946, that an article about himself in *Life* magazine, written by the Alsop brothers, contained inaccuracies. He enclosed for the president's perusal his note to *Life*'s editor, Wilson Hicks, calling the latter's attention to the alleged errors in fact. Truman's reply to Wallace was as follows:

June 7, 1946

Dear Henry:

Your note of the third, enclosing me copy of correspondence with Wilson Hicks of *Life* is all right. I was happy to receive it.

It seems that *Life, Time* and *Fortune* magazines take particular delight in garbling anything that either you or I have to say.

Sincerely yours,

[signed] HARRY S TRUMAN[19]

Of a writer for the *Kansas City Star*, the president once wrote: "I think maybe _____ has been scared of his physical condition and is on the road to reformation. He has told so many lies about me that he knows very well he can't pass the pearly gates unless he does something to offset that back record of his."[20]

In 1946 he complained of a conspiracy of newspapers and magazines guilty of bias in handling the news:

"*Time* and *Life* and the scandal press, represented by Hearst and the McCormick-Patterson axis, have been spending most of their time belittling the president. . . . The last issue of *Time* magazine, in a scandalous fabrication of untruths . . . charges that legislators are kept from the White House."[21]

Life magazine, when mentioned in a question at a press conference a month later, drew another criticism from the president:

Q: Mr. President, *Life* magazine said you were going to nominate General Eisenhower. Any comment on that?
The President: *Life* magazine knows a lot of things that I don't know, most of them not facts.[22]

On one occasion, the integrity of the *New York Times*, generally highly esteemed by Truman, came in for his criticism. He wrote an ardent supporter: "I am sure they won't publish your letter for the simple reason that it gives the facts which they don't like to make public."[23]

A favorite target of the president was the *Wall Street Journal*, as indicated in the following excerpt:

Q: Mr. President, the *Wall Street Journal* yesterday had a story that the administration had abandoned its hope of budget balancing, and that there will be no new taxes proposed for next year?
The President: Well now, the *Wall Street Journal* must have been standing behind the curtain somewhere that I know nothing about. No such arrangement has been arrived at.
Q: They didn't hear accurately?
The President: No sir, they did not hear accurately. They hardly ever do. (*laughter*)[24]

Publishers of newsletters and books were sometimes included along with newspapers in Truman's appraisal of unreliability in reporting: "The Whaley Eaton Service and Prentice-Hall outfit are just about as reliable as the *Washington Times Herald*."[25] When William Bradford Huie, editor of the *American Mercury,* published a somewhat scurrilous article in *Cosmopolitan* magazine entitled, "The Terrible-Tempered Mr. Truman,"[26] he received a reprimand from Mrs. Franklin D. Roosevelt for the inaccuracies that she saw in the piece. Apprised of her action, Truman wrote to her: "I am glad to get a chance to tell the *Cosmopolitan* author some of the facts. That is one of the most vicious articles that has ever been written with regard to my relations with you and President Roosevelt. Putting it mildly, there just wasn't one word of truth in it. You, of course, know that to be a fact."[27]

In a letter to Sherman Minton, shortly after his appointment by the president to the Supreme Court, Truman scored an old-time newspaper foe for its misrepresentation of the facts in its latest attack upon his administration: "You can rest assured that I don't pay the slightest attention to what the *Chicago Tribune* says. If they told the truth I wouldn't believe them, and you know they never do that."[28]

Truman demonstrated a genuine appreciation for factual reporting when he commended the series of five articles written by John Hersey for *New Yorker* magazine.[29] Although the articles were not devoid of occasional pointed criticism of the president, Truman stated: "I think John made a sincere effort to tell the truth, which is more than can be said about most columnists."[30]

The press' interpretation of Truman's fiscal program in the later years of his administration was a particularly touchy subject. While officiating at the laying of the cornerstone for the new General Accounting Office building in Washington, Truman commented on criticism of his spending policy as follows: "In a recent issue of a magazine which is circulated widely in this country and abroad, there appeared an article purporting to show that 'waste' and 'extravagance' were running wild in the federal government. Accompanying that article was a table of figures supposedly showing that nondefense expenditures of the government had increased anywhere from 100 percent to 1,000 percent between 1940 and 1950. It was just a pack of lies. This table was a typical example of what I once heard described as 'butterfly statistics'—statistics so meaningless that they seem to have been picked right out of the air with a butterfly net. And that is where these came from."[31]

Three months later, the *Chicago Herald American* published a report of department-by-department increases in expenditures, and Truman immediately sent a letter to Merrill C. Meigs, vice-president of the Hearst Corporation, with whom he had worked closely some nine years before while chairman of the Senate committee investigating the national defense program. Truman's letter stated in part: "Fred Bowman sent me a statement published in the *Chicago Herald American* that you sent to him. It certainly is one of the most misleading things that has been done by the *Chicago Herald American* and it is not by any means the only one. I am enclosing you a copy of the figures as they are. It has been my policy to use the existing Government Departments for the carrying on of the Defense Program and nearly all of the figures in the misleading column published in your paper are brought about by the Defense Program. I am sending you a copy of the exact report from the Budget which covers the situation. Of course, I don't expect any explanatory program to be published in the *Herald American*. It would never do to tell the facts, although I thought you might like to have them for your own information."[32]

When the only response to the president's letter turned out to be a curt reply on January 28 from Meigs, acknowledging receipt and advising that "since this is a matter for our editorial department, I am forwarding it to New York for the editors' attention," Truman dispatched a second note, considerably shorter and frankly bitter: "I knew very well I was wasting my time and yours to send a true document to the Hearst organization. I am sorry I bothered you but I am sending a copy of the Budget in brief which elaborates on the statement I sent you and I suppose it will be a waste of time on your part to read it and try and get the truth out."[33] Truman was convinced, apparently, as he wrote Fred J. Bowman, who had sent him the *Herald-American* report in the first place, that "of course, you wouldn't expect the Hearst papers to tell the truth about anything."[34]

Condemning another newspaper that was politically opposed to his administration, the president wrote to his administrative assistant, Edward D. McKim, early in 1952: "Ed Condon gave me a copy of your letter which appeared in the *Omaha World Herald*. I was certainly surprised when that lousy sheet went so far as to even publish your letter. It is a waste of time to try to get those people to understand the truth, but I am glad you tried anyway."[35] With an air of resignation, he commented to another friend: "It is funny what newsmen can make out of things that never happen."[36]

Truman became more positive in his conviction that the truth had little chance in the general press, particularly among the large-circulation magazines and the metropolitan newspapers. At an August, 1952, press conference, the following exchange took place:

> *Q.* Mr. President, do you plan to answer this *Saturday Evening Post* article of last week by Glenn Everett, the one that said in the 1948 campaign that you gave the farmers false information about grain storage shortages?
> *The President:* I haven't read the article and don't intend to read it, and of course I won't say anything about it. I don't very often read the *Post* because it's always wrong on most things. (*laughter*)
> *Q:* Well, Mr. President, to go back to the *Saturday Evening Post* . . .
> *The President:* (*interposing*) Why do you want to go back to that sheet, May [Craig]? (*laughter*)
> *Q:* Well sir, I was rather surprised. You said you never read it, but it was always wrong. Now, how do you know that? Do you get a briefing? Do you get summaries of things that . . .
> *The President:* (*interposing*) All I need do is look at the table of contents, May, and I know what's in it. And it's always wrong."[37]

Corresponding with a Kansas City acquaintance of long standing, Truman broadened his indictment against "untruthful" magazines: "You are exactly right about the *Saturday Evening Post*, the *Country Gentleman* and the *Readers Digest*. They don't want the truth because if they had the truth they wouldn't publish it."[38]

Truman seemed to object particularly to the practice of forecasting developments on the basis of reported facts. Ostensibly a man of action himself, he believed in coping with events as they presented themselves and was completely unsympathetic with what he considered speculation in the news. His frequent allusions to the subject reflect a genuine contempt for news reports that attempted to point to future developments. The excerpts listed below, taken from press conferences of 1950-1952, illustrate the strong feeling that the president developed in this direction toward the close of his Washington career:

Q: On the subject of Mr. Denham, Mr. President, have various calls which have been sounded by individuals for the recall of Mr. Denham been brought to your attention in any official . . .
The President: (*interposing*) I have seen them in the paper, but nowhere else.
Q: Nowhere else?
The President: Nowhere else but in the paper. Like a lot of other guesses that get into the papers. (*laughter*)[39]

Q: Mr. President, there are rumors around of the possibility of several ambassadorial appointments in the Latin American areas?
The President: That's right, there are rumors rife all the time. I have seen everything that is going to happen in the papers for the next two months, but then you had better wait until what the action is, before you decide that they are true. [sic][40]

Q: Is it [Korea] going beyond police action at this time?
The President: I can't answer that question, May [Craig]. That is what we are examining. We have exerted every effort possible to prevent a third world war. Every maneuver that has been made since June 25th has had in mind not to create a situation which would cause another terrible war. We are still trying to prevent that war from happening and I hope we may be able to prevent it. All these attacks and speculations and lies that have been told on

the members of the government have not helped that situation one little bit. There's a big one on the front page of the paper this morning, about Acheson. . . .[41]

Q: Mr. President, would you tell us one thing that we are all wondering. Are these stories true that you are going to run for the Senate in 1952? Are they inspired, or what?
The President: No comment, Bert. No comment. You can still speculate and draw your own conclusions. You wouldn't have any fun if you didn't have something like that to talk about. (*laughter*)
Bert Andrews: I would rather write about facts.
The President: Well, I hope you will continue to do just that, Bert. You won't have any quarrel with me if you do. (*more laughter*)[47]

Q: Do you have a candidate on the Democratic ticket, sir? (*continued laughter*)
The President: I wil tell you that later. I am not ready to make an announcement on that yet. Anyway, you fellows wouldn't have any fun.
Q: (*interjecting*) No sir.
The President: (*continuing*) If I was to tell you exactly what I was going to do, it would ruin the press conferences. (*continued laughter*)[43]

Q: Does the two-term limitation have any weight in your thinking about whether you will run again, even though you are exempt?
The President: The two-term limitation I think is all right, but you must understand that by a technicality I have only had one term. (*laughter*)
Q: But in actuality it is practically two terms.
The President: Well, you can translate it any way you want to. You and the *Post-Dispatch* will do a good job on it, I am sure. (*laughter*)[44]

Q: Mr. President, do you expect to touch on the Nixon fund on your coming campaign through California?

The President: Well now, you will have to wait and see. I suppose you will be along.

Q: I am anxious to go.

The President: I am not making any forecasts of what will take place on that trip because I don't think it would be as interesting to you. If you have something to speculate about, then you have a story to write, don't you see, whether it's true or not. (*laughter*)

Q: Mr. President, when you and Mr. Stevenson talked things over, presumably the election, did you decide why the Republicans won?

The President: No, I am leaving that up to you. You fellows know all about everything. I have seen you speculate on what I am going to do, what I haven't done, and what will be done in the future. Why don't you speculate on this which is past, and come up with the answer? You are perfectly capable of doing it. (*laughter*)[45]

Truman's often expressed concern about what he referred to as "all the lying slander you see in public life in this country today, and in the newspapers"[45] undoubtedly extended beyond temporary annoyances. He was obviously earnest in his fears for the integrity of American reporting and for its possible effects upon the recording of permanent historical information. He set forth these fears in a thoughtful letter to a Kansas City acquaintance. In part, he observed: ". . . I have had so much experience, and some of it exceedingly sad, with writers generally that I never believe half they write even when I am sure they are telling the truth. Some woman has written an article about Mrs. Truman for *Collier's* and it is about two-thirds hooey, even though it is intended to be a friendly article. It makes you wonder sometimes about the historical characters we read about in our school days, and makes us wonder if the historians may not have been in the same class with our jackleg reporters of today. I rather think they were. I remember reading somewhere that Herodotus once said that the man and the event hardly ever arrived at the same place at the same time, but a good historian would take care of that difficulty. I am rather inclined to believe that most of the things we read about didn't happen, but you can get enough of the real viewpoint where a research man examines all the documents to arrive at some grain of truth. For instance, Carl Sandburg's life of Lincoln comes as near containing the facts as any article about that great man, and Douglas Freeman's life of Lee is the same class, but there are very few individuals who had a man interested enough to dig up the facts. I was very glad to hear from you and I didn't intend to give you a dissertation on reporters and their unreliability—I think you understand them about as well as I do."[47]

More specifically, the president was fearful that the facts relating to the New Deal administration might be distorted through inaccurate reporting and that a false picture of the times might be preserved in the guise of historical data. "If we are not careful," he warned, "between the sabotage press and the columnists, we are going to have the same events happening to the history of Roosevelt's administration as happened to Jefferson's and Jackson's. It has taken one hundred years to arrive at the truth of Jackson's administration and more than that really to get at the facts of what Jefferson accomplished, and his philosophy of government."[48]

On at least one occasion, Truman urged definite action to offset the perpetuation of what he considered untruths. Writing to Senator Humphrey of Minnesota in regard to antiadministration charges, he suggested: "All those attacks should be individually met and placed in the Record, because if they are not some nutty historian of the future will decide that we didn't have any defense."[49]

In another brief "lecture" on this subject, Truman enunciated his own theories and ideas concerning truthful and objective reporting. He told Ambassador Bowers: "I wish some able literary person, like yourself, would make an analysis of the information service from which we now suffer in this country of ours. What we need more than anything else is a factual news service written by objective reporters and an editorial staff to write its own editorials on the editorial page—that would be an ideal press. I've never cared a great deal about what the editorial writers and columnists say about me on the editorial page if I can get a fair break on the front page in the news columns, but the newspapers have a habit of editing the news and writing misleading headlines, which is the worst form of deception. I wish you would think about the situation—your experience as a factual writer seems to me would fit you for just such an undertaking. Your Jefferson books, *The Tragic Era,* and articles you've written fit you to do a real service to freedom of speech on the modern publishers and advertising controlled U.S. press."[60]

Just how strongly the president felt the need for positive effort to instill into the press of the country the practice, as well as the principle, of truthful reporting is revealed in this declaration that he made in a letter to Thomas L. Stokes: "I am going to spend the rest of my life in an endeavor to cause a return to truthful writing and reporting."[51]

Thus the President chided and criticized the press — sometimes seriously, sometimes in a frivolous vein — for its failure to fulfill the basic function of reporting the news truthfully, accurately, and objectively. This failure on the part of the press, he said, was all the worse because it was deliberate. He saw misrepresentation in the news not as one of the occupational handicaps or hazards of journalism, but as a manifestation of an intention on the part of a "lying press" to distort, suppress, or misstate the facts. He would not be dissuaded from this belief, and toward the end of his Washington career he wrote with weary indignation: "I think it is time for all of us to put a stop to the press lies, which seem to be the policy and no accident on the part of the press."[52]

Chapter 12

WHOSE RESPONSIBILITY?

"I am asking them to use good judgment for the safety of the United States. I am not asking for any censorship at all."

REFLECTING ON THE OVERALL PERFORMANCE OF THE PRESS with respect to its manner of handling security information during the latter half of his presidential tenure, Truman concluded that, for the most part, the press had failed miserably in its responsibility to the nation. He summed it up in these words:

"When strategic material is as important to the welfare of the country, you'd think it would also be of enough importance to the people who own the information distributing agencies that they'd have enough sense to help protect the country. I told them that, and they didn't like it. They wanted to pass the buck to the government. If they'd got bombed it wouldn't make any difference if they sold more papers or not . . . this is a free country, and because it's a free country, they are the government. . . . They ought to have some feeling of responsibility as well as the fellow who's in the White House."[1]

During the first thirty-three months of Truman's administration, the question of security information or of press responsibility never came up. But with the addition of a more positive military policy early in 1948 as a means of meeting the increasing threat of Communist aggression in various sectors of the world, the president and his advisors became more conscious of the need for safeguarding information of a military or strategic nature. Truman himself seemed reluctant to invoke mandatory censorship regulations, at least in the early stages of his difficulties with an "irresponsible press." He advocated instead that the press exercise self-imposed restraint in publishing information affecting the national security, as illustrated in the following excerpt:

Q: Mr. President, has the matter of censorship of military developments come to your attention since last week?
The President: I have never heard of it. Nobody mentioned the subject to me at all. I don't think anybody is thinking about censorship.
Q: (interposing) Mr. President, . . .
The President: (continuing) I told you the last time, you gentlemen are just as patriotic as all the rest of the country in the protection of your own country, and its welfare is just as much in your hands as it is in mine.[2]

In this first recorded reference to the subject, Truman set forth the theme to which he clung with almost fanatic tenacity in every subsequent instance involving the handling of security information. To him, the formula was a simple one, requiring no more ingredients

than honest patriotism and good common sense. It was the responsibility of the press, he felt, to suppress any news or information that
might have a deleterious effect on the welfare or the military defense
of the country.

The president demonstrated what he meant by "common sense"
in answering a question aimed at secret negotiations between the
United States and Russia in 1948:

> *Q:* Mr. President, I think a request was made to the White
> House recently that the full minutes of our conversations with the
> Russians on the setup in Berlin be released to the public and
> that . . .
> *The President:* (*interposing*) They should not be released, and
> they will not be released . . .
> *Q:* (*continuing*) How about matters . . .
> *The President:* (*continuing*) . . . at this time.
> *Q:* (*continuing*) . . . various conversations we have had with
> the Russians on other matters that are touchy?
> *The President:* When you are trading on a piece of real estate, do
> you get out in front of a press conference and bargain, or do you
> try to reach an agreement and then announce it to the press con-
> ference?
> *Q:* Wouldn't the public have a better chance to evaluate . . .
> *The President:* (*interposing*) Well, we'll see about that.
> Whenever the—it is necessary to make a release, state all the
> facts as nearly as we can from our point of view; but if you are
> going to be successful in negotiations, you can't do it in a glass
> house.[3]

It soon became apparent, however, that the president's formula
of "patriotic forbearance" for handling security information was
subject to diverse interpretations. As global military strategy became
more complex, representatives of the press grew more confused as to
what constituted security information and—more particularly—who
in the federal government was authorized to define it as such.
Evidence of the growing confusion is apparent in the following lines
from a press conference, in which the president earlier condemned
congressional committee investigations of spy activities in the capital
as a "red herring":

> *Q:* Don't you think the American public is entitled to this infor-
> mation?

The President: What information?

Q: That has been brought out in these investigations?

The President: What useful purpose is it serving when we are having this matter before a grand jury where action has to take place, no matter what this committee does? They haven't revealed anything that everybody hasn't known all along, or hasn't been presented to the grand jury. That is where it has to be taken, in the first place, if you are going to do anything about it. They are slandering a lot of people that don't deserve it.

Q: Does that mean they won't get the information on Remington?

The President: They will get all the information that they are entitled to on Remington. They will not get any confidential information on him.

Q: Why was Remington asked to resign from the navy?

The President: I don't know anything about that. You will have to ask the navy about that. I can't answer the question because I don't know. I didn't even know he had been asked to resign.

Q: The navy puts it up to you, Mr. President?

The President: How's that?

Q: The navy puts it up to you, Mr. President?

The President: Well, I haven't the information available.[4]

It must be acknowledged that Truman fell heir to the responsibility of guarding what has been called "the world's biggest secret." As experimentation with the atomic bomb took on the proportions of a race for hemisphere survival, the urgency of a reliable security technique became indisputable.[5] The president did not equivocate with regard to his position on restriction of atomic information:

Q: Mr. President, have you under reconsideration the release to the public of the evaluation report of the Bikini tests?

The President: It will not be released. It's locked up in my safe and will stay there. It's a confidential report and should not be released.[6]

Signs of strain in the president's press relations as a result of increasing concern over security information grew steadily more apparent. In July 1949, a series of closed-door conferences at the Blair House on international policy regarding the use of atomic power— attended by the president, State Department officials, and members of the Atomic Energy Commission—piqued the curiosity of White House press representatives almost to a degree of exasperation.[7] The situation was discussed as follows in a press conference:

> *Q:* Mr. President, can you give us any information on what is going on in the atomic foreign policy?
> *The President:* No, I can't.
> *Q:* Mr. President, suppose you were a newspaper reporter and you were writing all this stuff, would you give us a little advice as to what is the relative importance of the story?
> *The President:* It is relatively unimportant. You see, it has been a habit of mine to hold conferences in the White House and in the Blair House on various subjects that affect the welfare of the country, and that has been going on for four years. And these conferences are on my personal invitation. This is the first occasion on which one of the persons who has been invited has leaked the fact to people that he was coming to the White House to see the president. I didn't like it, and I still don't like it.
> *Q:* (*interposing*) Well now, . . .
> *The President:* (*continuing*) I shall continue to have those conferences whenever I feel like it, and they will continue to be off the record.
> *Q:* This is one about the Blair House meeting. Do you have any contemplation whatsoever of telling the British how to make the atomic bomb?
> *The President:* No comment. I told you I wouldn't answer questions about the Blair House meeting, or anything in connection with it, or any rumors in connection with it.
> *Q:* Mr. President, here is one that you might answer. The man who leaked the news about the first Blair House meeting. Would you invite him to the second one?
> *The President:* I didn't have a second one.
> *Q:* Will you invite . . .
> *The President:* I will attend to that when it comes around.
> *Q:* Mr. President, do you know who he is?
> *The President:* Yes, Ma'am [May Craig], I do. (*much laughter*)
> *Q:* Who is he?
> *The President:* No comment. No comment. (*more laughter*)
> *Q:* Mr. President, you say in your earlier remarks on the mechanics of that meeting that you thought at some point we would agree that this was a relatively unimportant decision. Does that . . .

The President: (*interposing*) Just be patient until all the rumors are floored, then you will have the answer to that question.

Q: I wonder whether you could say now that it is — or at some future time that the whole thing will be disclosed?

The President: No, I don't intend to discuss it.[8]

Later, in the same conference, one of the reporters brought into sharper focus the general impression that the president's reticence on the subject had produced after Truman replied to another question as follows:

The President: I don't know anything about it. I think you fellows would know all about it. That is your business, to find out about those things.

May Craig: Sometimes, Mr. President, we can't investigate very easily, we are checkmated. (*laughter*)

The President: How? How do you get checkmated, Miss May? I never checkmate you.

May Craig: (*interposing*) Well . . .

The President: (*continuing*) I give you all the information.

May Craig: (*continuing*) . . . we were checkmated on the secrecy about the Blair House.

The President: I give you the information I can. There is no secrecy around the Blair House, Miss May, at all. I live there. It's my private residence.

Q: (*interposing*) Just the same . . .

The President: (*continuing*) Are there any secrets around your house where you live? (*laughter*)

May Craig: I am no president. (*more laughter*)[9]

It was about this time that two incidents occurred, which obviously convinced the president that at least part of the press was grossly irresponsible and which set the stage for drastic action later by the chief executive. Truman recounts the pair of incidents as follows: "The most glistening example was *Fortune* magazine publishing the location of our atomic energy plants, and the towns they were near to. I talked very coarsely to the editors of *Time, Life* and *Fortune*, and I told them I wished they would go to Russia and then publish the same information on Russia so that I could know as much about the Russians as they knew about us.

"They went around to these different places themselves and took pictures. And the Scripps-Howard papers published air maps of every great city in the country, and that was another case I quarreled about. They published these great air maps of Washington, New York, Boston, San Francisco and half dozen other cities—Detroit was another— all the great population centers and industrial areas. And these pictures themselves. And every single one of those things is in the Kremlin's military files, and we haven't got a single thing like that on Leningrad, Moscow . . . Stalingrad . . . Vladivostock. That was what I was quarreling about. It was worse than any spy ring. And in the name of a free press. I think I was right. And I think I still am."[10]

In a letter to former Secretary of the Interior Harold L. Ickes, Truman revealed just how strongly he felt about these disclosures by the Luce and Scripps-Howard publications. He wrote in part: "The original program inaugurated by President Roosevelt was intended to create the so-called hydrogen bomb. There wasn't any reason for all the conversation and foolishness that went on publicly about it, as the machinery had been set in motion to arrive at that conclusion in 1943. Some of our friends who like headlines do not seem to understand that national security sometimes depends on action and not conversation. Some of our high-hat slick magazines have published maps of the United States locating every defense plant that we have in the country, including the atomic plants.

"Our daily newspapers have published air maps of every big city in the country with its principal buildings marked and pointed out. I don't know what I wouldn't give for such information about the Soviet Union, but catch anybody doing anything like that in that country and tomorrow they would be shot or put in the gold mine on the Lena River, working at slave labor. We are immensely handicapped in our defense programs because of that attitude of our news hounds. Nevertheless, we have a very efficient actual defense set-up. It is not due to any cooperation and help of McCormick, Hearst, Luce, or Roy Howard."[11]

Truman's reason for including Hearst and McCormick is not specifically explained in the record, but it is understandable when viewed in the light of two considerations: (1) the generally recognized position of these two antiadministration journalists, whose papers tended to be isolationist and nationalistic, and thus a part of the "opposition press" and (2) Truman's propensity for sweeping generalizations.

The president's growing concern over leaks of classified information from within the defense establishment led him to take three decisive official actions within a twenty-month period, culminating in the famous Executive Order 10290 of September 24, 1951. One critic referred to that order as "by all odds the most controversial step by Mr. Truman affecting the press in 1951, and one of the most criticized actions he ever took."[12] The first of these three moves was an executive order issued February 1, 1950, "Defining Certain Vital Military and Naval Installations and Equipment as Requiring Protection Against the General Dissemination of Information Relative Thereto." It was, in essence, a restatement of President Roosevelt's prewar executive order of March 22, 1940, and merely called attention to the classifications of security information that had existed prior to the creation of a unified Department of Defense in 1947. There were mild repercussions on the part of the press to this pronouncement from the president.[13] The reaction of the working press was one of annoyance and grumbling, but nothing more than that, as illustrated in these lines taken from the press conference on the day following Truman's issuance of the order:

Q: Mr. President, yesterday you issued an executive order on the dissemination of information, and in it in the last paragraph you include military documents and reports which have been marked CONFIDENTIAL and RESTRICTED — also TOP SECRET and SECRET, etc. That classification RESTRICTED is the most general one I have ever seen.

The President: It is exactly a copy of the order that has been in effect all the time, Pete [Brandt], and the only reason that order was issued was that it conforms with the new Defense Act. There isn't any difference with this order and the one that has been in effect, . . .

Q: (*interposing*) The point was . . .

The President: (*continuing*) . . . that the order conform with the new law on the Defense Act.

Q: (*interposing*) Mr. President . . .

The President: (*continuing*) Unification — it's an order to make unification — to conform with the Unification Act, . . .

Q: (*interjecting*) Oh.

The President: (*continuing*) . . . that's all there is to it. That order has been in effect ever since I have been president.

Q: Is there any way to get a definition of RESTRICTED, so that the army officers would know what it means? In some places it refers to clippings.

The President: I can't answer the question, Pete. You will have to talk to somebody that uses RESTRICTED. I don't use it. (*laughter*)

Q: Well, every office boy seems to stamp RESTRICTED or CONFIDENTIAL, and I have seen many CONFIDENTIAL and RESTRICTED documents which had no reason whatever to be . . .

The President: (*interposing*) You never saw one come out with my signature on it. (*laughter*) You talk to them, now. That's their business, not mine. Those RESTRICTED documents are mostly military.

Q: Well, Mr. President, returning to this executive order a moment, would you interpret it for us?

The President: No, I won't try to interpret it for you, . . .

Q: (interposing) Well, Mr. President, . . .

Q: (*interposing*) Mr. President, . . .

The President: (*continuing*) . . . and that's final, and I don't intend to comment on it further. That order speaks for itself.

Q: (*interposing*) Mr. President, . . .

The President: (*interposing*) You can put your own interpretation on it.

Q: (*continuing*) . . . I have seen a picture of the North Pole taken from an airplane marked RESTRICTED.

Q: What?

Q: The North Pole—North Pole.

The President: A picture of the North Pole marked RESTRICTED. I can't comment on that, though. Take it up with the attorney general or with the military which is responsible.

Q: There is pretty much confusion about what we can write and what we can't.

The President: I am sorry about that. . . .[14]

The second move that Truman made to insure against an "irresponsible press" came late in the same year. On December 4, 1950, with a full-scale war in progress in Korea, he issued a memorandum to departments and agencies of the executive branch:

December 5, 1950

MEMORANDUM FOR:

The Secretary of State
The Secretary of the Treasury

The Secretary of Defense
The Attorney General
The Postmaster General
The Secretary of the Interior
The Secretary of Agriculture
The Secretary of Commerce
The Secretary of Labor
Chairman, National Security Resources Board
Administrator, Economic Stabilization Agency
Director, Selective Service System

In the light of the present critical international situation, and until further written notice from me, I wish that each one of you would take immediate steps to reduce the number of public speeches pertaining to foreign or military policy made by officials of the departments and agencies of the Executive Branch. This applies to officials in the field as well as those in Washington.

No speech, press release, or other public statement concerning foreign policy should be released until it has received clearance from the Department of State.

No speech, press release, or other public statement concerning military policy should be released until it has received clearance from the Department of Defense.

In addition to the copies submitted to the Departments of State or Defense for clearance, advance copies of speeches and press releases concerning foreign policy or military policy should be submitted to the White House for information.

The purpose of this memorandum is not to curtail the flow of information to the American people, but rather to insure that the information made public is accurate and fully in accord with the policies of the United States government.

[Signed]

HARRY S TRUMAN[15]

In a separate memorandum to the secretaries of state and defense, Truman said:

In addition to the policy expressed in my memorandum of this date to the heads of departments, concerning the clearance of speeches and statements, I wish the following steps to be taken:

Officials overseas, including military commanders and diplomatic representatives, should be ordered to exercise extreme caution in public statements, to clear all but routine statements with their departments, and to refrain from direct communication on military or foreign policy with newspapers, magazines, or other publicity media in the United States."[16]

It is clear that the president did not hold the press alone to be guilty of security violations. He was greatly disturbed by the laxity and carelessness that he saw inside the departments and bureaus of the federal government as well. In retrospect, he observed: "There are difficulties in every department in the government with leaks. It's a serious situation with the military, the State Department and with every other department in the government. We always tried to find them and head them off. But there are a great number of people who are employed in these departments and who have special friends who are reporters . . . or columnists. It is principally the columnists who publish the leaks. They get them from personal friends in the departments. It's like corruption in government — where it takes two people to make a leak — the reporter and the 'leaker.' And that's always a problem so long as the human animal is not perfect."[17]

September 24, 1951, the same day he issued Executive Order 10290, Truman explained in a memorandum to the secretary of defense how both the press and government officials were to blame for disclosures of top secret information important to the welfare of the United States. He wrote: "Attached is a complete file on our National Defense Program, published in the slick magazines and in our daily papers. I had the Central Intelligence Agency make a survey of intelligence which has been published by various branches of the government and they came up with the report that ninety percent of all our top secret information had been published in either the daily news-papers or in the slick magazines. It would be exceedingly helpful if we could have this same information from behind the Iron Curtain — but, of course, we can't get it. It seems to me that the urge to get on the front pages of the newspapers causes our Army, Navy and Air Force people to discuss for publicity, things that should never be talked about. I wish you would have a meeting with your civilian heads of the various departments and discuss this brochure which I am sending you."[18]

Thus, the record charts clearly the thinking of the president that led to the formulation of the blanket security order of September 24. Under that order, any agency that originated an item of security information was directed to mark it with the words *security informa-tion* plus one of four classifications: "top secret," "secret," "confiden-tial," or "restricted." The ten-page document specified the precau-tions to be taken in accordance with these classifications, ranging from the most stringent safeguards for "top secret" to minimum precautions for "restricted."

What the order actually amounted to was an extension of the regulations controlling security information in the State and Defense Departments to include the civilian departments and agencies of the federal government as well. It provided, for the first time, uniform standards of classifying and protecting security information through-out the Executive Branch.

In issuing the order, Truman stoutly denied that it carried any traces of censorship. "The American people," he declared, "have a fundamental right to information about their government, and there is no element of censorship, either direct or implied, in this order. The order applies only to officials and employees of the Executive Branch of the government. The public is requested to cooperate, but is under no compulsion or threat of penalty to do so as a result of this order. Furthermore, I have directed every agency to keep constant watch over its classifications wherever conditions permit. I expect each department head or his designated subordinate to investigate prompt-ly and carefully any alleged instance of unjustified use of security classifications. As the result of these policies, and as the result of the clear segregation of security from nonsecurity information, I hope that the American people will receive more, rather than less, informa-tion about their government as a result of this executive order."[19]

Although a press conference was held two days after Executive Order 10290 had been released for publication, not a single reference was made to it at that session.[20] It was not until the following meeting on October 4, after the order had stirred up somewhat of a tempest in the press from one end of the country to the other,[21] that the president's action was called into judgment by White House correspondents. By this time, they had felt the full impact of the order that so directly affected their work, and except for three or four minor digressions during the conference, they confined the questioning to a cross-examination of the president for almost two hours on his views concerning security information and censorship.

Truman demonstrated his awareness of the effect that his order had made upon the world of journalism by allowing himself to be grilled at length on the subject, to the almost complete exclusion of other matters. The result was one of the most interesting and most revealing press conferences — from the point of view of the student of journalism, at least — held by the president. For this reason, the transcript of that press conference is included here in full:

> *The President:* Please sit down. I haven't been late for a long time, but I thought I would keep you waiting for a little while. I know what you are interested in. You are interested in censorship. And I don't believe in it. So just to keep you busy, I am going to read you a statement.
>
> *Q:* Is that prepared for us?
>
> *The President:* Yes.
>
> *Q:* Yes sir.
>
> *The President:* Yes. (*reading, not literally*) "There has been considerable misrepresentation and misunderstanding of the Executive Order issued on September 24, 1951, relating to the handling of information which has been classified, in order to protect the national security."
>
> And right here I want to stop and tell you that Central Intelligence had Yale University make a survey, and that survey found — and they had no connection with the Government — that 95 percent of all our information was public property. (*continuing reading*) "This Executive Order represented an honest effort to find the best approach to a problem that is important to the survival of the United States of America. I issued the order with great reluctance, and only when I was convinced, after lengthy conversation, that it was necessary to protect the United States against its potential enemies. I think my record in defending civil liberties in the country demonstrates that I have no desire to

suppress freedom of speech, or freedom of the press. I would like for the public to understand what this order undertakes to do, and why it was necessary to issue it.

"In its simplest terms, the problem is what we should do to keep military and related secrets from falling into the hands of the enemies of the United States. I do not believe that any one could seriously contend that military secrets should be published in the newspapers, or that any one has a right or a duty to see that military secrets are published. I believe that everyone, including members of Congress and newspaper editors, should think twice before advocating a theory that would lead to that result. Whether it be treason or not, it does the United States just as much harm for military secrets to be given to an enemy through open publication, as it does for military secrets to be given to an enemy through the clandestine operations of spies."

There isn't any difference at all. (*continuing reading*) "On the other hand, I do not believe that protection of military secrets should be made a cloak or a cover for withholding from the people information about their Government which should be made known to them. I believe that everyone, including government officials, should try to prevent this from happening. It is easy to agree on these two objectives, but it was difficult to establish the means for accomplishing both of them.

"In those agencies of the government primarily concerned with national security matters, such as the Department of State and the Department of Defense, we have had for a number of years a system of classifying information to prevent its disclosure to unauthorized persons when it would be dangerous to the national security. This system has worked reasonably well, although it has not in all instances prevented the publication of information which aided our enemies against the United States, and in other cases it has been used to classify information which actually has no particular relationship to national security."

Those are the two things that we are faced with, how to prevent our military secrets from becoming the possessions of our enemies, and how to be sure that, in doing that, we don't cover up information that ought to be made public. (*continuing reading*): "In the present defense mobilization period, it has become necessary to make, in an increasing number of cases, military secrets available to executive agencies other than the military departments, in order that these other agencies might effectively perform their functions that are necessary in supporting the defense effort. It is also necessary for some of these civilian agencies — such as the Central Intelligence Agency, the Federal Bureau of Investigation, for example — to originate and protect some information vital to our defense.

"It should be readily apparent that military secrets in the hands of these other agencies should be protected just as much as when they are in the hands of the military departments. It would also seem to be sensible to provide that different agencies take the same kind of precautions to protect this information. It would not make any sense to have a paper containing military secrets carefully locked up in a safe in the Pentagon, with a copy of the same paper left lying around on the desk of a lawyer in the Justice Department.

"Now, the purpose of this executive order is to provide a common sense answer to these problems. It is to provide that information affecting the national security shall continue to be protected when it gets out of the hands of the military departments and into the hands of other agencies. The purpose is to provide that these other agencies shall provide the same kind of protection that is provided in the military departments.

"Another purpose of the order — and it is a most important purpose — is to provide that information shall not be classified and withheld from the public on the ground that it affects the national security, unless it is in fact actually necessary to protect such information in the interest of national security. In other words, one of the purposes of this executive order is to correct abuses which may have grown up by use of over-classification of information in the name of national security.

"I think this executive order represents a reasonable approach to a very difficult problem. I think it will work in the public interest, and I expect to watch it closely, to see that it is not used as an excuse for withholding information to which the public is entitled.

"It may well be that experience under the order will indicate that it should be changed. In that case, I will be glad to change it — and I will be glad to give consideration to reasonable suggestions for changes that are advanced in good faith.

"I would like to suggest to those who are seriously and honestly concerned about this matter, that they consider it objectively and with the interests of the United States uppermost in their minds. I would like to suggest that they consider how we can best accomplish objectives which all of us should be able to agree upon. I do not believe that the best solution can be reached by adopting an approach based on the theory that everyone has a right to know our military secrets and related information affecting the national security."

Now, I am going to hand you this — this in mimeographed form, and I hope every one of you will take a good look at it, and that you will give it to your editors and your publishers. And remember that 95 percent of our secret information has been revealed by newspapers and slick magazines . . .

Q: (*interposing*) Mr. President, . . .

The President: (*continuing*) . . . and that is what I am trying to stop.

Q: (*continuing*) . . . can you give us some examples of what caused this order?

The President: Yes. The most outstanding example was the publication in *Fortune* magazine of all the locations and the maps of our atomic energy plants. And then, in this very town — in every town in the country — were published air maps of Washington, New York, Chicago, San Francisco, Seattle, and other of our great cities, with arrows pointing to the key points in those towns.

Q: I think that information was given out by the departments . . .

The President: (*interposing*) Well, I don't care who gave it out. The publishers had no business to use it, if they had the welfare of the United States at heart.

Q: I don't know whether it was the military or atomic energy . . .

The President: (*interposing*) I don't care who gave it out, Pete [Brandt]. The publisher should be just as patriotic as I am, and I wouldn't give it out.

Q: The story was over the wire . . .

The President: (*interposing*) Well, I don't care about that . . .

Q: (*continuing*) . . . attributed to a military agency . . .

The President: (*continuing*) Yes, and if the military agency gives you that, and an atomic bomb falls on you on account of that, at the right place, who is to blame?

Q: Well, my — my experience has been that the editors did not make up these maps . . .

The President: (*interposing*) They did, in *Fortune* magazine.

Q: I mean, the Civil Defense Administration . . .

The President: (*interposing*) Well, the — they were air pictures of the great cities. And it's terrible. I wish I had them of Russia and their manufacturing plants. I could use them.

Q: Mr. President, when was that Yale survey made, sir?

The President: Oh, just a short time ago — just a short time ago.

Q: May I ask, Mr. President, right along the line of your effort to safeguard military and security information, what safeguards are there that the security officer will not be overzealous? As I recall, the first action taken under your executive order was the statement by the security officer of the OPS, who said that security information is anything which is embarrassing to OPS?

The President: And he had the carpet pulled out from under him, if you remember. (*laughter*)

Q: You are the one man to watch everything, except no one man can watch everything.

The President: No — that is correct — that is correct. And I hate censorship just as badly as you do, and I will protect you against that as far as I can. But the safety and welfare of the United States of America comes first with me.

May Craig: Well, Mr. President, . . .

Q: (*interposing*) As a corollary question, there was a speech on Capitol Hill, I believe by Senator Benton — although I am not sure — that each department which has a security officer also has a man who fights for release of information?

The President: Well, I don't know about that. I don't know about that. What is it, May [Craig]?

May Craig: Mr. President, have you weighed the importance of the free press in relation to military security . . .

The President: (*interjecting*) Yes, . . .

May Craig: (*continuing*) . . . as both important to . . .

The President: (*continuing*) . . . Yes.

May Craig: (*continuing*) . . . this country?

The President: Yes — yes. A free press is just as important as the — a free press is just as important as the Bill of Rights, and that is what is contained in the Bill of Rights.

May Craig: Yes sir. But do you not think you are giving dangerous power to civilian agencies to say what shall be given to the people?

The President: I am not so sure. We will have to wait and find out. If that is the case, why we will change it, as I said right here. (*indicating the statement*)

May Craig: Do you not think that censorship is always abused to a degree?

The President: I don't know. I have had no experience.

May Craig: I have, sir, and I find that it always is by the military.

The President: Well, I will ask Elmer Davis [formerly head of the Office of War Information in World War Two] what he thinks about that.

Elmer Davis: Is there any program for any training in uniform standards for the security officers?

The President: I hope there will—I hope there will be.

Mr. Short: (*to the president*) Mr. President, that was provided, sir. There is training in uniform standards by the ICIS, and the ICIS is going to review all of these classifications.

Q: Mr. President, . . .

Macon Reed: (*interposing*) Mr. President, did I understand you . . .

Q: (*interposing*) Didn't hear what Joe said, Mr. President?

The President: He said that there was provided in the order a training program for these men, and for uniform standards, and that training would be carefully supervised.

Macon Reed: Did I understand you to say, sir, that 95 percent of our secret information has been revealed by newspapers and slick magazines, and that is what I am trying to stop? Is that correct—is that correct, sir?

The President: That's right. That's correct. That's the answer.

Q: Mr. President, on this question of the maps, I wonder if we could recapitulate that just a little? Do we understand correctly that in event that a newspaper or magazine gets some information from, say, the Defense Department, do you think, sir, that the primary responsibility on whether that is published is on the publisher and not on the originating agency?

The President: There is no question about that, because they are very careful not to publish a lot of things that I say. (*laughter*)

Q: Mr. President . . .

Q: (*interposing*) Mr. President, just a technical question. What maps are we having reference to here?

The President: Air maps of the cities of the United States.

Q: Are you referring to any one in particular, or just some that have been published?

The President: If you will look back through the magazines, you will find—or the daily papers—the *News* here in Washington printed an air map of the city of Washington and pointed out the key places in it.

Q: Thank you very much.

The President: That is what I am worried about now. I am not trying to suppress information. I am trying to prevent us from being wiped out.

Q: Mr. President, to get the record clear, those maps indicating the vital points in cities, weren't they issued by the Civil Defense Administration?

The President: I don't know where they came from. I only know what I saw in the paper.

Q: Mr. President, I would like to clear up this 95 percent. You say the Yale—secret information has been disclosed. You would not have had that 95 percent disclosed that was already disclosed?

The President: No. There's a lot of it I wouldn't disclose, but the —95 percent of it has been made public, Pete [Brandt].

Q: Well, I know that the Central Intelligence and the others say that 95 percent of their information comes from magazines.

The President: That is correct.

Q: Yes.

The President: That is absolutely correct.

Q: As I understand the statement, that . . .

The President: (*interposing*) Ninety-five percent of our secret information has been disclosed.

Q: I think we are talking about two different things.

The President: Well, maybe . . .

Q: But is that . . .

The President: The *Post-Dispatch* and I are usually talking about two different things, Pete [Brandt]. (*laughter*)

Q: Not on military affairs. Not on military affairs. But the—this 95 percent of our—of our secret information which you want to keep secret has been disclosed?

The President: That is the information I have from Central Intelligence.

Q: Well, Mr. President, who classified that 95 percent as secret?

The President: The military.

Q: The military? Thank you.

Q: Mr. President, could you say . . .

The President: (*adding*) Military and State.

Q: (*continuing*) . . . could you say what is the unit of information? It is 95 percent of the facts or 95 percent of the documents or maps? How is the 95 percent figure arrived at?

The President: It takes into consideration all the things you mentioned.

Q: Mr. President, I am a little confused. Was that the Yale survey . . .

The President: (*interjecting*) That's right.

Q: (*continuing*) . . . that you are thinking about, that said that 95 percent of the secret information has been revealed?

The President: That's correct.

Q: Mr. President . . .

Q: (*interposing*) Mr. President, I would like to raise a case in point and get your reaction to it. Yesterday, Mr. Short announced on your behalf, another atomic bomb had been exploded, . . .

The President: (*interjecting*) That's right.

Q: (*continuing*) . . . and said that further details would not be given, because it might adversely affect our national security. Right after that, the Associated Press came through with a story quoting an unidentified source as saying that there had been two explosions, one of them a fizzle, and then quoting still later a congressman — also unidentified — as saying that the explosions had taken place in the last three or four days. Now, would you give some reaction to that, as a specific example of information over and above that which was released by the White House?

The President: I think that is an example.

Q: What was that, Mr. President?

The President: I said I think that is an example.

Q: Of what, sir?

The President: Of disclosing information that should not be disclosed.

Q: Well, Mr. President, . . .

Q: (*interposing*) Mr. President, . . .

Q: (*continuing*) . . . don't you think the Russians knew it! I mean . . .

The President: (*interposing*) They exploded it. Of course they knew it! (*laughter*)

Q: Yes sir, so why would it hurt our national security?

The President: Because we have got to find out what they are doing, May [Craig], so we will know what to do.

Q: I didn't get the last part? Disclosure of our means of detecting . . .

The President: (*interposing*) That's right—that's right. That's right—that is exactly right.

Q: Mr. President, how far did this Yale survey figure in the decision to put out this order?

The President: I didn't sign the order until I got it.

Q: Mr. President, some of this information comes out from Congress. Now the executive order doesn't apply to that. What about the responsibility of the publisher on information released by congressmen?

The President: I can't answer that.

Q: Mr. President, this may be—I may be simple-minded about this . . .

The President: (*interjecting*) No you're not, Smitty [Merriman Smith].

Q: (*continuing*) . . . but how did Yale know? (*laughter*)

The President: They made the survey.

Q: (*interjecting*) How did they get all this secret information?

The President: They made a survey and supplied it to Central Intelligence. That is how it came about.

Q: I just wonder what Yale was doing with that information?

The President: They got it out of the newspapers and magazines and sent it down here, and Central Intelligence came to the conclusion that they knew that 95 percent of it was disclosed.

Q: Mr. President, did the CIA recognize and agree with the Yale survey that 95 percent . . .

The President: (*interposing*) Yes. Yes.

Q: They agreed with it?

The President: Yes. They made the report to me.

Q: The CIA reported to you?

The President: Yes.

Q: Mr. President, recently the Defense Department gave out certain information about the Matador, also on these guided missiles, and so forth. That was published in probably every paper in the land. Was that the publisher's responsibility not to publish that?

The President: I think so, if they want to protect the country.

Q: Wouldn't it be better to tighten up over at Defense?

The President: That is what we are doing. I say, that is what we are doing, and that is what you are fussing about.

Q: Do you think publishers — if the publishers wanted to protect the country, they shouldn't have printed the pictures . . .

The President: (*interposing*) They ought to think about the welfare of the country, just the same as I do, Smitty, and I think most of them would, if they would stop and think about it.

Q: Mr. President, I don't want to defend editors, but . . .

The President: (*interjecting*) It's all right with me.

Q: (*continuing*) . . . these maps were used as part of the civilian defense program, to make the people alert to the dangers of atomic bombs.

The President: I agree, but then I don't think that it should have been made available to the Russians.

Q: Mr. President, do I understand that there was no A-bomb explosion in Russia that fizzled?

The President: I am making no inferences at all. I made the announcement yesterday, the only one that I can make.

Q: Mr. President, I would like to ask a question that I think maybe my editors are going to ask me if I don't ask you.

The President: All right, Bob [Nixon].

Q: Are you suggesting that perhaps — that — that the editors and publishers that we supply our news stories to, should ask — ask some agency in the government . . .

The President: (*continuing*) No, I am not, Bob. I am asking the editors and the publishers to take the same viewpoint of the safety of the United States that I take, and I am not asking them to ask anybody to help them do it. They ought to know.

Q: I know that many times we receive statements from members of Congress, for instance, and we go ahead and write stories about those statements. Perhaps many times a reporter feels that that information might be of a security nature, but if it is on the record up there on the Hill, there is nothing we can really do except to go ahead and put it out.

The President: That is up to you Bob. The safety of the country is in your hands just the same as it is in mine.

Q: Mr. President, do you think everyone in Washington talks too much?

The President: I wouldn't say that.

Q: Mr. President, I have a—if I may inject a political question which—we were down in the governors' co nference, and Jimmy Byrnes seems to have had some information that you were not going to run again, and—the burden of the office is too much . . .

Voices: (*interposing*) Louder—louder. We can't hear!

Q: (*continuing*) . . . the burden of the office is too much, and that the two-term constitutional amendment really shows that the people apply it to you, and in case you do run—I mean, he will oppose you; and his own candidates are Senator Russell, Senator George and Senator Byrd of Virginia?

The President: Jim didn't get his information from me.

Q: What's that?

The President: I said Jim didn't get his information from me.

Q: Do you think he is on the—do you think he has made a fair appraisal . . .

The President: (*interposing*) I have no comment on that.

Q: What's your comment on his candidates, sir?

The President: No comment.

Q: Do you think they would be good men for the presidency, sir?

The President: No comment.

Q: Mr. President, . . .

Q: (*interposing*) Mr. President, in your reading of the—of your written statement, parenthetically you said, as I got it, that the Yale survey found that 95 percent of the information had been made—of military information had been made public?

The President: Of our secret information. That covers everything.

Q: Had been made public?

The President: Not just military, but state and everything—that's right.

Q: Mr. President, there has been a controversy recently about the removal of crosses from thirteen thousand graves in Hawaii, and Mrs. Edith Mourse Rogers of Massachusetts has introduced a bill to force the army to restore those crosses to the graves. I wonder if that will be—if you have consulted, or what you think about it?

The President: No, I haven't. I haven't. I know nothing about it, Smitty.

Q: Mr. President, . . .

Q: (*interposing*) Mr. President, could I ask one practical question? What will happen to a reporter who prints something the government doesn't want printed?

The President: Nothing. We have had him print things that would cause our men to be shot in the back, and nothing was done to them, right in the middle of the war.

Q: Mr. President, could you give us some information about this White House conference, concerning which Mr. Stassen testified on the Hill, dealing with aid to China? There seems to be a little confusion . . .

The President: (*interposing*) I have no recollection of any such conference.

Q: You have no such recollection?

The President: No such recollection of any such conference.

Q: I would like to ask two questions that have been suggested by journalists visiting the conference this morning. The first question is, does the question of what line the Western Allies hold in Germany — that is, in case of attack — the Elbe to be held, or the Rhine on the French quarter — does that depend on whether or not the German people agree to contribute to their own defense?

The President: That is a military question, and I can't answer it.

Q: The second question: Do you favor a free election over all Germany on the subject of — as suggested by the Adenauer government?

The President: I can't answer that question, either.

Q: Mr. President, do you think that the continuing Russian A-bomb tests have made the danger of World War Three more imminent?

The President: I am not sure. I hope it hasn't.

Q: Mr. President, . . .

Q: (*interposing*) Mr. President, do the security rules apply to broadcasters and telecasters as distinguished from publishers?

The President: Oh yes, it should.

Q: You didn't mention it.

The President: I have heard broadcasters, and I listen to a lot of them talk about visits they have had to Korea, and reveal what our strategy is going to be. And you can't fight battles on that basis.

Mr. Short: (*to the President*) Mr. President, so far as the order itself is concerned, it applies only to officials and employees of the United States government.

The President: Joe wants me to make it perfectly clear that this order only applies to the officials of the United States government. My comments, though, apply to everybody who gives away our state secrets.

Q: Mr. President, I want to ask you, so there won't be any confusion, is the government going to decontrol meat?

The President: No. Period. We are going to enforce the rules against people who are disobeying the law under meat control.

Q: Well, is the OPS going to be aided by any other government agencies?

The President: Every agency of the government will cooperate with them.

Q: In the enforcement?

The President: Yes.

Q: Mr. President, as you must have known about this bomb for quite a time, is there any relationship between the fear of the new explosion in Russia and this executive order?

The President: No relation whatever. The order was signed before the bomb had gone off.

Q: As I remember it, that was released at the Pentagon — on the Matador — with photographs at the same time. The question was asked the White House later, was that one of the secret weapons that you have referred to?

The President: Which one was that? I don't know what you are talking about.

Q: Matador. As I understood your report, . . .

The President: (*interjecting*) Yes.

Q: (*continuing*) . . . there should have been no news printed on that?

The President: Yes.

Q: Well, now, when the Department of Defense hands us photographs and stories, are we supposed to censor that ourselves?

The President: Well, do you believe in saving the United States from becoming . . .

Q: (*interposing*) I don't think it should have been given out at the Pentagon.

The President: Well, that is your opinion, and you are entitled to it.

Q: Well, Mr. President, is the effect of what you are asking now, the — that the editors of the country impose a voluntary censorship?

The President: I am asking them to use good judgment for the safety of the United States. I am not asking for any censorship at all.

Q: Regardless of what was put out from the Pentagon?

The President: That's right — or anybody else.

Q: Mr. President, wouldn't that practically require the establishment of a security officer in every news room in helping to standardize their . . .

The President: (*interposing*) Well, I don't know how you can, when I read some of the papers. But I am just telling you what I think, that patriotism is universal, and the welfare of the United States is the first thing we ought to think about.

Q: Well, Mr. President, you told us at the news conference that this pilotless plane was one of the new weapons about which . . .

The President: (*interposing*) Did I? I don't remember it, Tony [Vaccaro].

Q: I was just wondering . . .

The President: (*continuing*) I don't remember.

Q: Mr. President, recently Senator McMahon made a speech in Congress in which he said among other things that a few billion dollars more spent on atomic weapons production can put such weapons on a mass-produced basis. That would make each weapon cost less than one tank now costs. Through that, the country could save a great deal of money in its defense efforts, and in effect could do away with our present conventional weapons, reduce our armed forces and make — make a great deal of savings in that way. Is there any shortcut to national defense?

The President: No, there is not.

Q: Mr. President, getting back once more to this 95 percent figure, may we have permission to quote this line: "Remember that 95 percent of our secret information has been revealed by the newspapers and slick magazines, and that is what I am trying to stop"?

The President: Yes.

Q: Mr. President, when Mr. Dulles left your office yesterday — when Dulles left your office yesterday, he indicated you might have some comment on his visit?

The President: Well, I sent for him to offer to make him ambassador to Japan, and he didn't think he should take the job because he thought he ought to try to save the Republican party from going isolationist. (*laughter*)

Q: Do you think that is a worthy objective?

The President: I certainly do. (*more laughter*)

Q: What was the question?

Q: What was the question?

The President: Bob [Nixon], they wanted to know what Mr. Dulles came to see me about, and I sent for him—sent for Mr. Dulles and told him that I would make him ambassador to Japan if he wanted to be, and he believed he couldn't take the job because he wanted to stay in civil life and try to save the Republican party from isolationism. (*much laughter*)

Q: Thank you, Mr. President!

The President: That's all right.

(*hurried exits*)[22]

This press conference devoted almost entirely to a discussion of security information was but one in a series of developments that constituted a chain reaction to Executive Order 10290. A chronology of the follow-up steps taken in the office of the president in the wake of the order would run something like this:

1. Executive Order 10290 was issued on September 24, 1951. Accompanying it was a letter to heads of executive agencies and departments explaining how the order was to be put into effect.
2. Also issued on the same date was a statement to the public explaining that the order was for security, not censorship, purposes.
3. On October 4, 1951, another statement was issued for public release defending the order, claiming it had been misunderstood and giving further explanations and reasons.
4. Also on October 4, after the president had allowed his press conference on that date to be devoted almost exclusively to the order, Press Secretary Short issued a statement clarifying to the newsmen some of the views which the president had expressed at the conference.
5. It was necessary for the president to order the recision of an Office of Price Stabilization memorandum issued on October 5 instructing the OPS staff to withhold any information that might be embarrassing. The OPS order was rescinded personally by the president 129 minutes after it was announced by OPS.
6. An exchange of correspondence between the president and Herbert F. Corn, president of the Associated Press Managing

Editors Association, was made public, emphasizing the strong division on attitude toward the order.
7. On January 12, 1952, announcement was made of the creation of the "United States Information Service Subcommittee on Executive Order 10290," which was set up to carry out the directions contained in the order.

Protests against the new ruling were loud and angry. Newspapers called the order "a dangerous instrument of news suppression," "a creeping censorship of a kind never before established in this country," and "An Evil Order."[23] An *Editor & Publisher* editorial on the subject was entitled simply "Blackout."[24] A cartoon entitled "Classified," drawn by Fred L. Packer of the *New York Daily Mirror*—which depicted Truman chiding the press with the remark, "You editors ought to have more sense than to print what I say!"—was awarded a Pulitzer prize as the best cartoon of the year,[25] and a Michigan newspaperman instituted a Senate investigation of the president's action.[26]

Despite these attacks, the president's order stood firm. He took little notice of them, with the exception of a column written by Arthur Krock of the *New York Times*, describing the press conference of October 4, 1951. He wrote Krock the following letter:

I've just read your column about my security press conference. You give me credit for the responsibility of the men who were the source of the information about which I talked. I wish that were true.

You newspapermen have a complex that anyone who tells you of any of your shortcomings is either ambitious to be a dictator or else he is an ignoramus. But you should take into consideration that we are no longer in the gay nineties of Ben Harrison, William McKinley, or Teddy, the Rough Rider.

We are faced with the most terrible responsibility that any nation ever faced. From Darius I's Persia, Alexander's Greece, Hadrian's Rome, Victoria's Britain, no nation or group of nations has had our responsibilities. If we could spend one year's military appropriations to develop the Euphrates Valley, the plateau of Ethiopia, the tableland of South America—if we could open the Rhine Danube waterway, the Keil Canal, the Black Sea straits to free trade, if Russia would be a good neighbor and use her military expenditures for her own economic development, I would not have to scold the publishers for giving away our military secrets. Wish you'd do a little soul searching and see if at *great* intervals the president may be right.

The country is yours as well as mine. You find no trouble in *suppressing* news in which I'm interested. Why can't you do a little safety policing?[27]

Truman's concept of press responsibility never deviated from the simple formula of judgment-plus-patriotism for handling all security information problems. When queried about the prospects of a truce in Korea by Christmas of 1951, he replied: "I don't expect anything until it happens. I do not want to be quoted on anything regarding Korea. Now, this situation is exceedingly delicate and dangerous, and it is your situation as well as mine, and anything that is done over here that embarrasses General Ridgway injures our bargaining position and may get some boys shot that otherwise wouldn't be shot. So keep still about Korea and the truce."[28]

Truman continued in the same bluntly earnest vein after being asked if his remarks about Korea were off the record: "Yes, it's off the record—it's off the record. I just want you to use the same judgment that I have to use as a citizen of the United States for the protection of our forces in Korea. It is up to you just as well as it is to me, to see that those boys don't get shot in the back."[29]

The only logical inference that can be drawn from the data is that the president never consciously advocated censorship, in any form in which he understood the term, as a weapon to use against an antagonistic press. This is not to deny the dangerous implications that may have existed in the security order, as catalogued and reviewed on many occasions by the sincere protagonists for freedom of the press.[30] But the evidence is that the president had no desire to impose a harsh censorship on the press as a retaliative or punitive measure.

In no other document, perhaps, did Truman set forth his views so cogently as in a letter to the Criminal Law Section of the American Bar Association four days before the issuance of Executive Order 10290. Addressing Arthur J. Freund, chairman of the group, the president expressed an understanding of the largeness of the problem, which was seldom revealed in his other comments on the subject of personal rights and national security. Particularly in the following excerpts does he demonstrate a recognition of the basic distinction between oppression by censorship and protection of the public welfare through the regulation of security information:

The great peril of Soviet aggression which confronts the United States and, indeed, all free nations today makes it necessary that we continually scrutinize our national security measures . . . to make sure that they are entirely adequate for the critical times in which we live. The federal government is doing that and will continue to do so. As I have pointed out in the past, however, the greatest contribution that the United States has to make to its own citizens and to the world is the heritage of freedom — freedom of speech, freedom of religion and freedom of political belief. That heritage is not only the object of all our protective security measures, it is also the basic source of our true overall national security.

Although the nation has always united against any external peril, blind obedience to authority has never been characteristic of Americans. Rather, they have been questioners, doubters, experimenters, and very often articulate and vociferous dissenters. This attitude is perhaps our unique and most valuable national asset. It has promoted our moral and spiritual welfare. It has made possible great material advances. It has forced discussion, examination and reexamination of policies on every level. The free interchange of opinion and criticism thus made possible is in a very real sense the most important element of national security we possess, for it provides a greater likelihood that we will take the right course than does any system in which policies are determined by a few leaders whom none dares criticize.

The fact is—and what an object lesson there is for us in that fact—that the repressive security measures of the police states do not promote their overall national security. On the contrary, they hurt it. They hurt it because the dictators of those countries have thereby made certain that they will not receive any opinions which do not conform with their own preconceived opinions—that even the intelligence reports which they receive about the strength and vulnerability of other countries will be slanted to conform with the party line view about those countries, however distant that may be from the real facts, lest the men who prepare those reports be suspected of being too friendly to foreign powers. Thus, in their mistaken zeal to promote their security by excessive police measures the totalitarian countries have actually undermined their security by making certain that their national policy decisions will be the product of the intuition or hunches or biases of the dictators rather than actual facts and full discussion.

Full discussion can take place only in an atmosphere of freedom —an atmosphere in which a different, or even an unpopular idea does not render the motives and patriotism of its proponent suspect, as would be the case in a totalitarian country. This national asset must be preserved. Unfortunately, the very crisis which requires that we take action to protect our security generates fear and suspicion. Because of this, there appears to be a growing confusion as to what are wise and appropriate security measures and what are measures that have little or no merit in terms of security, but which may and often do inflict irreparable harm upon innocent individuals and at the same time gravely injure real national security by enforcing conformity of political expression and thought. Too many Americans have not made a sufficient distinction between the two. . . .[31]

In addition to pointing out the democratic approach to security regulations, Truman acknowledged the precise nature of the problem in which the factors of press responsibility and press freedom had to be maintained in a delicate balance. He appealed, in closing, to the lawyers for continuing study and recommendations regarding the subject:

All these measures and proposed measures should be given critical, constructive, and public consideration by the bar to help our people and the authorities involved determine whether they are reasonable and practical methods of maintaining security or whether their potentialities in terms of stifling freedom of expression outweigh their utility as security measures. Searching scrutiny of this character by able and fair-minded lawyers will greatly contribute toward enlightening the whole nation as to how we can best strike the difficult balance between security and individual rights in these trying times.[32]

Reduced to the simple language more typical of the president, Truman said of the controversial security order three years later: "All I was trying to do was protect the country, and if you'll read the order carefully, you'll find that there wasn't any censorship in it. It was the only way. This was an effort to stop the leaks that had been the bane of our lives in the State and Defense departments. We always had trouble with 'leakers.' An attempt was made with this order to put a stop to it. I just made up my mind to see what we could do with an order."[33]

Leaving the problem, then, at the doorstep of an "irresponsible press" where, in his opinion, it had originated, Truman concluded: "If I had had the cooperation of the press, I would not have needed to issue it."[34]

Chapter 13

OF SPECIAL INTEREST

"[The *Wall Street Journal*] is the special interests publication, published in New York City every day. They use half their editorial columns giving me hell, because I am for the people."

A QUICK REVIEW OF THE POLITICAL CAREER OF HARRY Truman is sufficient to disclose the recurrent antipathy toward "special interests" that characterized his out-and-out New Deal-Fair Deal philosophy while president and that seemed to permeate his thinking in nonpolitical situations as well.[1] Especially during the campaign of 1948 was his animosity toward special privilege brought out in bold relief when he told audience after audience: "There is just one issue in this campaign—it's the people against the special interests." What Truman meant by "special interests" were those minority groups of society deemed to represent the wealthy, influential class opposed to the welfare program of his and Roosevelt's administration. Included in the catchall term were corporations, big business, lobbyists, Wall Street financiers, advertisers, private utilities, and miscellaneous other interests representing private capital.

Perhaps it was natural for the president to link this opposition with that of the press when, in 1948, he faced what appeared to him to be a combination of these elements militating against his nomination and election. It was not until that year that he apparently decided that the communication media of the country had sold themselves to the moneyed interests and that he employed for the first time as president the term "kept press."

In his diary, Truman made the following entry on July 15, 1948: "I called a special session of Congress. My, how the opposition screams. I am going to attempt to make them meet their platform promises before election. That is according to the 'kept' press and the opposition leadership 'cheap politics.' I wonder what 'expensive politics' will be like. We will see."[2]

Within a matter of weeks, Truman carried the charge against the press from the privacy of his diary to the public platform. The first instance in which he openly linked the newspapers and radio with special interests occurred in Hillsboro, Texas, where he spoke to a large crowd from the rear platform of his special train: "You know, 90 percent of the press in this country are against the president of the United States because he believes in the welfare of the people; and 90 percent of the radio commentators are against the president because they know that he believes that the government of the United States should be a government for the people and not for the special interests."[3]

This was merely the beginning. At Paula Valley, Oklahoma, he said of the *Wall Street Journal*: "That is the special interests publication, published in New York City every day. They use half their editorial columns giving me hell, because I am for the people."[4]

Hinting that the special interests were resorting to paid advertising campaigns to vitiate the integrity of the nation's newspapers, Truman declared at a rally in Louisville: "The NAM spent a million and a half on newspaper advertising. . . . A special clip sheet with NAM propaganda went to seventy-five hundred weekly newspapers and to twenty-five hundred columnists and editorial writers."[5]

This was not the first time that Truman had expressed suspicion of an unholy alliance between newspapers and free-spending advertisers,[6] but it was the first time he had done so in a public address. A week later, he again charged that newspapers were in league with the space buyers: "The newspapers and the million dollar propagandists misrepresent the president. They are trying to tell you that I don't know what I am talking about, but I am going to prove to you before I get through with this campaign that I do know what I am talking about. I think the majority of the people will know it, too, when I get through in spite of all the propaganda they can put out. That is why I have come to see you. That is why I am trying to give you a chance to know the truth."[7]

In one of his strongest indictments of the press, Truman told an audience in St. Louis that "the smear campaign on your president" had begun when his twenty-one-point message on domestic policy had gone to the Congress on September 6, 1945, and that a united attack was launched against him by headline writers, columnists, radio commentators, and editorial writers "not because they believed anything they said or wrote, but because they were paid to do it."[8]

As Truman neared the end of his 1948 campaign trail, he fired the following Parthian shot on his way back to Washington: "They say that the radio commentators and the newspapers would not be against me if I hadn't stepped on the toes of so many big corporations and so many lobbies."[9]

In his introduction to the State of the Union message to the Eighty-first Congress in January 1949, the newly elected president vigorously condemned venality in the press: "Now, I have no bitterness in my heart against anyone — not even the bitter opposition press and its henchmen, the paid columnists and managing editors, and the bought and paid for radio commentators. . . . You have learned that the people do not believe in the kept press and the paid radio."[10]

There is evidence that Truman never deviated from his belief that newspapers and radio were controlled by the special interests through advertising subsidies. In 1949, he renewed the criticisms that had characterized his references to the press during the preceding year, warning at a Jefferson-Jackson Day dinner in Washington: "The special interests are on the job year in and year out—seven days a week, twenty-four hours a day. They work through their lobbies and pressure groups, through the editorial pages and the columnists and commentators they control . . . This one-sided barrage of propaganda seems overwhelming at first. There are no full-page ads on our side. In fact—all we have on our side is the people. Thank God for that!"[11]

An attempt by a Washington correspondent, who later became Truman's press secretary, to get Truman to name some of the special interests to which he referred so often, drew the following unrewarding answer from the president: "It would not be difficult to name them, Joe [Short, of the *Baltimore Sun*], but then I don't think I need to name them for a reporter of the *Baltimore Sun*. They know the special interests and support them all the time."[12]

A year later, Truman was writing to a confidential adviser, Max Lowenthal: "If you will study the press attacks on Washington and Jefferson, Jackson, Andrew Johnson, Grover Cleveland, and Woodrow Wilson, you will see that there is not much difference in the patter of the 'kept press' then and now. It never bothers me when I think I am doing right."[13]

In 1952, Truman complained on more than one occasion about the advertising campaign that was being conducted by the light and power companies of America through their trade association to re-sell the principle of "free enterprise" and to combat and discourage "creeping socialism" in the form of government participation in the public utility business. He asserted in a Chicago speech in March: "You can hardly pick up a newspaper or a magazine these days without seeing an expensive full-page advertisement denouncing the 'socialism' of our public power program. Incidentally, the cost of these ads is mostly paid for by the taxpayers, because the costs of such advertising are deductible from income taxes. It looks to me as though that advertising campaign itself is pretty close to 'socialism,' because the taxpayers finance so much of the cost."[14]

After making this observation, the president described the real threat that he saw in paid institutional advertising: "I want to say right here that this propaganda campaign is one of the most cynical and dangerous developments in many years. It is cynical because it assumes the people of this country cannot be trusted to decide on the basis of facts what is best for their own welfare. It assumes that the way to get things decided in a democracy is through big, expensive advertising campaigns in magazines and newspapers, and a big, expensive lobby in Washington."[15]

Truman appeared to be troubled because the media allowed their space and time to be purchased by the private utility industry, without realizing or acknowledging the inherent dangers of which the president warned. He called attention to the situation again in May of 1952, concluding his remarks with a stinging accusation of treasonable conduct on the part of the advertisers and, by implication, the journalistic media as well: "The private power companies are spending millions of millions of dollars on this campaign. They are sponsoring nationwide radio programs which cost them many thousands of dollars every week. They are running full-page ads in the big magazines, month after month. Do you know that just one full-page ad in Mr. [sic] Clare Booth Luce's *Life* magazine costs $17 thousand? And in one big corporation-controlled *Saturday Evening Post*, it costs $12 thousand. They are turning out pamphlets and leaflets and canned editorials by the score, and spreading them around the country. . . . This is nothing less than an attack on the fundamental principles of our democratic country. Instead of letting people make up their own minds on the basis of the facts and the truth, this private power company propaganda is deliberately designed to conceal the facts and to manipulate people's opinions by appealing to their emotions and not to their reason."[16]

Reflecting on the 1952 campaign, Truman reasserted his conviction that an active conspiracy existed between the press and the business interests and that one was just as culpable as the other: "There was not a single metropolitan newspaper, except the Cox papers, that was editorially favorable to the continuance of the most prosperous administration in the history of the United States. Why, I could never understand. I suppose it was the pressure of the advertisers."[17] The truth of the matter seemed to be that the opposition had more money to spend for advertising, and Truman was inclined to impugn the press for accepting it. There is evidence that he appreciated advertising when applied in behalf of Democratic goals and policies. When a group of citizens in the East placed an advertisement supporting national compulsory health insurance in the *New York Times*, the *Washington Post*, and the *Washington Star,* Truman wrote to one of the sponsors: "It certainly was a fine piece of work and I can't tell you how much I appreciated it. I think we are going to get that health program through eventually."[18]

Speaking to the Advertising Council in 1946, two years before his organized assault against the "kept press," the president professed a genuine respect for the power of advertising: "You know, you may not realize it, but the psychological effect of your advertising, properly applied, is much more powerful than the editorial of any newspaper. Many more people get ideas from properly and well-written ads than they do from reading the editorial page. Although there are some great editorial writers in this country, their influence is not nearly so great as pictures and statements that are made on the advertising pages of those same publications."[19]

In his remarks to the same group three years later, he expressed a whimsical concept of the function of advertising, but showed that he appreciated what advertising might accomplish for the federal government: "I find that there are two definitions of advertising. If a politician is on your side and he gets headlines, that is favorable advertising; if he is on the other side and gets headlines that are not in your corner, he is a publicity hound. There is a distinction and a difference there. But the work which has been done for the government on behalf of the government by this organization has been strictly, I think, in the public interest. I always remember the top-notch one—the bond sales department of the Treasury, what a magnificent job was done all during the war in the sale of these bonds. That was advertising at its best, I think.

"And then there are plenty of instances where merchants and large advertisers have contributed immense space to the bond sales, and to the inauguration of the draft, and to a number of other things during the war, which I myself was instrumental in instigating. And I found that those advertisements—if you want to call them that—were exceedingly helpful in getting the job done."[20]

Not only did Truman admit the power for good that was inherent in advertising, but on one occasion he even had kind words for the "special interests" by whom he felt most of the advertising was financed. Two years after the bitter 1948 campaign against big business, when war broke out in Korea, he wrote the chairman of the board of directors of the Standard Oil Company as follows: "I have always known that when the country is faced with difficulties the men in charge of great business organizations are always ready to do whatever is necessary to meet the situation. I came in close contact with them in the Second World War, and I am thoroughly convinced that all of them are patriots."[21]

Judging by the mere weight of the testimony, however, it must be concluded that such expressions of esteem for either the media of advertising or those who used them to promote their own interests represent aberrations from the true course of Truman's thinking. As a master politician, Truman recognized in advertising a powerful weapon, but it was a weapon that he considered to be largely under the control of the enemy camp. Therefore, he wasted little time in theorizing about its possible virtues and depended upon other endowments more readily available for his use. He advised Chester Bowles, who was planning his gubernatorial campaign in Connecticut, in a letter postscript as follows: "P.S. Don't spend a lot of money on advertising! In spite of tours and Bill Benton's experience that line political advertising just doesn't bring in the votes. Handshakes before election day and precinct workers on that day to see that the voters come to the polls win elections."[22]

The last reference to the "kept press" appears in a handwritten note by the president that he jotted down on a piece of hotel stationery at the Statler Hotel in Buffalo, where he spoke on October 10, 1952, on behalf of Adlai Stevenson's campaign for the high office. Truman wrote: "Had a grand reputation and an enthusiastic meeting here yesterday. The kept press tried by every hook and crook to make it appear that the visit was not a success. The morning and afternoon sheets which pose as newspapers are owned by the same outfit and controlled by antiadministration interests. . . ."[23]

To the end, Truman maintained his contention not only that the press was "kept" by financial interests, but that the people felt the same way he did and demonstrated it by voting for him. Bringing this concept down to a specific case, he summed it up this way: "Most high-hat politicians overlook the fact that the voters are just the everyday people and that everyday people . . . don't care very much what the [Kansas City] *Star* and the big bankers think. They are interested in the welfare of the nation, and I think that is one of the reasons that I've been able to go from precinct to presidency in one short life."[24]

Chapter 14

MASS MEDIA MOTIVES

"The object of the sabotage press now, of course, is to make a scoundrel out of Roosevelt, if they can, and naturally I am not going to allow that to happen."

THE MOST CONSISTENT CHARGES THAT TRUMAN LEVELED
at the opposition press were that it was guilty of "sabotaging" his administration, his friends, his foreign policy, and his political objectives. As he conceived it, the antagonism of the general press to his
program transcended the bounds of partisan opposition and
threatened the very framework of the government's domestic and
foreign operations. To the "sabotage press," he attri¹uted motives
and methods ranging from character assassination to treason.

In some of his earliest references to the "sabotage press," the new
president deplored the smear techniques that he found newspapers using against the reputation of the late President Roosevelt and his New
Deal policies. He wrote Wayne Morse of Oregon: "We have a
sabotage press in this country whose principal aim in life has been to
discredit the Roosevelt Administration and whose present approach is
to smear him after he is dead."[1] When a friend sent Truman a copy of
an editorial from the *Chicago Tribune*, which appeared to view
Truman in a favorable light as compared with his predecessor, the
president made a discerning observation: "I know I am wrong when
the *Chicago Tribune* tries to give me credit for something, and if you
read the editorial carefully, you will find there was no credit intended
—it was merely their chance to throw a little mud at a dead
president."[2]

Applauding a complimentary article on Roosevelt written by
Jonathan Daniels for *Liberty,* Truman commented to the author: "I
wish that you and all his friends would continue to see that these
friendly articles are published. As you know, it's the policy of the
Hearst and the McCormick-Patterson press to smear the whole
Roosevelt family when they have an opportunity, and the only way in
the world to offset it is by articles such as yours. It is a fine article, and
I don't know when I have read one I enjoyed more."[3]

The president again cited what he considered one of the basic
aims of the opposition press in the following paragraph from a letter
written November 9, 1945: "The object of the sabotage press now, of
course, is to make a scoundrel out of Roosevelt, if they can, and
naturally I am not going to allow that to happen."[4] This habit of
discrediting the late president, however, was the least of the faults
that Truman found in the press. More annoying to him were the current attacks upon the personnel of his own administration. He complained to a correspondent early in 1946: "The American press has no
patience with a public official no matter what he does, and you have
had enough experience in public life not to let that bother you."[5] In a

letter just one week later, the president drew attention to a specific case: "Take Harry Hopkins as an example — you'd think to read the sabotage press now that he was a sort of saint in his lifetime. That same press pictured him as the lowest devil in hell."[6]

Members of the Advertising Council were approached by the president in 1949 for their cooperation in combatting the harmful effects of such criticism, which, Truman claimed, was keeping qualified men out of government service. He stated: "Now we are faced in the aftermath of war with a situation that is equally important, and one in which you can do an equally good job. It is just as important that people understand the functions of their government in times, such as these, as it is in wartime. It is much harder to get their cooperation. It is a difficult job here to get good men to assume the responsibilities which are inherent in government. They are underpaid, and in addition to that they are not only underpaid and have a difficult time finding living quarters in the capital city — or in any other center where government is established — but they have to take an awful beating. You will find that whenever a man comes to work for the government, he is a fair target for the commentators and the columnists who like to misrepresent the facts — and there are a great many who spend their whole time misrepresenting the facts. They have a tremendous amount of advertising when they do it — not all the right kind of advertising, in my opinion. . . .

"And I am doing everything I possibly can to discredit the people who are forever throwing mud at public servants. There are a great many fine men who have been driven out of public service because they couldn't stand the continual mudslinging that goes on in a lot of these columns. I have in my own staff men who are continually made the target of these people, not for any good reason but simply because they think that spreads out their listeners."[7]

As time went on and Truman felt that press interference with the proper staffing of his administration continued, his denunciation of this form of "sabotage" became more caustic. Incensed by newspaper attacks on his friend and appointee William Boyle, he remarked: "You can rest assured that the dirty columnists headed by Duke Shoop, Walter Winchell, and Pearson will do everything they can to smear Bill Boyle. That is customary with anyone who happens to be in any way connected with me in a confidential manner."[8]

In September 1950, Truman extended this particular criticism of the press to include some of the federal lawmakers as well: "The difficulty these days is to keep good men in high places because of the unjustified attacks made on them by lying columnists and others. In fact, there seem to be just as many men who murder the truth in the Senate as there are writing columns for the newspapers."[9]

Truman obviously resented deeply these attacks on the members of the presidential family and seemed to feel that they were invariably motivated by political aspirations alone. He often took the position that, while the criticisms of the newspapers did not bother him personally, he felt that the opposition press was doing the country a disservice by resorting to such a strategy for blocking his program. He expressed these sentiments on one occasion as follows: "I never give the slightest weight or attention to the brickbats that are thrown my way. The people that cause me worry are good men who have to take these brickbats for me. Very seldom are direct attacks made on the president himself, except by such morons as _____ and his minions, but there have been a number of excellent men who when fighting my battles have been ruined—take for instance Jim Forrestal, Louis Johnson, and a dozen others I could name who have been unmercifully mistreated for no good reason at all. I don't care what they say about me because it has all been said, and there is nothing new that can be hurled at me, but it does make it very difficult to obtain men of ability who generally are thin-skinned in such matters."[10]

The unshakeable loyalty of Truman for his friends and appointees has frequently been cited as one of his most identifying traits of character. One observer remarked that "he is slow to give trust and friendship to people, but his loyalty once given is not lightly taken back. Usually this is good, but there have been more than a few times, especially with regard to personnel problems around the White House and in the executive departments, where the results are not too happy for Mr. Truman, and probably, not for the country."[11]

When asked at a press conference in 1951 if he had any intention of asking Frank E. McKinney to leave the National Democratic Committee, the president replied: "I certainly don't. Mr. McKinney suits me down to the ground. I don't put people in places or ask them to serve in places and then pull the rug from under them the first thing anything happens that the newspapers don't like. It pleases me when they don't like it, because I think it's right."[12]

Writing a former Senate colleague during the final year of his presidency, Truman gave evidence that his attitude toward the "sabotage press" was unchanged from what it had been when he had taken office in 1945: "It has been the policy of the lying columnists and the newspaper editors to initiate attacks on people in the presidential family. You remember they started off on John Snyder.

When that didn't work they transferred their affections to Harry Vaughn, and now they have gone to work on the attorney general. They are setting plans to do the same thing to Bob Lovett, secretary of defense, and to Oscar Chapman, secretary of the interior. They find that the president is not an easy man to intimidate."[13]

It is apparent that Truman looked upon the attacks against his administration as a cumulative effort on the part of the opposition press and not as a series of isolated instances. When a supporter sent him a copy of an antagonistic editorial from the *Huntington* (West Virginia) *Herald-Advertiser,* Truman drew attention to what he considered a conspiracy within the press: "This is part of a propaganda program, the backbone of which consists of McCormick, Hearst, Patterson, and United Press outfit. I don't think there is any reason to get excited about what they are trying to do—they have been trying that sort of an approach on me ever since I became president. They never got anywhere with it, and I don't think they ever will."[14]

An editorial in the *Washington Post*[15]—which advocated the creation of a "commission on national security" composed of citizens and designed to end witch-hunting and irresponsible accusations by such bodies as congressional investigation committees—aroused Truman's suspicion and provoked him to write Philip L. Graham, publisher of the *Post*, as follows: "I read with a great deal of interest the editorial in your May 22 issue of the *Washington Post*, and I am inclined to think that there is an effort to set up a second Congress and Executive Department for the purpose of going around the elected representatives of the people. It is an interesting procedure. It seems to me that if you newspapermen would sit down and analyze the situation for all it is worth and then get behind the domestic and foreign program which this administration advocates we could accomplish something. . . .

"Understand, of course, that it was a most terrible disappoint-ment to all the big guns of the press of the United States when the people decided that they were satisfied with the present incumbent of the White House and it has been the policy of the vast majority of the press ever since that election to do everything possible to discredit the policies which the people want implemented. I am sorry this is the case but I suppose editors and publishers are human just as are politicians."[16]

Broadening his definition of the journalistic cabal whose objec-tive, he said, was to wreck his administration, the president itemized for Senator William Benton some of the specific instances that caused him greatest concern: "There is a concerted effort on the part of the wire services, Associated Press and United Press to discredit whatever the administration forces try to do. If you will analyze the manner in which they handled people who are members of the administration you will see what I mean. For instance they speak of the Democratic organization in Illinois as the Kelly-Nash Machine; they speak of Green's unspeakable organization in Illinois as the Governor Green Organization.

"When the *Saint Louis Post-Dispatch* made an unfounded attack on Bill Boyle and got nowhere with it, they blew it up sky high on the wire services and gave it to every paper in the country. When the *Milwaukee Journal* and the *Madison* (Wisconsin) *Capital Times* state the facts on McCarthy and his income tax escapades, the wire services inform the *Milwaukee Journal* and the *Capital Times* that they must make an investigation to be sure of the facts, but they didn't wait to be sure of the facts with regard to Mr. Boyle, as he happens to be a Democrat and head of the Democratic National Committee.

"You will find if you will study the lines followed by these press people that they are just as guilty of sabotaging the news as *Pravda* and *Izvestia* in Russia. Of course, they are not going to be able to get away with it any more than they did in nineteen hundred and forty-eight, and before this thing is ended, you and I are going to teach them a lesson."[17]

In expressing his conviction of "concerted effort" by certain blocs within the opposition press, Truman was not without the backing of some organized research and counsel on the part of his own advisers. An unsigned memorandum that came to the president's desk on April 19, 1951, sounded a dramatic warning:

The president has probably noticed that the Scripps-Howard newspapers, in recent weeks, have been sharpening their attacks against the administration. There is good reason to believe that this is the opening campaign in a real journalistic war against the Truman program. On Wednesday April 18, the managing editors of *Farm Journal* and *Pathfinder* magazines, both owned by Joe Paw, were summoned to Philadelphia, where they were given orders to step up criticism of the administration. *Pathfinder,* with a circulation of approximately 1,250,000, mostly rural, all mail subscriptions, no newsstand, has been quite liberal toward the administration over the past several years. *Farm Journal,* the largest of its kind in the field, has upwards of over 3,500,000 circulation.[18]

In a retrospective analysis of the antiadministration conduct of the "sabotage press," Truman added the names of other offenders: "There was an effort on the part of a certain segment of the press to discredit the administration in any manner they could. The truth had no weight with Scripps-Howard, Hearst, or the McCormick-Patterson axis for the simple reason that their objective was to discredit the president in everything he did, right or wrong."[19]

The evidence would indicate a concept in Truman's mind of the "sabotage press" as embracing, at one time or another, the major portion of the general press. He clearly demonstrated a tendency, at times, to sweep most segments of the American press—if not all—under this label when they appeared to criticize unjustly the personnel and the policies of his administration. Thus he concluded that an organized press conspiracy was on foot throughout the almost eight years of his presidency.

One of the purposes of this conspiracy, according to the testimony of the recorded data, was to create division between the president and his advisors, or to set one faction in the administration against another. In the two following excerpts from letters to his friends, Truman assures them that he is impervious to such an approach: "You can rest assured that I never let press comments or statements affect my attitude toward my friends. It is a policy of the press, of course, to create a breach or a misunderstanding between members of the same party, particularly under conditions such as exists now. I have had too much experience to allow it to affect me so don't worry about it."[20]

"It seems to be the objective of our newspaper friends to stir up trouble between friends, particularly if they can misrepresent a report of mine. They take extreme pleasure in doing just that. I am not easily swayed by what the newspapers say or what they write about so don't you worry about my attitude toward a good Democrat like you are."[21]

Early in 1952, when General D. Eisenhower's political star was steadily rising, the president wrote him as follows: "I had a press conference the other day[22] in which many questions were asked me and I tried to answer straight from the shoulder. I have had a platter made of that press conference and I am sending to you because I want you to know exactly what took place. As usual, the news hounds are trying to drive a wedge between us. As far as I am concerned that will never happen."[23] Two weeks later, he followed up that overture with another assurance: "You can rest assured that no matter what the professional liars and the pathological columnists may have to say, you and I understand each other."[24]

Proclaiming once more his unswerving loyalty to the dictates of his party regardless of any criticism, Truman complained to an associate in the summer of 1952: "The newspapers have made it a disgrace for a man to stick by the platform on which he is elected. A man who runs out on his political promises is a hero to nearly all the press. That is not my brand of politics."[25]

The retiring president found himself in a delicate position as the Democratic party began to build up a head of steam for the 1952 campaign. It was a position that the press made more difficult, as Truman explained to Senator Benton: "I don't know exactly what my situation will be with regard to the coming campaign as I have to be exceedingly careful not to use the presidential office to overshadow the presidential candidate. It is going to be somewhat of a tight-rope walk to keep that from happening because you know 87 percent of the papers, that is the metropolitan papers, are trying to do everything they can to create difficulties between the Democratic nominee and the president."[26]

As can be seen, most of Truman's allegations against the "sabotage press" were based on the more general aspects of political opposition. There are some references, however, to particular issues on the domestic scene in which the attitude of newspapers convinced him that his accusations were justified. He refers, for example, to such an incident in the following entry in his diary during the second month of his tenure as president: "Had dinner on the south porch all by myself. It is a beautiful outlook across the White House lawn to the Jefferson Memorial with the Washington Monument rising just to the left of the picture. And the sabotage press, represented by Mr. _____, did everything possible to prevent the building of the Jefferson Memorial. It makes a lovely picture from the south porch."[27]

One of the chief executive's most famous slaps at the press was his allusion to the *Chicago Tribune* and the *Spokesman Review* as the "two worst papers" in the country.[28] The immediate provocation was the stunt of collecting "bundles for congress," for the purpose of ridiculing and defeating a bill establishing a pension program for senators and congressmen. Truman came to the defense of the Congress and denounced the Washington newspaper for attempting to wreck the program.

The *Chicago Tribune,* on this occasion at least, was apparently branded on general principles alone, but the effort of the *Spokesman Review* to "sabotage" the congressional measure (which was eventually approved) was never forgotten by the president. Sometime later he wrote in a letter: "You remember the time we voted a pension system and then a good-for-nothing newspaper out in Washington caused us to throw it overboard. That shouldn't happen."[29] And several years later, referring to the same incident, he said: "The press doesn't defend Congress. Whenever it's possible to say something mean about them, they do it."[30]

Truman also resented the objections raised by one paper to his proposal for architectural improvements to the Capitol and to the White House, as revealed in the following remarks: "A little pinheaded congressman from Iowa interested the *Washington Star,* and the House beat the bill. We still have a red sandstone center to the Capitol of the greatest republic in the history of the world, and one of the three great domes of the world hanging in the air! What an accomplishment for a pinheaded congressman and a newspaper! That same 'great' newspaper tried the same tactics when I was making the south front of the White House architecturally correct—but, the 'great' paper didn't have a pinheaded congressman to legislate—and it failed in its wrong purpose."[31]

It was not in matters involving government personnel or domestic policy, however, that the "sabotage press" wreaked the greatest harm, Truman maintained. Newspaper intervention in the administration's diplomatic relations with foreign countries appeared to him to be the cause of damage that was serious and far reaching.[32] He expressed quite eloquently, in a letter to Congressman Lodge on the subject of the Italian colonial situation, his anxiety over this danger: "As in all foreign relations, the water can be very easily muddied and the interests of the people who live in the colonies badly injured, if the matter is worked out in the newspapers. As you know, it is impossible to carry on diplomatic relations with headlines."[33]

To Elmer Davis, his former director of the Office of War Information, the president suggested that "if the news mediums would spend more time supporting the policies which are slowly and gradually becoming successful, it would be a lot easier to run the government and establish a foreign policy that in the end will work."[34]

Newspaper criticism of the conduct of the Korean conflict in its early stages provoked Truman to draw an interesting contrast, at one of his press conferences, between the loyalty displayed by General Douglas MacArthur and the near-treasonable attitude of the press:

> *Q:* Mr. President, are you now in complete agreement with General MacArthur on Formosa?
> *The President:* Let me tell you something that will be good for your soul. It's a pity that you columnists and reporters that represent a certain press service can't understand the ideas of two intellectually honest men when they meet. General MacArthur is the commander-in-chief of the Far East. He is a member of the government of the United States. He is loyal to that government. He is loyal to the president. He is loyal to the president in his foreign policy, which I hope a lot of your papers were—*wish* a lot of your papers were.[35]

Six months later, however, after the Far East commander had been relieved of his duties, the president looked upon the performance of the press as quite consistent with that of the general. This is demonstrated by the following memorandum which Truman sent to Charles Wilson (of General Electric) concerning a fling at pamphleteering by Charles Wilson (of General Motors):

April 11, 1951

MEMORANDUM FOR: Charles E. Wilson, Director
                Office of Defense Mobilization

FROM: The President

Attached is a pamphlet put out by the General Motors. It is almost as bad from the sabotage of the policy as MacArthur's performance—yet these people have profited more by the policies which we have pursued in the last six years than any other organization. This is 100 percent isolationism and one of the difficulties with which we are faced.

I thought maybe you might have an opportunity to discuss the foreign policy situation with Charles Wilson of General Motors. There isn't any difference in this gentleman's performance and Fulton Lewis'—they are both for the complete wreck of the foreign policy which we are trying to pursue—that is support of the United Nations and the endeavor to get peace in the world by negotiation instead of bullets.[36]

When asked at a press conference if he saw any reason for modification of the bipartisan attitude on foreign policy, Truman replied, "Why, certainly not. Of course there isn't any reason, except in Bertie McCormick's mind, or Hearst's. They are isolationists, if you remember."[37] On another occasion, the president was asked what he thought about newspaper reports that "a wave of isolationism" was rising in the United States. His answer was: "I don't think there is any wave of isolationism, outside of the *Chicago Tribune* and those papers."[38]

Elaborating on the subject of isolationism in the press, Truman later explained: "The newspapers in control in the Middle West—Hearst and the McCormick-Patterson axis—have always been isolationists and have made it appear that they represented the thinking of the people of the Middle West, and they don't represent it at all. The people of the Middle West understand international affairs as well as the people on either coast do, and a vast majority of them in the 1920s were for the League of Nations, and a vast majority in the present day are strong for a going United Nations to establish world peace. They're no more isolationist than any other section of the country."[39]

The gravest charge that the president directed at the press with regard to its interference in international affairs appears in one of John Hersey's five "profiles" of the chief executive. Truman is quoted as linking newspaper attacks on his foreign policy directly with Communist China's decision to invade North Korea: "What has appeared in our press, along with the defeat of our leaders in the Senate, has made the world believe that the American people are not behind our foreign policy—and I don't think the communists would ever have dared to do this thing in Korea if it hadn't been for that belief. Why, J_____ [a newspaper publisher] had an editorial just yesterday claiming that he was personally responsible for the defeat of our foreign policy. He *boasts* about it! And the result is the news [about the Chinese Communists' invasion of Korea] we get this morning."[40]

Throughout his administration, the "sabotage press" was looked upon by the president as one of the chief irritants in his diplomatic program.[41] In his final year, his complaint still was that "on the foreign situation, nobody knows exactly what things mean when they come out in the papers."[42] His campaign speeches for Adlai Stevenson in the same year contained numerous references to the members of the opposition press as "the confusers."[43]

In the "sabotage press," then, Truman recognized a persistent enemy that stalked both the domestic and the foreign programs of his administration. In his political concepts and convictions, he was perhaps as positive and as uncompromising as any man who has ever occupied the White House. Therefore, he had no patience with, or trust in, those newspapers which represented to him the strongly entrenched political concepts of "black Republicanism." As illustrated in these pages, he fought back at this contingent of the opposition press with whatever ammunition he could find—sometimes his shots were like rifle bullets at a favorite target like the *Chicago Tribune*, which to him was "the Bertie McCormick sabotage press,"[45] and at other times they could be more accurately described as shotgun blasts aimed in the general direction of the whole American press.

Chapter 15

THE POLITICS
OF PUBLICITY

"They [publishers] don't see any
threat to our political system in having
almost all the newspapers on one
side."

THE EVIDENCE PRESENTED THUS FAR ESTABLISHES TENA-
ble grounds for the conclusion that at the very heart of much of the
controversy and division that existed between the president and the
"opposition press," there was, more often than not, the element of
politics.[1] Although the various and diverse manifestations of his basic
conflict with the press frequently can be linked with specifically identified incidents and situations that are seemingly nonpolitical in
character, a thoughtful study of the man and the president suggests
that his interest in politics was a prime catalyst in the chemistry of his
relations with other men in general[2] and with the American press in
particular.

The highest political aspirations of Truman's life were at stake in
the presidential election of 1948. His defeat was predicted almost
unanimously by the popular polls, the press, and even professional
politicians. Only Truman himself seemed completely confident of a
victory over Dewey in November. He scoffed at the public opinion
polls and at press opposition and developed his own "whistle-stop"
technique to garner a plurality of 2,135,747 popular votes and a victory in the electoral college of 303 ballots over 189 for Dewey.

Just three days before the election, *Editor & Publisher* had
reported that, in terms of circulation, daily newspaper support was
eight to one in favor of Dewey.[3] In the state of Missouri, fourteen
dailies supported Dewey with their combined circulations of
1,326,397, while Truman had the backing of thirteen with an aggre-
gate circulation of only 44,569.[4] His victory, therefore, was hailed as
a triumph over the opposition of the great majority of American
newspapers, as well as a surprise win over his Republican opponents.

Although many critics, like Pollard, considered the 1948 election
a turning point in Truman's career, which "gave him a degree of self-
assurance and downright self-confidence that amounted to cocksureness and approached the aplomb of Franklin D. Roosevelt himself,"[5]
Truman denied consistently that it caused any change in his attitude
toward the press or toward anyone else. His defeat of a candidate who
had enjoyed overwhelming press support came as no surprise to him;
it was a pattern with which he was almost callously familiar, as he
stated in 1953: "I had been through four statewide campaigns in
Missouri in which the attitude of the press and the figures they would
publish would show that I didn't have a Chinaman's chance to win,
but I beat them every time."[6]

Although the president was, of course, jubilant in his hour of
triumph, the record of his subsequent comments about the press

would not reveal an attitude of gloating or derisiveness inconsistent with the sentiments he had expressed during the years prior to the 1948 election. The following exchange, for instance, is illustrative of the fact that his relations with the working press continued to be characterized by the good-natured give-and-take that was typical of pre-election press conferences:

> *Q:* (*continuing*) Frank Knight, *Charleston* (West Virginia) *Gazette.* To what do you attribute the fact that newspaper editors polled are pretty bad in picking presidential winners? (*laughter*) *The President:* I will tell you exactly what is the matter with them. They don't know anything about politics. (*laughter*) And I am trying to tell you to learn something about it.[7]

Teasing a group of publishers and editors who called on him for a special conference at the White House, the chief executive said: "I thought maybe the weather would clear up and we could have a meeting in the rose garden of the White House, and I would be able to shake hands with each one of you and express my appreciation for what took place last fall. (*laughter*)"[8]

The president did not decline the opportunity, however, to make political hay out of the experience and to interpret his victory as a repudiation of press influence in American public affairs. He told delegates to a CIO-PAC rally: "If you remember, in 1948, 85 percent of the medium — what they call the free press — was in the other corner, and it became necessary for the candidate to see that the majority of the people knew the facts and the truth."[9]

In his keynote speech before the Democratic National Convention in 1952, Truman could not resist using the experience of four years earlier as a political expedient with which to poke fun at the "opposition press": "Now, these Republicans have nearly all of the newspapers and magazines on their side. They may have, and probably will have, public opinion polls — as in 1948. Well, the pollsters and the press in 1948 acted like Kipling's monkey convention, and the head of the whole simians made a statement, and made a statement, and made a statement. And he kept on making that statement. Finally, the concourse said, 'It must be so, we all say so. It must be so, we all say so.'

"It turned out a little differently in 1948. You know, those pollsters and press men should have conferred with the people, instead of voting monkey meetings among themselves."[10]

It was to be expected, in light of Truman's experience with the press in 1948 and in consideration of the fact that he remained the titular head of his party in 1952, that "Republican control of the press" was slated to become one of the issues of the Democratic campaign. But it was the party candidate himself and not Truman who provided the catchwords with which to spearhead the assault on the opposition press. In a widely publicized talk on the subject of press responsibility in politics, Adlai E. Stevenson — an able phrase-maker and former newspaperman — warned Oregon publishers against the dangers of a "one-party press" in the following terms: "I am in favor of a two-party system in politics. And I think we have a pretty healthy two-party system at this moment. But I am in favor of a two-party system in our press, too. And I am, frankly, considerably concerned when I see the extent to which we are developing a one-party press in a two-party country."[11]

Truman was delighted by Stevenson's lecture to the newspaper profession.[12] He wrote the Illinois governor two days later: "I've been following your tour across the country. I heard your Denver speech, read the one in Minnesota, and was particularly interested in what you had to say about the press in Portland, Oregon. You gave them just exactly what they needed. Every old columnist in the business has been trying to alibi for the press — the *New York Times* has a column-and-a-half editorial. Arthur Krock has a column, the *Herald-Tribune* has an editorial, as does the *Washington Post* and the *Evening Star,* and so does the *Baltimore Sun.* Their alibis, however, don't hold water. You stuck the rapier into the spot that was tenderest and where it needed to be stuck."[13]

Stevenson's label of the Republican-dominated publications as the "one-party press" became a byword with the president, who employed the term frequently during the two months following the Portland speech. His first use of the tag in public occurred on the third day after its origination by the Democratic nominee, when Truman opened his press conference with a review of statistics regarding presidential support by the newspapers:[14]

The President: You know, at the Chicago convention, I said the Republicans have nearly all the newspapers and magazines on their side. Governor Stevenson, the other day, in Oregon, had something to say on this situation. I agree with what he said, and would like to add just what I mean by Republican control of the press. In 1948, only 10.3 percent of the 1769 daily papers . . .

Q: (*interposing*) Mr. President, would you mind repeating that figure again?

The President: Sure Tony [Vaccaro]. Only 10.3 percent of the 1769 daily papers in this country supported the Democratic candidate, and almost all the big circulation magazines were pro-Republican. I don't think the situation has changed much since then. . . . In New York, only 4 percent of the papers were for the Democrats. In Pennsylvania, 1.5 percent. In Illinois, 3.4 percent. In Ohio 4 percent. In California 4.8 percent.

The one-party press situation is, of course, particularly tough for Democratic congressional candidates, who get even less opportunity to state their case in their local Republican papers than does the Democratic presidential candidate. Now, I do not expect that listing these figures will result in any switches from the Republican to the Democratic party. Newspapers — especially daily newspapers — have become big business, and big business traditionally has always been Republican.

I suggest that Americans bear this in mind, and add a dash of salt to every Republican helping of news, especially in those many papers and magazines which do not give a fair balance of news between the two major parties. If Democracy is to work properly, the people must be able to read and hear not only the Republican story but the Democratic as well. Our newspapers, magazines, radio, and TV have a great responsibility to be fair in this and all other campaigns.

I want to add a comment to that, that I don't think it makes much difference what they do. I have had some experience with the situation for over thirty years, and as far as I can remember, I never had the support of the metropolitan press in Missouri when I was running for the Senate, and I never asked for it. In 1948 I read you the figures, and I think it is a rather pitiful situation, the small amount of political influence that the great free press of the United States has.[15]

In deploring the "small amount of political influence" exercised by the American press, Truman overlooked a significant historical fact — the fact that a "national press" has never existed in the United States. This is stated more explicitly — and more accurately — by Mott, who found that "there seems to be no correlation, positive or negative, between support by a majority of newspapers during a campaign and victory in a presidential canvass."[16]

Mott's study revealed that, in thirty-seven presidential campaigns, from 1800 to 1952, the winner had the support of a majority of the press in only eighteen instances, and in nineteen cases he had a minority of the press behind him.[17] Truman's experience in 1948, therefore, was nothing new or startling in American history. Neither, Mott concludes, is the small and decreasing newspaper support of a victorious presidential candidate in recent years indicative of a "progressively perilous situation," as Harold L. Ickes once observed. Mott's explanation is as follows: "It would be perilous if newspaper support today meant a refusal to report the other side. Jackson's press was trained 'to wheel and fire at the word of command' and to ignore the Whigs except to vilify them. Today, nearly all papers print the speeches and leading pronouncements on both sides, and many present columnists with conflicting views. And this in spite of the fact that they have 'come out' for one candidate or the other.

"Whatever the American newspaper may have been in the past, and whatever sentimentalists may wish to believe it to be now, it is today primarily and basically a purveyor of news. It is a *newspaper*, and it is founded upon the Jeffersonian doctrine that if the people have the news, they will know what to do about it. That is democracy. Newspapers have never controlled electoral decisions. That would be undemocratic and perilous indeed. The chief critics of the press in the first half of the nineteenth century agreed that usurpation of popular rights was the newspapers' greatest sin. Now they say that failure to enforce their preferences shows that they have lost their old power. Both sets of critics have been misled by a failure to understand the proper function of a newspaper."[18]

Mott concludes this illuminating analysis with a statement by Roy Roberts, publisher of the *Kansas City Star,* to members of the American Society of Newspaper Editors: "Primarily the newspaper's business is not to win elections; it is to print a *newspaper*. . . . If it were winning elections, you ought to add an election department to your paper, set up a political machine, put in your precinct workers."[19]

Putting it another way, the editor of the leading newspaper trade magazine wrote: "If the Democratic candidate wins, newspapers will get more of the same old 'loss of influence' criticism. If the Republican candidate wins, newspapers will be accused of unfairly promoting the 'propaganda' of the GOP."[20]

Truman's attitude toward the "one-party press" in the 1952 campaign was understandably that of the politician rather than of the scholar or journalist. Stevenson's apt phrase became, in the campaigning president's hand, a new barb with which to puncture the hide of the Republican elephant. At Boston, for instance, he declared of the opposing party: "They began to attack their political opponents, and government employees who resisted their demands, even their critics in the press—as communists. And every time they did it, the one-party press gave them a headline—increasing their appetite for more headlines."[21]

As the race entered the final heats, Truman lashed out at the Republican-controlled press in the old style. Referring to his "whistle-stop" technique, he told an audience in St. Paul: "This has enraged the Republicans. It has infuriated the one-party press. In lofty editorials from coast to coast, I have been accused of 'mud-slinging.'"[22] Later in the same address, the president elaborated on the point: "And the very newspapers that had praised Dewey, four years ago, when he rejected this same association [with Republican candidate Chapman Revercomb of West Virginia], hurled cries of 'foul blow' at me, for even bringing up the subject. The comparison was all in Dewey's favor. Perhaps that's what upset him so. Perhaps that's what disturbs the editors. Maybe they are all secretly ashamed of this man they now support.

". . . Instead of hurling epithets at me, they should be calling on their favorite candidate to face up to the grave defects in his own course of conduct and in his party's record. But that, I fear, the Republican politicians and the one-party press will never do. The last thing in the world they want to do is to face the facts. . . ."[23]

The next complaint was registered in Chicago, where Truman accused the partisan press of publishing falsehoods:

"When I stayed in Washington and took no part in the campaign, the Republican candidate and the one-party press felt free to vilify me as a traitor and as a corruptionist. When I replied and carried a campaign of truth around the country, their only retort was to accuse me of slander and abuse. The Republican leaders and the Republican press are desperate in this campaign. From the beginning, they had planned to win by using the Big Lie and the Big Doubt. When these tactics were exposed, there was nothing they could do but cry 'foul.'"[24]

In his last campaign speech as president—and his final address outside of Washington—Truman once more singled out the one-party press for his St. Louis audience: "Now another element in this strange and wonderful campaign is the press of the country. Most of the daily newspapers in this country are Republican. Only about 10 percent of the circulation is Democratic. Governor Stevenson has called this the one-party press. The two-party system is all right for the common people, but not, apparently, for the publishers of newspapers. They don't see any threat to our political system in having almost all the newspapers on one side."[25]

Truman concluded with the following interesting remarks, part of which were *ad libitum*: "And there are a few publishers I want to compliment, too. There is one in this town. The *St. Louis Post-Dispatch* and I have at last managed to agree on one thing—and that is the election of Adlai Stevenson. You don't know how much satisfaction it gives me, to have converted that paper to do right just once."[26]

This is the only recorded instance in which the president expressed any satisfaction with the policies of the independent *Post-Dispatch*. The year before, when the newspaper's investigation of the St. Louis Internal Revenue office had resulted in the conviction of Collector James P. Finnegan on a charge of misconduct in office, the following exchange had occurred between Truman and a *Post-Dispatch* correspondent at one of the President's press conferences:

> *The President:* Well, what would you do under the circumstances?
> *Q:* In the case of Finnegan? (*laughter*)
> *The President:* Of course, I know what the *Post-Dispatch* would do to any Democrat, they would cut his head off every time they had a chance.
> *Q:* (*interjecting*) We would do the same for a Republican.
> *The President:* (*continuing*) I am not so sure.[27]

Another time, Truman recorded this statement: "Of course, I never expected the *Post-Dispatch* to support any Democrat, particularly for a national office. They keep up their subscription list by being against Democrats on a basis of character assassination."[28]

Truman's loyalty to his party was matched by his fealty to those newspapers that he considered to belong to the alleged 10 percent minority support. He once declared, "I am not against any Democrat who can win the nomination and be elected"[29]—and by the same token, he apparently was not against any newspaper that would support wholeheartedly the Democratic party. A sampling of the data is sufficient to illustrate his frame of mind toward proadministration publications.

To the general manager of the *Chicago Times* before its merger with the *Sun,* Truman wrote: "I know you will make a good paper a better one."[30] For Jonathan Daniels, whose *Raleigh* (North Carolina) *News and Observer* was a champion of Truman policies in the South and whose biography of the chief executive was the first ambitious literary treatment of the thirty-third president,[31] the following note of approval was written: "Thanks a lot for your note enclosing editorials from your good paper on fear and Russia. As usual, you are as right as you can be."[32]

To the editor of a loyal Missouri newspaper, Truman wrote in 1949: "I hope your good paper remains a supporter of the administration."[33] Of a Democratic newspaper in Montana, the president told a Great Falls audience: "Here in Great Falls, you are fortunate in having a fine newspaper, the *Great Falls Tribune*. I wish there were more *Great Falls Tribunes* around the country so the people could get the truth."[34]

One of the most loyal newspaper groups in the Republican stronghold of Ohio were the newspapers of Democratic Governor James M. Cox. In 1951, Cox received the following letter from the president:

July 9, 1951

Dear Governor:

I have just had a chance to read some of the editorials from your good papers and I can't tell you how grateful I am for the manner of their approach to the politics I have been trying to pursue.

Your editorials clearly set out exactly what my objective is — peace in the world and prosperity at home. A just and lasting peace — economic well-being for all segments of our population. This has been my continuing policy. I am very happy that there is one levelheaded publisher in the United States who fully understands that program.[35]

At his January 31, 1952, press conference, when a reporter stated, "Mr. President, I have a request to ask you a couple of questions from the *Mexico,* Missouri, *Ledger,*" Truman interrupted him to say: "That's a good paper . . . a nice country daily . . . a very good paper, and a friend of mine."[36] The mid-Missouri newspaper, through its father-and-son editors (Robert M. White and Robert M. White II), had established its reputation throughout the state as one of the Democratic administration's most ardent and vigorous supporters. It attracted considerable attention in 1953 by touting Truman as the logical choice to fill the vacancy then existing in the presidency of the University of Missouri.

The last occasion on which the president publicly showed what he meant by a "good" newspaper was during an address at Scranton in which he mentioned extemporaneously: "You have a good newspaper with the courage to give you the facts, in the *Scranton Times.* And I want to say to you that that sort of newspaper is decidedly in the minority these days."[37]

Thus it would appear that, to Truman, the appraisal of the merit of any newspaper was, to a large degree and a priori, contingent upon the political complexion that it showed. This is not to imply that "good" and "bad" were terms he applied to newspapers in synonymity with the terms "pro" and "con," but there can be no doubt that the brand of politics he ascribed to a publication was a primary consideration in his personal evaluation of that particular publication.

Accordingly, whenever a favorable comment appeared in an organ of the "one-party press," Truman was likely to doubt its integrity. He told a friend who had forwarded him a copy of an editorial from the *Wall Street Journal,* which complimented the fiscal progress made by the Truman administration during the reconversion period: "Of course when the *Wall Street Journal* takes a notion to be kind to me I rather look upon it with suspicion."[38] And of a news story clipped from the *St. Joseph* (Missouri) *News-Press,* he said: "It surely was a favorable one to come from that good-for-nothing old Republican paper."[39]

"When the *Cleveland Press* compliments anything I do," the President commented in 1951, "I am inclined to think I have been wrong. They have about the meanest disposition of any newspaper outside the Hearst press I know of."[40]

As a concluding illustration of Truman's characteristic wariness, which had been sharpened by thirty years in the arena of politics, the case history of his relations with the *Denver Post* is enlightening. In a series of letters to Maple T. Harl, chairman of the Federal Deposit Insurance Corporation, the president acknowledged receipt of a number of editorial and news clippings from the *Post*, which Harl sent him from time to time, as indications that the Denver newspaper, under the management of Palmer Hoyt, was swinging from the Republican to the Democratic column. The chronology of Truman's comments in these letters, dated from February 2, 1949, through September 12, 1952, provides an interesting picture of the reluctant transition in the attitude of the man from the fabled "show-me" state: "I wouldn't put too much faith in what that dirty sheet in Denver would do. It is sort of like expecting something tangible from Mr. Stalin. The editorial comment, however, was good."[41]

"I hope the gentleman is really vaccinated, but I doubt it very much."[42]

"I am beginning to weaken a little bit on that *Post* . . . looks like they might eventually get right, but don't count too much on it."[43]

". . . I think Hoyt right down in his heart is a Democrat and always has been, but until this last time I am sure he always voted the Republican ticket."[44]

"It does look as if Mr. Palmer Hoyt has found out what makes the world go around. I am happy that that is the case."[45]

"It looks as if this fellow has gone all out — I hope that is true."[46]

"I think that Palmer Hoyt always has been a little on the liberal side, and he is beginning to find out that is about the only place he can land and be consistent with himself."[47]

"I was happy to read the editorial from the *Rocky Mountain Journal* about the 'objectivity' of the *Denver Post*. It is about as objective as any of the Republican press, I imagine."[48]

The last of the above comments indicates that, as far as Truman was concerned, the *Denver Post* was the big fish that almost got caught but slipped off the hook. This is borne out by a final reference in August of 1952, when Truman wrote Harl: "In my opinion, the *Denver Post* and the *Rocky Mountain Journal* are in the same class with the *St. Louis Post-Dispatch* and the *Kansas City Star* — they don't mean a thing to me."[49]

If the president was a practical politician, as the foregoing excerpts suggest, he was also a patient one. The burden of withstanding, for almost eight years, the opposition of what he figured as 90 percent of the country's newspapers left him in as good a humor with the working press as he had shown with them in 1945.[50] He never gave any indication of real bitterness toward these representatives of the press, as Hoover had done toward the end of his term of office. He continued his press conferences without interruption in either the regularity of meeting or the accustomed good-natured digs at the reporters and their newspapers. In one of the final sessions with the press, he drew attention to his attitude toward partisan journalism with a jibe that was characteristic of most of the preceding 321 press conferences:

> *Q:* Mr. President, on this New Year's Eve, do you plan any personal resolutions to make . . .
> *The President:* (*interposing*) About the only resolution I can think of is, I hope the Lord will give me power to prevent me from swearing at the newspapers. (*laughter*)
> *Q:* Mr. President, have you been more impelled to swear . . .
> *The President:* (*interposing*) What's that? What's that?
> *Q:* Have you been more impelled to swear lately than usual?
> *The President:* No. I have always been in that same frame of mind when it comes to the vast majority. You see, 90 percent have always been against me.[51]

Chapter 16

A MATTER OF
OPINION

"The editorials in the press never
bother me one way or the other. I
never pay any attention to what they
think or say, and never expect to."

TRUMAN MAINTAINED A REGULAR VIGILANCE OVER THE individual positions and the general course taken by the editorial pages of America's leading newspapers and magazines.[1] His attentiveness to the expressions of editorial opinion in the nation's press from the beginning of his administration is further attested by the following entry in the diary of his first director of the Bureau of the Budget, Harold D. Smith: "I entered the president's office as soon as I arrived at the White House. My principal purpose was to discuss the navy budget recisions. The president was glancing over some editorial clippings, and he remarked that he was just looking at 'the day's poison.' He commented on the arguments that are developing as to which direction he is going, to the left or to the right."[2]

The chief executive spoke to exclusive groups of newspaper editors on at least six occasions.[3] One of these was a press conference for members of the American Society of Newspaper Editors in the fall of 1947, at which Truman said, "I make it a point to read a great many editorials. They are most of them, thoughtful and well written, and are exceedingly useful to the welfare of the country. I can't say that for all of them, but that is true in any business, there are people who are outside the pale. And you have that to contend with, just as I do in politics."[4]

The president evidenced a high regard for the work of some individual editorial writers — particularly the contributions of his friend Jonathan Daniels, of whom he wrote: "I am hoping that Jonathan will be able to make arrangements to be in the White House family when everything is arranged. He and I have discussed the matter and, as you know, he is responsible for a large part of the editorial work on the *News and Observer* at Raleigh. I think he is one of the ablest of the editorial writers. He is writing an article on Mrs. Truman, so I understand, which will come out in *McCall's* very shortly, and I am sure it will be a wonderful piece."[5]

Not untypical of his occasional correspondence with newspaper editors is the following letter, which Truman sent to his hometown paper:

September 5, 1950

Dear Frank:

I read your editorial in the thirty-first of August issue headed "As Others See Us." I think you really hit the nail on the head and as a newspaperman I think you are beginning to understand just what I have been up against nearly all my life.

The feature writers are never too anxious to state the facts as they are. They are always trying to find something that they call "make a story" — consequently the fair approach is hardly ever reached.

I enjoyed your discussion on the subject very much.

Sincerely yours,

[signed] HARRY S TRUMAN[6]

In the great majority of instances, however, the president's comments were considerably less affable and his criticisms of the nation's editorialists more pronounced. He obviously resented their assumption of what he considered the role of armchair statesmen and strategists. In a sarcastic reference to this "Monday morning quarterbacking," Truman complained: "Of course, there isn't a newspaper editor in the United States who doesn't know how to run the government better than the president does."[7]

So strongly did the president feel about the editorial intervention of newspapers in government affairs that he included this statement in the introduction to his State of the Union Message to Congress in 1949: "We have the greatest republic in the world if we remember that the people elect us to do what we think is right and not what some . . . misguided editorial worker tells us to do."[8]

Writing to one of his advisers, Max Lowenthal, on the history of editorial attacks against heads of state for decisions that were later proved sound and in the best interests of the country, Truman said: "You will remember, and I know you can remember all the editorial writers jumping on Wilson for his sending Funston into Vera Cruz and Pershing into Northern Mexico. I don't think anybody remembers those of the present day. It is the business of the president to meet situations as they arise and to meet them in the public interest. There are at least 176 instances parallel to what we face today. . . ."[9] And, less than three weeks later, he wrote Lowenthal that "it has become apparent that slanted comments by broadcasters and distorted editorials is the policy."[10]

Truman came to the conclusion in 1951 that "editors are peculiar animals—they throw mud and bricks at you the whole year round—then they make one favorable statement which happens to agree with facts and they think they should be hugged and kissed for it."[11] The editors gave cause for further offense to the president, as revealed in his note to the chief editorial writer of the *Boston Post*: "On several occasions I've written letters of thanks to editors of newspapers and very few of them have found time for a courteous acknowledgment. Therefore, I treasure yours most highly."[12]

Truman's reaction to the editorials of certain publications varied from enjoyment to disgust, as he told Arthur Krock in 1949: "I enjoy immensely reading the editorials of the *New York Times,* the *Baltimore Sun,* the *Washington Star,* the *Washington Post* and others. The McCormick and Hearst editorials are not fit even for publication, let alone for reading matter."[13]

In a number of the references by the president to the "opposition press," the Scripps-Howard newspapers are often placed in the same category with the publications of Hearst and of the "McCormick-Patterson axis." There appears to have been a more civil state of relations, however, between the president and Roy Howard, and an effort was made at reaching points of agreement between the policies of Truman's administration and the editorial policies expressed by the Scripps-Howard group. Truman invited Howard to visit him at the White House for a personal discussion on foreign affairs, but the publisher was preoccupied at the time with the strike situation on his *New York World-Telegram and Sun* in the summer of 1950 and wrote the president an apology for his inability to accept the invitation. Truman replied in a cordial letter:

July 26, 1950

Dear Roy:

I appreciated very much your letter of the twenty-first and I am sorry that you were unable to come in after I had invited you to come and have a conversation about the international situation.

There are a lot of things in connection with the far eastern situation that you should know when you write articles and editorials on it. . . . It is too late now to discuss that matter but I'll still let you in if you decide to come to the White House on your own steam.

Sincerely yours,

[signed] HARRY S TRUMAN[14]

The appearance of an editorial by Edward J. Meeman in the *Memphis* (Tennessee) *Press-Scimitar* of September 4, 1950, precipitated considerable embarrassment for Senator Estes Kefauver of that state. The editorial, entitled "We Need a Perfect Leader," pointed out the obvious strengths of President Truman and asked him to overcome his weaknesses to become the "perfect leader." A constituent of the senator rushed a clipping of the editorial to Kefauver requesting that it be brought to the attention of the president and commenting, "In the meanwhile, some of us will be praying earnestly that Mr. Truman will be guided aright in his reaction to this editorial." Kefauver complied with this request and soon received this reaction from the chief executive: "I am returning Dr. Diehl's letter to you which enclosed the editorial from the *Memphis Press-Scimitar*. I read the editorial with a great deal of interest, and it is, of course, the prerogative of any editor to tell any public official how he ought to do his job. The funny part of the editorial was that referring to socialized medicine and deficit financing. Socialized medicine has nothing to do with the Public Health Program which I have been advocating, to arrange matters so everybody can have proper medical care when he needs it.

"The American Medical Association and Scripps-Howard are responsible for socialized medicine propaganda lies which have been made a whipping boy to beat the health program. They had similar scare words to beat the Social Security, the Securities and Exchange Act, and several others of our great legislative reforms in favor of the common everyday man. As far as deficit financing is concerned, I've never been for deficit financing. That situation was brought about entirely by the Eightieth Congress and the pinheaded approach to government financing advocated by the Scripps-Howard press. Of course, they have been so nasty in their editorial policy toward me that a 'halfway all right editorial' is something to write home about."[15]

The president added a postscript in longhand which said, "I've made the above perfectly clear to Roy Howard in a personal interview," thus indicating that Howard had made an appointment to talk matters over with Truman.

This was not the reaction that Kefauver expected, and he expressed remorse at not having read the editorial more discerningly and in its entirety. In a letter to the president, Kefauver explained: "I read about one-half of the editorial and it seemed to be very good in that it expressed confidence in you as president and in your earnestness. . . . I regretted I did not read the last part of the editorial, and I did not subscribe to the statements contained therein at all."[16]

With the indulgence of one who accepted as his responsibility the proper indoctrination of less experienced aspirants to party leadership, Truman eased the embarrassment of Kefauver in the following note: "The Scripps-Howard outfit has never been in my corner and they never did write a favorable editorial without putting a 'cracker' on it that ruined the favorable part of it. I am glad that I got a chance to call that to your attention."[17]

The complete disintegration of whatever good relations might have been built up between the president and the Scripps-Howard chain, finally, is hinted in Truman's remarks to the editor of the *Washington Daily News* subsequent to that newspaper's publication of an editorial entitled, "The Korean Stalemate," in its issue of November 28, 1952. Truman wrote: "The attached editorial—it contains a double-barreled barefaced lie which I've marked with a red line. . . . Of course, truth means not one thing to Roy Howard or your snotty little *News*—but these are the facts."[18]

The *Press-Scimitar* editorial was not the only one that had a "cracker" on the end of it, as far as Truman was concerned. This was a common practice with some newspapers, as he told the minister of his church in Washington: "Sometimes such papers as the *Richmond Times Dispatch,* the *Washington Star*, and *Life* have to admit that everything can't be wrong with this administration. Usually though, when they do admit it, they wind up with a 'cracker' on the end of the editorial that knocks out all the good part."[19]

As an example, Truman cited an editorial in the *Washington Post* of July 5, 1952, which commended his administration on its maintenance of a stable economy. The "cracker" in this instance was in the caption of the editorial, as Truman pointed out in a letter to one of his economic advisers: "There is an editorial in the *Post* this morning on the subject. It really is painful to them to have to admit that what we have done is the correct thing. The subject of the editorial is 'Successful Patchwork.' I think the policy has been anything but that."[20]

Another reference to a *Post* editorial reveals general dissatisfaction on the part of the president with what he read: "The *Washington Post*, this morning, has one of their usual nasty editorials. . . . It has become almost chronic with them to take a shot at me whenever they get a chance. . . . The *New York Times* has an editorial which states more nearly the facts."[21]

Truman did not always express an appreciation of the editorial pages of the *New York Times*. It appeared to him that an unfair amount of biased opinion was expressed there as in other newspapers. On one occasion in particular, he objected to adverse editorial comment on Schlesinger's book on the MacArthur episode,[22] which he felt to be deserving of a more considerate appraisal: "I had read the *Saturday Review of Literature*'s article about it and had also read the review of the *New York Times* and the *New York Herald Tribune*. The *Saturday Review* was fair, the other two were very much slanted — the *Times* particularly so. The editors of these great dailies are like the editor of *Look* — anybody who says the president is right is 'wrong.'"[23]

Recalling his relations with the *Kansas City Star,* Truman made it clear that "I never had any difficulty with the management of the *Star*. It was only on their editorial page that they attempted to skin me."[24]

His rapport with the editorial writers of the other metropolitan newspaper of his home state was hardly less salutary, judging from the following comment: "When the *Post-Dispatch* prints a favorable editorial about me, I always search my soul to find what I've done wrong."[25]

The editorial that bothered Truman more than any other that was published during his two terms in office was one that appeared in the February 13, 1951, issue of his arch newspaper enemy, the *Chicago Tribune*, and which advocated the impeachment of the president. "When the time comes for the impeachment of Truman," the editorial argued, "the articles of the bill will fall into two classes, each backed by overwhelming evidence. One is Truman's violations of the Constitution, which he is sworn to uphold and defend; the other is his

repeated sponsorship and protection of grafters and influence ped-
dlers in his official family, including the White House circle."

The editorial charged further that "Truman's institution of
Pendergast spoils politics in the White House has brought the
presidency to its lowest position in history. His military aid, Major
General Vaughn, accepted bribes, one of which was passed on to Mrs.
Truman. Vaughn's friend, Maragon, now in prison, peddled influence from the White House with Vaughn's assistance." After other
allegations of corruption in the White House, the *Tribune* editorial
concluded with this statement: "Truman is crooked as well as in-
competent. That is sufficient ground for the impeachment of any
official."

The president was understandably indignant. He dispatched a
memorandum to the United States attorney general in which he intimated serious considerations of libel proceedings against the
Tribune: "In the main editorial in the February thirteenth issue of the
Chicago Daily Tribune, they had the nerve to make the statement that
Truman is a crook which I think is libel and criminal libel at that. I
wish you would get copies of that editorial, read it carefully, and then
proceed with whatever action is necessary to get the right result. Not
only is it libel to myself but it brings Vaughn and Mrs. Truman into
the picture. . . . I don't think we ought to sit still any longer and let
these things pile up. . . . I hope . . . that you will analyze the
editorial to which I refer—then go after these people with hammer
and tongs."[26]

Despite the fact that Truman sought legal grounds for ascertain-
ing the libelous nature of these attacks, the evidence is that he had no
personal desire to prosecute his maligner in the courts. This conclusion is based on his remarks several weeks later, in which he appears
to have adopted an attitude of philosophical forbearance. He wrote
to a friend: "I am wondering if all the libelous statements, particularly
this one and several others that we are familiar with, could not be kept
until sometime in the future when we could make use of them not for
gain but for historical purposes. There have been only two or three
presidents who have been as roundly abused and misrepresented in
certain sections of the press as I have."[27]

That the president managed to maintain this attitude is borne out
by the subsequent facts. He did not pursue the idea of instituting a
libel suit against the *Tribune* or against a number of other journalists
and publications whose attacks against him might very well have been
actionable in a court of law. It is perhaps significant that Truman

could write in 1949: "The editorials in the press never bother me one way or the other. I never pay any attention to what they think or say, and never expect to."[28]

The following headline appeared over an article in the November 15, 1947, issue of *Editor & Publisher*: "Truman Dislikes the Columnists." An exploration of the record of the president's comments regarding this contingent of the "opposition press" furnishes grounds for belief that the *Editor & Publisher* caption was somewhat of an understatement. Such an observation constitutes at best only a generalization. Only by examining the data itself can an accurate picture be drawn of Truman's relations with the columnists.

It has been shown that Truman made distinctions between the "working press" and "opposition press." Just how he would classify the newspaper columnist, who could logically be a member of the working press and at the same time be identified with the opposition, is not clear. Perhaps the most helpful explanation is that given by Helm, who was a close acquaintance of the president and a Washington correspondent for the *Kansas City Post-Journal*. Helm defines in the following elementary fashion the kinds of newspapermen with whom the president had to deal:

"One kind—the largest group—is the reporter. He reports what is said and done, doesn't fight the news or quarrel with it. He may agree with everything a politician says or he may not believe a word of it. It makes no difference; if he is a good reporter he sends an accurate story to his newspaper, uncolored by his personal views. . . . Such newspapermen make up the great majority of the capital's correspondents. With these Harry Truman had no quarrel.

"Another kind of Washington newspapermen is the columnist. Generally he has been a working reporter. He signs his stuff and slants it toward his own viewpoint or the bent of the editors who employ him or buy his writings. . . . He writes opinion largely, editorials rather than straight news. Correspondents of that sort are usually hard-working fellows with a flair for turning a happy phrase. Because they generally are fair and unprejudiced, Truman does not feel he has suffered at their hands, with one or two notable exceptions.

"A third kind of newspaperman is the pundit. . . . Some of these writers who have been high in official life are really not newspapermen at all; they are has-beens making money out of the fact that once they were prominent. . . . Such writers are apt to develop into public scolds, and as a rule don't last long in the writing business. . . . Truman feels he has been misrepresented grossly many times by that sort of newspaperman."[29]

Truman did not go to such lengths in classifying the newsmen. To him, columnists were something apart from the working press, as he conceived the terms. He drew this distinction, for example, during the course of informal remarks at William Jewell College in 1946: "There is not a single great newspaper in the United States that could operate if it did not have these workmen down here in front of me today to do this work. They can't all be managing editors. They can't all be top-notch columnists to tell the president what he ought to do. (*laughter*) Somebody has to sit in the front row and do the work."[30]

When writing to his cousin, the president referred to both reporter and column-writer in less complimentary terms, but drew a distinction nevertheless: "You are exactly right about the wolves and the nitwit columnists."[31] (His use of the first of these labels is explained in an earlier chapter.[32])

As far as the president was concerned, there were two general classes of columnists. In his own colorful language, he described these as "ivory-tower" columnists and "gutter-snipe" columnists, making the following distinction: "One writes from an ivory tower and the other writes from the gutter, and not one of them tells the truth except by accident."[33]

By the first of these appellations, the president apparently meant those columnists who specialized in analytical comment and prognostication in the field of public affairs. He referred specifically to Arthur Krock of the *New York Times* as one of the "ivory-tower" columnists: "To give you an example, Arthur Krock of the editorial staff of the *New York Times* spent a lot of effort writing two whole columns on the Electoral College and what he thought I was trying to do to it. Until I saw the matter in his column, I had never heard of the proposition. He quoted a certain southern senator who had been to see me and to whom I had made no commitment of any sort, to the effect that I thought the Dixiecrat votes in the College should be cast for the Democratic candidate. In fact, I don't want them. All Mr. Krock would have had to do would have been to call the White House and confirm the statement that he was supposed to have attributed to me. Of course, if he done that he could not have written his column and the space would have been vacant, or he would have had to think up something else which maybe would have been true."[34]

Critics were included in this category of columnists. Truman had this to say about a drama critic on the *Washington Post*: "I notice one of the 'ivory-tower' critics in the *Washington Post* this morning has some 'funny' remarks—I might say 'phony' remarks about the acting. I've found that critics usually are picked from frustrated people who have made a failure in the things they criticize."[35] (His famous letter to the *Post*'s music critic is treated later.[36])

Judging from the number of references by the president, it must be concluded that he considered the "ivory tower" was far less crowded than the "gutter." Within the confines of the latter definitions he placed the "gossip" and "scandal" columnists, whose chief purpose, he felt, was to "dig up dirt" on persons in public life or to fabricate scandals rather than to analyze and report facts. Helm states: "But what I do know from his own lips is his conviction that a part of the American press has never given him a break. He feels that some newsmen are sent to the White House to dig up scandal rather than news."[37]

In one of his allusions to a columnist whom he placed in this class, the president shed further light on his meaning of the term: "He had no grounds on which to base what he said but he is a kind of 'gutter columnist' and always has been. Like most of that class the truth means very little to them—they are trying to sell a bill of goods."[38] And in another, he observed that a certain journalist's "so-called 'news column' is a 'gossip column' and most of the gossip is untrue, but everybody reads it because everybody likes a little scandal once in awhile."[39]

Truman never ceased to deplore what appeared to him to be unseemly conduct on the part of such writers. It was immediately after his twenty-one-point message to Congress of September 6, 1945, which set forth the long-range domestic program of social legislation that his administration was to pursue, that "the vast majority of scandalous columnists began to throw bricks at me and to belittle me," Truman told a friend who had reported an error in the press to him. "And I have a notion that from whomever your quotation came had never an lyzed the situation on his own initiative. It is interesting and I hope some means may be found to offset such a miserable approach to the welfare of the country."[40]

After the chief executive had suffered a minor physical ailment for which he was temporarily hospitalized in 1950, he wrote a friend: "Don't worry about my health—it is so good it is shameful. Some of the reporters and columnists spend their time trying to find something the matter with me, but they don't succeed very well."[41]

In one of his most amusing flights of whimsy on the subject, Truman recorded the following memorandum: "I have just made some additions to my Kitchen Cabinet, which I will pass on to my successor in case the cow should fall when she goes over the moon. I have appointed a secretary for columnists. His duties are to listen to all radio commentators, read all columnists in the newspapers from ivory tower to lowest gossip, coordinate them, and give me the result so I can run the United States and the world as it should be. I have several able men in reserve besides the present holder of the job, because I think in a week or two the present secretary for columnists will need the services of a psychiatrist and will in all probability end up in St. Elizabeth's.

"I have appointed a secretary of semantics—a most important post. He is to furnish me 40 to 50 dollar words. Tell me how to say yes and no in the same sentence without a contradiction. He is to tell me the combination of words that will put me against inflation in San Francisco and for it in New York. He is to show me how to keep silent —and say everything. You can very well see how he can save me an immense amount of worry."[42]

The evidence is clear, however, that the president, throughout his administration, remained seriously aware of what was being written in various newspaper columns. When the subject of Byrnes' resignation, for instance, was brought up in a press conference, some revealing information on Truman's attitude on the columns was brought to light:

Q: Mr. President, does your comment about Secretary Byrnes infer that he is not going to resign?

The President: He has never had any intention of resigning, and he is not going to resign, either on his own initiative or by request.

Q: Mr. President, I am curious—I think we all are—as to why you voluntarily brought that up as the first thing in the press conference? Have you been hearing rumors yourself?

The President: Oh, yes. All the gossip columns are full of it. Of course, I never believe the gossip columns, but then a lot of people read them.

May Craig: How do you know what's in them? (*laughter*)

The President: Somebody presents them to me, usually.

Q: Did you say you never read them?

Q: (*interposing*) You don't *believe* them.

The President: I didn't say I didn't read, I said I didn't *believe* them.

Q: Excuse me.

The President: That's all right. That was a good question (*more laughter*)[43]

Following his visit to Fulton, Missouri, with Winston Churchill for the prime minister's famous "iron curtain" speech, Truman wrote in a letter: "We had a nice meeting at Fulton and I think everybody enjoyed it. It gave the columnists a chance to have many spasms — both happy and unhappy, so it was worth something just for that."[44]

In his political speeches during the 1948 campaign, the president drew the attention of his audiences on a number of occasions to the "misguided" columnists, as in the following example: "It is perfectly legitimate for me to come out here and talk to you and let you see me, and let you find out for yourselves whether I am just the kind of a bird that these columnists say I am. I have had, as I told you, a wonderful time. The welcome that has been given me since I have left Washington has surprised me as much as it has the newspaper columnists."[45]

Truman stated his general view of newspaper columnists in no uncertain terms when he told the postmaster of St. Joseph, Missouri: "I appreciate the fact that you are against all columnists — so am I. Most of them are wrong all the time and the rest of them are wrong about 50 percent of the time."[46] And in even stronger language, he declared that "radio commentators and columnists I think are the bane of our free press."[47]

As an incumbent in December 1952, Truman was approached by Silliman Evans, publisher of the *Nashville Tennessean,* with a serious offer of a new career for the retiring president — as a columnist! While Truman expressed the same contempt of the profession that he had shown all along, it is interesting to note that, in his reply to Evans, he did not deny the possibility of such a development in the future: "Matt handed me your letter of November twenty-fourth regarding the possibility of my going into the columnist business. There have been all sorts of rumors and stories about what I am going to do and what I am not going to do after I get out of office — they range all the way from writing a book, teaching school, raising yellow legged chickens, and even getting so low as to write a column. I haven't made up my mind what I am going to do as yet and it will be some time before I do.

"If anything resembling the suggestion you make comes up, you of course will be right in the front rank of those under consideration."[48]

Any discussion of Truman's relations with newspaper columnists is likely to bring to mind certain rebukes of a rather indelicate nature that the president applied at times to individual journalists — the most famous of which, perhaps, was his "s.o.b." remark about Drew Pearson.[49] Such epithets were no more than recurrent symptoms of his attitude toward columnists and editorial writers in general.

Chapter 17

MORE BARK
THAN BITE

"You might tell the gentleman . . .
that if he comes out with a pack of
lies about Mrs. Truman or any of
my family his hide won't hold shucks
when I get through with him."

How did Truman, the man, react to the presence of a rather substantial and relentless volume of adverse criticism in the media? The opposition was real. One observer fixes the recognizable beginning of press criticism of the president as the day on which he announced his "Fair Deal" administration program. "The message of the president of the United States to the Congress, on September 6, 1945, amounted to the termination of a presidential honeymoon by the man who was enjoying it."[1] according to Jonathan Daniels, a newspaperman who served two presidents as press secretary.

He continued: "Truman himself believed that he made his own position clear — perhaps too quickly clear — with his message on September 6, 1945, after the Japanese surrender. Part of his purpose in that speech had been to let the big publishers, who had been praising him . . . know that they had not taken him into camp."[2]

It is significant to note that Truman himself was interested in the subject of presidential reaction to press criticism. His knowledge of historical precedents gave him comfort and guidance — and some forbearance — in this aspect of his official experience as it seemed to in many other phases of his career.[3] This is demonstrated in the philosophical attitude expressed in the following paragraphs: "Most presidents have been subjected to abuse and misrepresentation. Those who were treated the worst by the public press were Jefferson, Jackson, Lincoln, Grover Cleveland, and Woodrow Wilson, and it is interesting to observe the reactions of those presidents to the vicious attacks that were made upon them. . . . I've stood quite a bit of abuse myself, but it doesn't bother me like it seemed to have bothered those gentlemen. I have always been of the opinion that lies will answer themselves and that turned out to be true with all the presidents."[4]

He pointed out another parallel in a note to a writer on the *St. Louis Post-Dispatch*: "The attack on Mr. Lincoln didn't have any more effect on his re-election than the attack on the *Post-Dispatch* had on me in 1948."[5]

When the subject of journalistic abuse of presidents popped up at a press conference, Truman spoke of his own reaction in untypically guarded statements, as if fully aware of his position in the "president's pulpit."

Q: You said that George Washington was the most abused man by the press. Do you consider that the press abuses you? (*laughter*)

The President: Oh no, the press doesn't abuse me. The press is very kind to me. (*more laughter*) I have no quarrel with the press. Never have.

Q: (*interposing*) Mr. President . . .

The President: (*continuing*) But you ought to read those things, you will—they are just as interesting as can be. You should see what was said about Washington and Jefferson, and John Quincy Adams and Andrew Jackson. And I believe the man who got the worst treatment besides George Washington in the press was Grover Cleveland. . . .

Q: You are not saying that you have got some bad treatment from the press?

The President: No, I didn't say that—I didn't say that.

Q: We can draw that inference.

The President: Any inference you want to draw, that is your conclusion, not mine.[6]

If, as Daniels suggests, September 6, 1945, represented the go-ahead signal as far as press criticism of the president was concerned, the attack apparently did not take Truman by surprise. On the contrary, he seemed to expect it and was prepared from the beginning to weather whatever the storm had to offer. As he wrote to a friend: "The barrage of criticism on my personal affairs, of course, is to be expected. I have had it before—I have lived through it, and it hasn't hurt, but it is a very great satisfaction to find people in the country who understand the situation. . . . You won't find legitimate news services doing any of this sort of backdoor stuff and, as I said before, it will not bother me in the program which I have set my mind to carry out."[7]

Consistent with his established attitude, Truman made the following entry in his diary on January 1, 1947: "Came back to the White House at 8:45 A.M. New Year's Day. Read the morning papers as usual. Some gave me hell and some did not. It makes no difference what the papers say if you are right."[8]

Later in the same year, the president, replying to a communication from a Texas newspaper publisher, showed his resentment to inconsiderate and unenlightened criticism, but made it clear that he would ask no quarter of his attackers:

"You no doubt have been at a ballgame when the shortstop would make a home run in an early inning and fail to catch one out in the field later. He is a hero the first time, and they throw pop bottles at him the second time. He needs sympathy in both instances, but seldom gets it, so I never pay any attention to bricks which are thrown my way or to compliments which come my way. Neither of them means anything in the final analysis when a job is to be done. All the president can do is get the basic alignment of facts that he can and make the best decision of which he is capable in the public interest, and let the river take its course, and that is what I do.

"People think apparently that the president is made out of cast iron and that he can work eighteen hours a day for three hundred and sixty-six days a year. If he decides to get away from it for a few days' rest, then there is a chance to throw more bricks. That makes no difference either to me."[9]

Truman's resistance obviously stiffened as the eventful years passed. A White House historian testified to this in the following passage from a full discussion of the abortive Vinson mission to Moscow in 1948: "Everyone, including the president, recognized that the idea would be heavily criticized by the opposition press. But this did not greatly worry him."[10]

On the day that marked the beginning of his sixth strenuous year as chief executive, the inevitable question was asked at a press conference, and an answer was returned that revealed an unruffled spirit and a stubborn good humor in the face of criticism:

> *Q:* Do you think the first five years are the hardest? (*laughter*)
> *The President:* That is an easy thing for a person to say. The first five years have been rather difficult, but the country is still on its feet. I think it's in fine shape. Of course, it couldn't possibly be that the executive is to be credited with that situation. That just took place. It would have taken place if we had had a moron on the job, according to the way the general attitude of some of the press is. (*laughter*)[11]

The same attitude of defiance is manifest in Truman's remarks to Max Lowenthal a year later: "Don't you worry about the attacks and slanted editorials that are being written about the president – that is customary and will continue to be customary as long as we have a complete opposition press. . . . It makes no difference what the president does, it is wrong, but when it comes time for the people to understand the situation, the president can take care of himself, so don't you worry about it."[12]

As the president neared the end of his tenure in office, he began to wonder what criticisms the press would overlook in attacking him and his administration. "The only thing that is missing in this controversy," he penned, "is the fact that they haven't yet thought to blame me for the defalcations of all the bank officials and bank clerks who have gone wrong, but I am sure they will get around to it before November."[13]

Later in 1952, Bedell Smith showed Truman a copy of the famous editorial written by Benjamin Franklin Bache in his *Philadelphia Aurora*[14] on the occasion of President Washington's retirement from office, which said in part: "It is a subject of greatest astonishment that a single individual should have carried his designs against the public liberty so far as to put into jeopardy its very existence. Such, however, are the facts, and with these staring us in the face, this day ought to be a jubilee in the United States." Truman was greatly amused by the piece, and commented in his reply to Smith that "conditions never change so far as the presidency is concerned."[15]

The testimony of recorded statements presented earlier[16] indicate that Truman strongly resented attacks on his "presidential family" of appointees and advisers. The excerpts presented in this chapter suggest that he considered purely personal criticisms as far less reprehensible. An attack on his person obviously disturbed him less than recriminations against the loyal men who had to take the "mud and brickbats" for him.

There was one other type of criticism that literally enraged the president on more than one occasion and for which he never forgave the offender. In his own words, as quoted in one of the few private interviews handed out during his career, Truman explained it as follows: "When you come down to it, there's just one thing I draw the line at, and that's any kind of attack on my family. I don't care what they say about me, I'm human. I can make mistakes. Any man can make mistakes, even if he's trying with all his heart and mind to do the best thing for his country. But a man's family ought to be sacred. There was one columnist who wrote some lie about my family when I was in the Senate, and instead of writing him a letter, I called him on the phone, and I said, 'You so-and-so, if you say another word about my family, I'll come down to your office and shoot you.' He hasn't printed a whisper about them since."[17]

In one of his earliest letters to his mother and sister after becoming president, Truman expressed his annoyance at the sudden publicity to which his family had been subjected because of him. He warned them against letting their guards down before a relentlessly prying and critical press. The letter reads:

April 29, 1945

Dear Mamma and Mary:

Received your letter with the one from Dr. Graham in it and was glad to get it. Hope you and mamma have not been bothered too much. It is a terrible—and I mean terrible nuisance to be kin to the president of the United States. Reporters have been haunting every relative and purported relative I ever heard of and they've probably made life miserable for my mother. I am sorry for it, but it can't be helped.

A guard has to go with Bess and Margaret everywhere they go—and I don't like it. They both spend a lot of time figuring how to beat the game, but it just can't be done. In a country as big as this one there are necessarily a lot of nuts and people with peculiar ideas. They seem to focus on the White House and the president's kin. Hope you won't get too badly upset about it.

Between the papers and the nuts they surely made life miserable for the Roosevelt family. Maybe they can have some peace now. I hope so.

I must caution both of you to take good care of your health. Don't let the pests get you down. I'm writing this before breakfast—before anyone is up.

Love you both.

[signed] Harry[18]

When the president got wind of a proposed article by a *Chicago Tribune* reporter delving into the personal affairs of the first lady, he issued a vigorous warning in the idiom typical of the Midwest: "There isn't a word of truth in that *Chicago Tribune* venture. You might tell the gentleman . . . that if he comes out with a pack of lies about Mrs. Truman or any of my family, his hide won't hold shucks when I get through with him."[19]

The debut of his daughter, Margaret, into the public entertainment field made Truman more attentive to what the press had to say about his family. He admitted his apprehensiveness of the attitude that the unfriendly press might adopt toward his daughter and expressed his appreciation for the kind treatment accorded her on one occasion by the publisher of the *Kansas City Star* in a note to that newspaper's Washington correspondent: "My pretty daughter has been shoving me off the front page and I am glad of it. She made quite a hit here the other night, as she did in Kansas City. Tell Roy [Roberts] that I appreciate most highly his kindness to her. I don't care a lot what you and Roy say about me but I am a little touchy about my family."[20]

It was the review written by the *Washington Post*'s music critic, Paul Hume, on the day following Margaret Truman's Washington concert in Constitution Hall that provoked what was perhaps the angriest response recorded by the president's hand and precipitated a noisy controversy quite out of proportion to the importance of the incident.[21]

Hume's review of the performance was frankly derogatory, and included such aspersions on Miss Truman's ability as: "There are few moments during her recital when one can relax and feel confident that she will make her goal, which is the end of the song. . . . She is flat a good deal of the time. . . . She cannot sing with anything approaching professional finish. . . ."[22]

The day after the publication of Hume's criticism, the journalist received the following letter written in longhand by the president:

I have just read your lousy review of Margaret's concert. I've come to the conclusion that you are an "eight ulcer man on four ulcer pay."

It seems to be that you are a frustrated old man who wishes he could have been successful. When you write such poppycock as was in the *back* section of the paper you work for it shows conclusively that you're off the beam and at least four of your ulcers are at work. Some day I hope to meet you. When that happens you'll need a new nose, a lot of beefsteak for black eyes, and perhaps a supporter below.

Pegler, a guttersnipe, is a gentleman alongside you. I hope you'll accept that statement as a worse insult than a reflection on your ancestry.[23]

Numerous attempts were made, after the White House had confirmed the letter, to account for the president's behavior. Hume considered it an "outburst of temper" due to the strain of the current world crisis.[24] Pegler called it "the nasty malice of a president."[25] A psychologist speculated on the chemistry of letter writing as an emotional outlet,[26] and others suspected that it was allied to the grief that Truman felt in the loss of Press Secretary Ross, who had died on the day of the concert.

While all of these conditions may have played some part in the action, it is believed, in the light of the accumulated data, that Truman's retaliation to the critical review was an entirely normal and consistent reaction, rather than some psychosomatic manifestation of accumulated pressures. He simply did not like attacks on members of his family and did not intend to tolerate them. He felt, himself, that no further explanation was necessary, as he reflected a few days later: "Margie held a concert here in D.C. on December 5. It was a good one. She was well accompanied by a young pianist named Allison, whose father is a Baptist preacher in Augusta, Georgia. Young Allison played two pieces after the intermission, one of which was the great A-flat Chopin Waltz, opus 42. He did it as well as it could be done, and I've heard Paderewski, Moritz Rosenthal, and Josef Lhevinne play it. A frustrated critic on the *Washington Post* wrote a lousy review. The only thing, General Marshall said, he didn't criticize was the varnish on the piano. He put my baby as low as he could, and he made the young accompanist look like a dub.

"It upset me and I wrote him what I thought of him. I told him he was lower than Mr. X and that was intended to be an insult worse than a reflection on his ancestry. I would never reflect on a man's mother because mothers are not to be attacked, although mine was.

Well, I've had a grand time this day. I've been accused of putting my baby, who is the apple of my eye, in a bad position. I don't think that is so. She doesn't either—thank the Almighty."[27]

The reverberations of this criticism of his daughter's performance seemed to endure longer, as far as Truman was concerned, than any other specific press attack aimed in his direction while he was president. A week after the concert, he wrote to a sympathizer: "I appreciated very much yours of the tenth and I am sorry that the incident about Margaret's singing upset you. Don't let it. That fellow is no good and that is the end of the thing. He . . . never made a contribution of any kind to the welfare of his country. I think he is inhibited some way or other, but I told him exactly what I thought of him, and I still feel the same way."[28]

To Hollywood actor Edward Arnold, whose performance in the play, *Apple of His Eye*, was much appreciated by Truman, the chief executive wrote a sympathetic note of his own in which he referred once more to the incident. "I certainly did enjoy the show," he said, "and I think the critics treated you like that 'nut' did Margaret when she sang here."[29]

Almost two years later, Hume's original criticism of Miss Truman and her accompanist, Herman Allison, was recalled with renewed vigor by the president, who was little disposed to accept compliments from his attacker: "That good-for-nothing critic here in Washington, who said so many things about Margaret and your son, finally had to come out and admit that he might not have been just exactly right in what he said. They tell me that he put on a television show and played one of Margaret's records and then made the statement that the president was the most musical one who had been in the White House. I don't know whether that is a compliment or not, but it is a little bit different from what he said about Margaret and Herman, Junior. As you remember, General Marshall said the critic criticized everything but the varnish on the piano, and that was the only thing in the show that needed criticism."[30]

An incident of less significance involving the Swedish press and his daughter in 1952 demonstrated the same readiness on the part of the president to slash back at what appeared to him to be the universal truculence of journalists. Stockholm newspapers obviously overplayed an account that Miss Truman's Secret Service escorts manhandled Swedish photographers and newsmen.[31] Truman assured Leonard Lyons of the *New York Post* that "there was absolutely nothing to the incident except what the press made of it. I had a complete report with a statement by the Swedish police who were present that nothing happened."[32] He recorded his personal feeling about the matter more graphically in his diary, writing: "When she arrived, the Swedish sabotage press created an incident. I was surprised to learn that the Swedish 'free press' is just as discourteous, irresponsible, and untruthful as our own publisher's press."[33]

Truman's reaction to criticism was almost invariably a positive one, as can be seen from the foregoing examples. The statement, "I never believed in running away from a fight," was often attributed to him in politics and is obviously applicable to his relations with the press. John Hersey quoted the president as saying in 1951, "I'm saving up four or five good, hard punches on the nose, and when I'm out of this job, I'm going to run around and deliver them personally"[34] to journalists who had maligned him.

Whether this is actually what Truman said is not clear, however. This was the conversation recorded in a press conference following publication of the Hersey article:

Q: Mr. President, along the same line, who are those four or five people that [John] Hersey said you are going to punch in the nose? (*more laughter*)
The President: I have no comment to make on that. As I said awhile ago, I haven't read the article and I know nothing about the . . .
Q: This is the Hersey piece.
The President: Yes, I know — and I don't intend to read it — I am not interested in it. People have a right to say what they please about me if they want to. I have no objection.[35]

After reading Yankovich's *Libel and Contempt,* Truman wrote David Noyes, who had presented the copy to the president for the author: "What I've read in the book is very interesting and maybe I'll have some lawsuits after I get out of office as a result of reading it."[36] There is little reason to believe, however, that Truman had any intention of prosecuting a grudge. While there is every indication that he had no notion of taking press criticism lying down, his efforts at vengeance were never anything more than verbal retaliation.

Undoubtedly it was Truman's reaction to and defiance of press criticism that touched off what Pollard called "one of the biggest hornets' nests of his career."[37] Truman's historic seizure of the steel industry the week before his three hundredth press conference brought down a torrent of criticism from segments of capital, labor, politicians, and the press. Truman stoutly maintained his position on the "inherent powers" vested in the chief executive by the Constitution even though the Supreme Court eventually held against him. Publishers and editors from all over the country had assembled in Washington for the annual conventions of the American Society of Newspaper Editors and the American Newspaper Publishers Association, and approximately five hundred twenty newsmen were crowded into the National Museum auditorium for the president's press conference on April 17, 1952. Official reporter Jack Romagna missed the name and publication of the journalist who asked the fateful question:

> *Q:* Mr. President (*name and paper inaudible*), if you can seize the steel mills under your inherent powers, can you, in your opinion, also seize the newspapers or/and the radio stations?
> *The President:* Under similar circumstances, the president of the United States has to act for whatever is for the best of the country. That's the answer to your question.[38]

Speculation on the possible implications of the president's reply challenged, in both intensity and volume, that which had followed in the wake of the security order of September 21, 1951.[39] Once again, Truman found it necessary to talk the matter over with correspondents at the press conference a week after his remark had been circulated:

> *The President:* Please be seated. I have a word or two for you before we start the questions. There has been a lot of hooey about the seizure of the press and the radio. As I told you last week, the president of the United States has very great inherent powers to meet great national emergencies. Until those emergencies arise a president cannot say specifically what he would do or would not do. I can say this, that the thought of seizing press and radio has never occurred to me. I have difficulty imagining the government taking over and running those industries. . . .
> *Q:* Mr. President, may we quote that word hooey?
> *The President:* Well, . . .
> *Q:* (*interposing*) Mr. President, may I interrupt and say may we quote the whole thing?
> *Q:* (*interposing*) Yes sir, that's what . . .
> *Mr. Short:* (*interposing*) Let's see about putting the whole thing on the record.

The President: The—my press secretary would like to edit it before he puts it on the record, and I have no objection to its quotation if it works out all right.

Q: Mr. President, how about the word *hooey*, pending that?

The President: Well, let's "pend" it.

Q: Sir?

The President: Keep on "pending" it.

Q: Mr. President, (*inaudible*) last Saturday night Casey Jones made his attack on you—I would like to have a copy of the transcript of what you said about press and steel to give my bosses.

The President: Well, I will leave that to Mr. Short. I think you can get it. . . .

Q: Mr. President, you say that during an emergency you have very great inherent powers to act. Are there any limitations at all over a president's acts during an emergency?

The President: Well, you had better read your history and find out. There are a lot of presidents who have had to make decisions in emergencies, and if you will read history you will find out why they had to make them. But it did not hurt the republic. In fact, it made the republic better.

Q: Mr. President, there never was any statement by you that— even by implication—that you intended to seize any newspapers or radio stations . . .

The President: (*interposing*) Not at all.

Q: (*continuing*) . . . was there, sir?

The President: Not at all.

Q: Mr. President, just to really nail that one down . . . (*laughter*)

The President: (*interjecting*) All right, nail it, Smitty [Merriman Smith].

Q: (*continuing*) Actually a number of people, particularly among the editors at your press conference last week, got the idea that—when you were asked that question about whether it would be proper to seize the press and radio—that you were implying that you had those powers. Now, were you answering the point on steel, or to press and radio?

The President: I was answering the point of the welfare of the country, Smitty, and that is what is at stake.[40]

While it is evident that Truman entertained no serious idea of taking over the journalistic media by presidential fiat, he remained firm in his conviction that it was within his rightful power to do so in emergency situations. As a case in point, he cited the following: "Lincoln not only ordered out 75,000 volunteers, he took over several newspapers when they published treasonable articles . . . but his objective was always the same—that was to save the union and keep this a free republic from the Atlantic to the Pacific."[41]

Truman's occasional denials of the existence of any press influence appear to have been another manifestation of his determination to fight criticism with criticism. Otherwise, it would be difficult to reconcile such negative testimony with the numerous affirmations he gave to the power of the mass media over the behavior of citizens. One of his first refutations of press influence appears in a letter written December 1, 1948, in which he also invents a new name for his enemies, the newspaper columnists: "I sincerely hope that the election returns will be a body blow, particularly to the worst of the fact murderers. Whether it will be or not, I don't know. The election, however, is conclusive proof, that when the American people know the truth, neither press nor radio influences them."[47]

While Truman attested frequently to the fact that he was an avid newspaper reader, he consistently denied that they had any appreciable influence on his thinking. When he was advised by Governor Smith of Missouri that the four metropolitan newspapers of the home state were not supporting his administration, the president replied: "I appreciated very much your letter of the 28th, and don't get it into your head that I arrive at my conclusions by reading newspapers."[43]

Quite the opposite opinion is expressed by Allen and Shannon, two of Truman's earliest and perhaps harshest critics: "The clearest manifestation of his insecurity was the ready manner in which he responded to forceful suggestions from the press. If newspapers suggested that Herbert Hoover's great talents as an 'elder statesman' should be made use of, Truman obligingly dug the battered great engineer out of moth balls and sent him around the world on a food survey. If newspapers raised a clamor that a Republican be put on the Supreme Court to keep it 'balanced,' Truman obediently appointed Republican Senator Harold Burton. It was as if Truman, uncertain in his own mind what his course should be, looked to the newspapers for guidance and was reassured by their plaudits."[44]

No real evidence or documentation is produced by Allen and Shannon to convince the reader that their conclusion regarding such causal relationships is anything more than conjecture on their part. Like the majority of criticisms in *The Truman Merry-Go-Round*, this one appears to be extremely biased.

Truman's most explicit denial of the effectiveness of either criticism or support by the press appears in the advice he gave to Governor Chester Bowles of Connecticut when Bowles was running for re-election in 1950: ". . . and another thing that I think I can advise you on is the influence of the press on the general public in the United States. The press has lost its influence due to the fact that it pays lying columnists to write editorials and slant the news in the headlines. I think this statement was conclusively proven in 1948. With 90 percent of the press rabidly opposed to a candidate for president, he won the election. People just didn't put their trust in the press. If I were in your place, and Connecticut no larger than it is, I'd make it my business to get into every precinct in the state and talk to the people individually, and just let the press go to hell."[45]

Truman's reaction, then, to press criticism was generally to criticize the press. This was the method that his political experience had taught him, and he seemed surprised at the excitement and resentment that his retaliative reactions produced in the press from time to time. He was frankly disgusted with the unwillingness or the inability of newspapermen to "roll with the punch" as he was expected to do. In his own words to a Florida journalist, the president said: "I find in my dealings with distinguished newspapermen they are all thin skinned — they like to give a public man hell but when he comes back a little, they find it hard to take."[46]

In one of the most candid and most thoughtful letters that he ever wrote to a representative of the press, Truman expanded on this subject as follows: "I can't tell you how very much I appreciated your note of the thirtieth of September. *Editor & Publisher* and one or two of the sabotage sheets controlled by Hearst and McCormick take the attitude that I have a bitter and resentful attitude toward the press. That isn't true at all. Nobody, as you are well aware, has had to take it or been more able to take unjust criticism than I have. But that is a two-way street, particularly when I am president of the United States and can get a hearing on what I have to say.

"One of the difficulties with most of the press people is that they are too thin skinned. They are like the dollar-a-year men who were down here in Washington when the war was going on. They have been in the habit of criticizing public officials, sometimes unjustly. But when public officials actually give the members of the press something constructive to think about they should take it too."[47]

Several years later, reflecting on his vicissitudes with the press, he drew the same conclusion in these words: "Well, I always used to say that they can give it out, but they can't take it. They're thin skinned. And it gave me a little bit of pleasure that it hurt them so bad."[48]

There is insufficient data to validate the claim that Truman developed a tendency toward a persecution complex. Pollard quotes "a long-time Washington reporter" as saying: "Rather recently, it seems to me that I have detected in Mr. Truman the beginnings of a feeling of persecution. Newspaper criticism, for example, he often considers unfair. . . . He feels pretty sure of himself, and anyone who criticizes him does so, he thinks, out of evil motives. The interesting thing is that I have seen the same thing in two other presidents, Roosevelt and Hoover. I think it is an occupational malady which comes upon any man after he has had several years of adulation."[49]

Regardless of the provocations that Truman saw in the press comment concerning him, in his reaction to criticism, malice apparently played no part at all. He felt that 90 percent of the press, like the Republicans, were "out to get him," and he fought them both with the same tactics that he felt they were using against him. But morose bitterness does not appear to be a characteristic of his reaction toward the press, and there is no instance on record of his attempting to "get revenge" — as mentioned before — through any exercise of official or legal prerogative.

In his relations with the men and women of the "working press," the president's reactions to the attacks of the mass media apparently produced no more than temporary tiffs, and no lasting effects are discernible. The same "long-time Washington reporter" quoted above confessed that "practically everyone has a personal liking for Mr. Truman. This applies to newspapermen as well as to everyone else. They may disapprove of him or criticize him with their intellectual faculties, but on the human front they feel warm toward him. I do not know anyone, either pressman or other, who feels anything except personal warmth for Truman the man."[50]

Others have testified that Truman demonstrated a spirit of forgiveness in his reaction to press criticism.[51] Clemens, for example, related the following incident: "At the White House Correspondents' Association dinner, Truman spied one of the newsmen who had ribbed him rather unmercifully about his dining out. But characteristically he bore the fellow no ill will and shouted a cheery greeting: 'I'm still eating on the cuff, as you see.'"[52]

An even more revealing episode is narrated by Helm, one of Truman's newspaper critics in Washington for about eighteen years.

He tells of a Kansas City journalist whose attacks on the president culminated in a front-page editorial flaying Truman for his attitude on current legislation and holding him up as a traitor to his home state. Helm continues: "The incident had a sequel, wholly unexpected, that put Harry Truman in a new light in my eyes and regard. The editorial writer left the paper not long after he had written that editorial. Months later I heard he was in financial straits; then for a long time I heard nothing of him. 'What became of him?' I asked Truman about a year later. 'Why, I heard he had a job in Kansas City.' 'A job with the *Star*?' 'No, I believe not.' 'With some other publication?' 'No; he was out of the publishing business.'

"That was always the teasing tack Truman would take with me when he tried, in his overwhelming self-effacement, to withhold from me something that might reflect credit on himself. So I bored in. 'Have you heard of him recently?' 'Fairly recently.' 'How recently?' 'Within a couple of weeks, I should say.' 'Do you know where he's working?' 'Yes.' 'Where?' 'Oh, he has a little job with the county.'

"That, of course, meant Jackson County whose affairs Truman had directed before coming to the Senate. 'A little job with the county,' I repeated. 'Did you, by any chance, get him that job, Harry Truman?' 'No, I can't say I did,' Truman replied in evident embarrassment. 'All I did was to recommend him for it.'"[53]

As far as press criticism is concerned, Truman's reaction was louder than his action.

Chapter 18

Pluses and Minuses: A Recap

"Every time a remedy is suggested for the debauchery of the free press they charge us with trying to strangle the free press, when the facts in the case are we are trying to maintain the free press."

BECAUSE THE WHOLE RECORD OF THOUGHTS AND RE-
marks and reflections of Harry S Truman during his tenure as president of the United States, as they related to his experience with the
mass media of communication, added up to a considerable volume of
data — sometimes contradictory — it may be helpful to summarize the
material presented in the foregoing chapters. The following encap-
sulations are for that purpose:

(1) Truman demonstrated a marked awareness of the existence
of the press and its importance in American life.

(2) Truman's consciousness of the influence, the attitudes, the
affairs and the condition of the press is illustrated by more than 644
significant references that he made to the press in his public and
private utterances.

(3) Truman read newspapers extensively, intensively, and
regularly and kept himself informed on what was in public print as
well as the content of broadcast news.

(4) Truman devoted more of his time and attention to the newspaper than to any other medium, with the possible exception of
books.

(5) As a student of history, Truman exhibited considerable
familiarity with the history of the press and an active interest in the
biographies of American newspapermen.

(6) Despite some testimony to the contrary, Truman evidenced a
genuine respect for the general influence of the press on the thinking
of the public.

(7) On occasion, Truman paid high tribute to the press, indicating some degree of admiration — momentarily, at least — that
went beyond mere respect for press influence.

(8) Truman viewed the press as comprising two distinct
segments, which he labeled the "working press" and the "opposition
press."

(9) Within the classification of the "working press," Truman included reporters, correspondents, photographers, and others
employed primarily in the newsgathering function.

(10) Truman's relations with the working press were generally
excellent. The data reveal the existence of an easy, intimate, and predominantly friendly relationship with the men and women of the
press with whom he came into regular contact.

(11) Truman preserved the tradition of the regular White House
press conference — the president's primary contact with the working

press — and maintained it without interruption throughout his ninety-three months in office.

(12) Truman enjoyed a wider acquaintance among working newspapermen than any of his predecessors, and the first of his 324 press conferences broke all attendance records.

(13) Truman's proclivity for short, quick answers to questions by reporters and visiting newsmen tended to make his press conferences much briefer than those of President Roosevelt.

(14) Truman's answers were characterized by frankness and directness. Although he made frequent use of "no comment," he rarely resorted to evasion of questions that he did not wish to answer.

(15) Truman seldom made use of prepared answers suggested to him by his advisers in anticipation of questions that might be put to the president in press conferences, except when the information was of a strictly technical nature.

(16) The finality and rapidity with which Truman customarily answered questions led to occasional slips, which later required clarification.

(17) While such incidents were sometimes embarrassing to Truman, there is little evidence to show that they were as painful as his critics usually made them appear to be, and Truman felt that the press often made little effort to give fair representation to the real intent of his statements on such occasions.

(18) Truman's tiffs with the working press were usually good-natured and of minor importance.

(19) The two major disputes with the working press, in which the element of humor was apparently lacking, grew out of Truman's violation of the custom of not giving exclusive presidential interviews and his issuance of Executive Order 10290 restricting security information. The tiffs resulting from these actions, however, did not seem to have a lasting effect on the press conferences.

(20) Truman's interest in the press conference was demonstrated by the innovations he had made in the mechanics of the conference. His introduction of the budget seminar and his alteration of the location and procedure of the press conference represented some of the first changes since the administration of Woodrow Wilson.

(21) In his general appraisal of the press conferences as an institution, Truman expressed great appreciation of its value and genuine enjoyment in the regular rough-and-tumble sessions with representatives of the working press. He heartily endorsed the

perpetuation of the practice as a wholesome institution for both the president and the press.

(22) Although two of his press secretaries died in office, Truman was fortunate in having men in that position who contributed substantially to his relations with the press. However, his relations were consistently maintained largely on the basis of his own personality rather than through the intermediary influence of a press secretary.

(23) Press Secretary Charles G. Ross occupied a unique position because of the great esteem in which he was held by Truman and by the news profession.

(24) Truman's relations with the news photographers as with other contingents of the working press were uniformly good. Cameramen found him an unprecedentedly willing, cooperative, and accessible subject.

(25) In contrast to his pleasant relations with the working press, Truman consistently exchanged recriminations with the owners, editors, publishers, columnists, and others whom he considered to be part of the "opposition press."

(26) Truman accused the opposition press of falsification and distortion of the facts, which he attributed not so much to carelessness or accident as to deliberate prejudice and a bent for lying.

(27) Truman objected to speculation and prediction in the news. He evidenced a distaste for "interpretative" reporting and decried the lack of objective reporting in most of the country's newspapers.

(28) Truman's concept of government was thoroughly Jeffersonian in that he believed if the people know the truth, they will act in the best interests of the majority and thus preserve the democracy. He charged that the press was failing to provide the people with the truth.

(29) It was this conviction, Truman maintained, that prompted him to undertake the "whistle-stop" tours of 1948 in an effort to "give the people the facts" in person.

(30) An especial concern expressed by Truman was that misreporting of current events by a "lying press" might induce permanent distortions of the truth in the recorded history of the times.

(31) Truman felt that the press was irresponsible in its handling of information involving the national security.

(32) It was the failure of the press to exercise proper judgment and to accept the patriotic obligation of self-imposed censorship, Truman held, that led to his official attempts to strengthen protection

of government security information, culminating in Executive Order 10290.

(33) Without denying the dangerous implications of prior censorship that press leaders recognized in Executive Order 10290, there is no evidence to indicate that Truman personally advocated censorship, in any form in which he understood the term, as a retaliative or punitive measure against an antagonistic press.

(34) The fact that the controversial security order continued throughout the remainder of his term and into a Republican administration without revocation affords grounds for Truman's argument that the order was not extreme in its provisions or partisan in its purpose.

(35) Truman accused the opposition press of conspiring with "special interests" — by reason of the latter's ownership, financial control, or subsidization of the newspapers and radio through purchases of advertising — in an economic combine, which was inimical to the policies of his administration.

(36) Truman expressed an appreciation for the power of advertising on occasion, but he continued to voice contempt for its effectiveness as used against him politically in the "kept press."

(37) The press was also guilty, Truman charged, of exceeding the limits of partisan opposition to his program and undermining the framework of the government's domestic and foreign operations.

(38) The deleterious aims and effects that Truman ascribed to the "sabotage press" included the following: to destroy the reputation of the late President Roosevelt; to discourage, through "smear attacks" and "character assassination," the procurement of qualified persons for appointment to responsible positions in Truman's administration; to create discord between Democratic party leaders for the purpose of disrupting and defeating the Truman program; to interfere in the normal domestic responsibilities of the federal government; and to enforce isolationistic and other policies, which Truman considered to be Republican-inspired, into the foreign affairs of the United States government.

(39) Truman castigated the American press in general as a "one-party press." He maintained that he had never had the political support of the newspapers in any stage of his career and that 90 percent opposed him during most of his presidency.

(40) Truman's partisan interests were inseparably bound up with his attitudes and feelings toward the press. He sometimes expressed

genuine approbation of newspapers and journalists who appeared to be supporters of the Democratic party, but he was wary in his appraisal of newspapers and journalists of whose political complexion he could not feel certain.

(41) Truman deplored the "small amount of political influence" exercised by the opposition press, indicating that he may not have fully considered the proper function of a newspaper (as defined by the authorities quoted in several of the earlier chapters of this book).

(42) Truman's unprecedented political victory in 1948 did not noticeably affect his relations with the working press or change his attitude toward the opposition press. The data indicate that the experience served to confirm, rather than to change, his conviction of the lack of political influence exercised by the opposition press. Except for the few instances when he chided the ineffectiveness of the "one-party press," there is no record of a gloating attitude inconsistent with the recorded testimony of his relations with the press from the very beginning of his succession to the presidency.

(43) Truman manifested less respect for general editorial comment in the press than for the reportorial function. He repeatedly observed that he did not care what the newspapers said in their editorial pages if they would print the facts accurately in their news columns.

(44) Truman criticized newspaper editors as meddlesome, discourteous, unprincipled, two-faced, unconscionably biased, and perpetrators of libel. He conceded, however, that the editorial writers of the nation represented a great power for good and that some few did not abuse that power.

(45) Truman held the column-writing function of journalism in low esteem, with few exceptions.

(46) Truman classified columnists loosely as either frustrated critics, who wrote from "ivory-tower" positions of self-assumed authority, or gossip mongers, who purveyed unreliable or scandalous information for mercenary or undistinguished motives.

(47) Because of his knowledge of historical precedents, Truman asserted, he was enabled to maintain a philosophical reaction to press criticism. He apparently expected, as the thirty-third president, to receive a certain share of journalistic abuse from the time he entered office.

(48) Truman regarded attacks on his person as less reprehensible than criticisms of his appointees and advisers.

(49) Press criticisms aimed at the members of his family were to Truman completely inexcusable and intolerable.

(50) Truman's overt reaction to press criticism was generally to criticize the press. In the exchange, he found newspapermen too "thin skinned," and scoffed at what he considered their inability to take criticism as well as to give it.

(51) Although Truman considered himself to be one of the most maligned of presidents, he made no efforts beyond verbal retaliation to "get revenge."

(52) There is no evidence in the record that Truman developed a tendency toward a persecution complex, as some authorities have suggested. While Truman admitted that his feeling might have been different had he enjoyed the support of a more representative portion of the press during his political career, his testimony bearing on this subject reveals no suggestion of lasting bitterness or malice. To the contrary, his prevailing mood seemed to be one of cheerful resilience or, at the least, philosophical acceptance of press opposition. As he candidly stated to a home-state newspaperman, "I have talked with the people you mentioned in your letter and they seem to have an opinion that the president is against a free press. I don't know how we are going to overcome that, and I fear very much that we can't."[1]

Appendix

SIGNIFICANT
REFERENCESS
TO THE PRESS

REGARDLESS OF WHAT CONCLUSIONS MIGHT BE REACHED concerning Truman's attitude toward the press, there can be no doubt that he recognized the role of the newspapers of the United States as an extremely important one in the life of the nation. He was manifestly conscious of a press that demanded the attention of the highest officials of government because it commanded the attention of the American public. The record reveals that the president devoted a good deal of attention to that press himself.

Throughout his tenure as president, Truman made many references in public and in private to the American press—some of which undoubtedly never made their way into the permanent record. Although a number of the allusions were recorded in his personal notes or in miscellaneous isolated documents, a painstaking survey of all the Truman papers shows that the overwhelming portion—perhaps 90 percent—of his recorded references to the press originated from three prolific sources: press conferences, speeches, and letters.

Before too much importance is attached to the position that the press occupied in Truman's thinking while in office, it is necessary to ascertain the approximate proportion of his utterances, at least in these three major categories of his recorded communications, that he devoted to the subject. This is done in the following paragraphs and is illustrated in the accompanying tables.

It should be understood that not all of Truman's recorded references to the press are tabulated here. The attempt was made, in collecting the data, to exclude mentions of the press that are obviously unimportant or inconsequential to this study; the objective was to ferret out significant references or comments of the president that would be of value to an understanding of his press relations. For example, the president wrote many thank-you notes to individuals who sent him newspaper clippings, but such routine acknowledgments are not tabulated as significant references to the press.

Furthermore, the word *reference* does not signify the mechanical appearance in the record of a key word or phrase such as "publisher" or "freedom of the press." As used in this study, a reference is any expressed thought that the president formulated in a word, a sentence, or perhaps several hundred words. Regardless of form or length, therefore, his preserved thoughts that tend to shed some light on his relations with the press constitute significant references.

Table 1 lists the number of press conferences held each year and indicates the number of significant references to the press that were made by the president at these conferences. Truman conducted a total of 324 press conferences during the time he was in office, and on 206 occasions he had something to say about the press.

It will be noted that 162 conferences were held during each term of office, but that a total of 144 significant references were made during the second term as compared with only 62 during the first. This suggests that Truman became increasingly preoccupied with thoughts about the press during his second administration.

Table 1
Significant References to the Press Made
by President Truman in Press Conferences

Year	Conferences	Number of Conferences	Significant References
1945	1 – 40	40	12
1946	41 – 93	53	21
1947	94 – 131	38	14
1948	132 – 162	31	15
1949	163 – 209	47	32
1950	210 – 248	39	30
1951	249 – 287	39	35
1952	288 – 320	33	44
1953	321 – 324	4	3
	Totals:	324	206

An actual count of the manuscripts of the president's speeches delivered between April 2, 1945, and January 20, 1953, revealed a total of 1,101 public performances. Speeches of the chief executive are classified according to the White House filing system as "addresses," "remarks," "messages," and "toasts."

The "addresses" are speeches of major importance delivered before recognized bodies or the public at large. They are frequently broadcast and usually receive the widest publicity. The "remarks" of the president are generally shorter and less formal. These may range from an impromptu talk to a group of visiting teachers in the Rose Garden of the White House to a rear-platform spiel on a cross-country campaign tour. "Messages" are addresses made before the Congress and are almost exclusively devoted to a discussion of legislation requested by the president and to the annual State-of-the-Union report. The "toasts," of course, are the routine tributes paid by the president, usually at social functions.

In table 2, the breakdown of Truman's speeches is presented along with the number of significant references made to the press. As shown in the figures, the totals of speeches delivered in the election years of 1948, 1950 and 1952 exceed those for the nonelection years, and the number of references to the press is also relatively higher for those three years. It is particularly noticeable that 1948 was a peak year for both "remarks" (which included 263 "whistle-stop" speeches) and "significant references," indicating an intensification of the president's attention to the press during his own campaign for office.

The 118 references which Truman made to the press in his public speeches take on added significance when it is realized that these are instances in which the president is expressing his views not to a personal friend or to a selected group, but to great crowds of people and, sometimes, to the entire nation. What he might have said of the press over an international radio broadcasting network must be considered on a different basis from the remarks he may have made to a reporter at a press conference. This is why, throughout this book, attention has been given to the background or the context from which significant references are drawn.

The personal letter seemed to have been Truman's favored medium of communication as chief executive—so much so that he was known as a "letter-writing president." Near the close of his second term, he remarked to a Kansas correspondent, "It doesn't seem possible that you have received a hundred letters from me since I've been president, but if you say that is a fact it must be."[1]

Truman frequently resorted to letters to friends or to opponents to unburden his mind and, consequently, to reveal most clearly some of his otherwise unexpressed feelings. From the first letter he wrote on the day after he became president to his last one before retiring from the office, his writing is characterized by a style that is consistently

Table 2
Significant References to the Press Made
by President Truman in Public Speeches

Year	Addresses	Remarks	Messages	Toasts	Number of speeches	Number of "significant references"
1945	18	18	1	1	38	4
1946	17	48	2	0	67	8
1947	24	47	2	7	80	16
1948	58	343*	3	3	407	32
1949	27	62	1	5	95	13
1950	41	106**	1	3	151	13
1951	37	82	1	6	126	8
1952	59	66***	7	1	133	13
1953	1	0	3	0	4	11
Totals:	282	772	21	26	1,101	118

* About 263 were campaign speeches.
** About 57 were campaign speeches.
*** About 23 were campaign speeches.

homey and personable, direct and unequivocal, brief to the point of abruptness, and genuinely earnest in tone.

Truman produced a total volume of personal letters estimated at 31,650. A careful search through the entire collection revealed a total of 320 significant references to the press.

Table 3 illustrates a trend comparable to that revealed in the charting of his press conferences and public speeches—i.e., a gradual increase in the number of significant references through the two administrations. The table shows that, with the exception of 1947, the steady upward curve from 20 references in 1945 to 81 references in 1952 is uninterrupted.

Table 3
Significant References to the Press Made
by President Truman in Personal Letters

Year	Letters Written (approximate number)	Significant References
1945	3,400	20
1946	3,500	29
1947	3,700	24
1948	3,900	30
1949	4,500	36
1950	4,200	44
1951	4,300	53
1952	4,000	81
1953	150	3
Totals:	31,650	320

NOTES

References to the statements of President Truman can be found in the original documents (press conferences, personal letters, public speeches, etc.) that are housed in the Truman Library in Independence, Missouri. Other sources are indicated in the bibliographical data accompanying each footnote. Personal interviews referred to were between the former president and the author during 1954, either at his offices in the Federal Reserve Bank Building in Kansas City or at his home, 219 North Delaware Street, in Independence.

CHAPTER 1: APPETITE FOR NEWS

[1] Frank McNaughton and Walter Hehmeyer, *This Man Truman* (New York: McGraw-Hill, 1945), p. 79. Copyright 1945 by McGraw-Hill Book Co. Used by permission.

[2] J.T. Salter (ed.), *Public Men In and Out of Office* (Chapel Hill: University of North Carolina Press, 1945), p. 3.

[3] Robert S. Allen and William V. Shannon, *The Truman Merry-Go-Round* (New York: Vanguard Press, 1950), p. 34.

[4] White House Press and Radio Conference no. 36, Dec. 4, 1945.

[5] Harold D. Smith, personal diary (photostatic copy in the Truman Collection), entry of Feb. 18, 1946.

[6] Charles Van Devander and William O. Player, in the *New York Post* (Sept. 26, 1946), p. 12.

[7] Cyril Clemens, *The Man from Missouri* (Webster Groves, Mo.: International Mark Twain Society, 1945), p. 7.

[8] Personal letter to George H. Mead, 131 North Ludlow St., Dayton, Ohio, Dec. 28, 1946.

[9] Personal letter to Brigadier General Frank L. Howley, 7811 Froebel Rd., Philadelphia, Penn., Feb. 14, 1950.

[10] Personal letter to Mary W. Dawson, 171 West 12th St., New York, N.Y., Apr. 17, 1947.

[11] Personal letter to A.A. Berle, Sr., 27 West 44th St., New York, N.Y., Apr. 5, 1948.

[12] "New HST Note Pats Joe Palooka," *Editor & Publisher*, 83 (Dec. 23, 1950), p. 12.

[13]Personal letter to George Lichtenstein, Sun and Times Company, 211 W. Wacker, Chicago, Ill., July 20, 1948.

[14]White House Press and Radio Conference no. 187, June 30, 1949.

[15]Truman Asks Original of Shoemaker Cartoon," *Chicago Daily News* (July 17, 1951), p. 10. (Cartoon was "There Goes Margaret's Father," by Vaughn Shoemaker).

[16]Address at 35th Division reunion, Little Rock, Ark., June 11, 1949.

[17]Remarks at breakfast of National Cartoonists Assn., Washington, D.C., Nov. 6, 1951.

[18]White House Press and Radio Conference no. 124, Oct. 17, 1947.

[19]Personal letter to C.S. Huntington, 66 Pinckney St., Boston, Mass., Feb. 6, 1948.

[20]Personal letter to Governor Forrest Smith, Jefferson City, Mo., March 6, 1950.

[21]White House Press and Radio Conference no. 124, Oct. 17, 1947.

[22]Ibid., no. 289, Jan. 10, 1952.

[23]"Harry S Truman, 'Mr. Citizen,'" *American Weekly* (five installments), Sept. 20, 1953, through Oct. 18, 1953.

[24]*Kansas City* (Mo.) *Times.*

[25]Ibid., Section 1 (Sept. 20, 1953), p. 6.

[26]Ibid., p. 8.

[27]Ibid., Section 2 (Sept. 27, 1953), p. 10.

Chapter 2: Of Precedents and Presidents

[1]Personal letter to Robert E. Hannegan, Washington, D.C., Apr. 15, 1947.

[2]Address to the Gridiron Club, Washington, D.C., May 11, 1947.

[3]White House Press and Radio Conference no. 111, July 19, 1947.

[4]Remarks to a group from the National Association of Radio News Editors in the executive office of the president, Nov. 13, 1947.

[5]Remarks at the dinner of the Order of the Ahepa, Washington, D.C., Mar. 29, 1948.

[6]Personal letter to George E. Phillies, 1064 Ellicott Square, Buffalo, N.Y., Apr. 9, 1948.

[7]White House Press and Radio Conference no. 134, Jan. 22, 1948.

[8]Ibid., no. 186, June 16, 1949.

[9]Ibid.

[10]"The victims of the gag laws must be freed; they will be freed by the organized power of the people. This will of course not be done by President

Truman, who called attention to the similarity between the current repression and the repression of the 1790s. Who more than he is responsible for this era of repression?" William L. Patterson, *The Reign of Witches: The Struggle Against the Alien and Sedition Laws* (New York: Civil Rights Congress, 1952), pp. i-ii.

11Westminster College, Fulton, Mo., under auspices of John Findley Creon Foundation, Apr. 12, 1954.

12Personal interview, Kansas City, Mo., Aug. 19, 1953.

13James E. Pollard, *Presidents and the Press* (New York: Macmillan, 1947). Used by permission.

14White House Press and Radio Conference no. 144, Apr. 23, 1948.

15Personal letter to Clarence W. Bearry, Jr., U.S. Court House, Chicago, Ill., Sept. 22, 1950.

16Personal letter to Stephen B. Gibbons, Bergenlin Ave. and 32nd Street, Union City, N.J., Nov. 17, 1950.

17Remarks at Masonic Breakfast, Washington, D.C., Feb. 21, 1952.

18White House Press and Radio Conference no. 257, Mar. 15, 1951.

19Ibid.

20William Hillman, *Mr. President* (New York: Farrar, Straus and Young, 1952), p. 90. Reprinted by permission of Farrar, Straus and Girous, Inc. Excerpts from *Mr. President* by William Hillman, pictures by Alfred Wagg. Copyright ©1952 by William Hillman and Alfred Wagg.

21Personal interview with the author, Kansas City, Mo., Aug. 31, 1954.

22Remarks at Masonic Breakfast, Washington, D.C., Feb. 21, 1952.

23Ibid.

24There is no evidence to indicate either that Washington declined the race for a third term because of newspaper opposition or that the oft-heard version, quoted by Truman, of the report on Lincoln at Gettysburg, has any referent in historical documents. Neither "event" is recognized in the most comprehensive journalism history, Frank Luther Mott's *American Journalism,* rev. ed. (New York: Macmillan, 1950).

25Hillman, *Mr. President,* p. 3. Reprinted by permission of Farrar, Straus and Girous, Inc. Excerpts from *Mr. President* by William Hillman, pictures by Alfred Wagg. Copyright ©1952 by William Hillman and Alfred Wagg.

26White House Press and Radio Conference no. 300, Apr. 17, 1952.

CHAPTER 3: CREDIT WHERE DUE

1Remarks at FAO Conference, Washington, D.C., Oct. 2, 1945.

[2]White House Press and Radio Conference no. 42, Jan. 11, 1946.

[3]David M. Noyes, former presidential adviser, in conversation with the author, Kansas City, Mo., Aug. 20, 1954. This is also pictured in "Mr. Truman after Five Years: Sizing Up His Faults and Merits," *U.S. News and World Report* (Apr. 14, 1950), p. 16.

[4]David M. Noyes, former presidential adviser, in conversation with the author, Kansas City, Mo., Aug. 20, 1954.

[5]White House Press and Radio Conference no. 48, Feb. 15, 1946.

[6]Radio address, Washington, D.C., June 29, 1946.

[7]Letter from Senator Frank P. Briggs to President Truman, Dec. 18, 1946.

[8]Personal letter to Frank P. Briggs, U.S. Senate, Washington, D.C., Dec. 28, 1946.

[9]White House Press and Radio Conference no. 102, Apr. 10, 1947.

[10]"President Asks Aid of Press," *Editor & Publisher,* 80 (Apr. 26, 1947), p. 10.

[11]Radio address, Washington, D.C., Oct. 30, 1947.

[12]Personal letter to Burton K. Wheeler, Southern Bldg., Washington, D.C., Jan. 7, 1948.

[13]Personal letter to Burton K. Wheeler, Southern Bldg., Washington, D.C., Jan. 31, 1948.

[14]White House Press and Radio Conference no. 124, Oct. 17, 1947.

[15]Address to American Society of Newspaper Editors, Washington, D.C., Apr. 17, 1948.

[16]"He was alive, alert, fresh and outspoken, and sprinkled his talk with humor. It was an entirely different Truman from the picture in the minds of the editors who knew him only from reading about him and reading his canned 'copy' in their offices. When he finished, they rose and applauded enthusiastically—a really tremendous ovation for such a group —and turned to one another to express their amazement at what they had witnessed." Thomas L. Stokes, "Harry Truman, Politician Extraordinary," *New York Times* magazine (May 7, 1950), p. 13.

[17]Remarks to the American Society of Newspaper Editors, Washington, D.C. Apr. 17, 1948.

[18]Rear platform remarks, Everett, Wash., June 9, 1948.

[19]Personal letter to Robert M. White II, *Mexico Ledger*, Mexico, Mo., Oct. 6, 1949.

[20]Address to National Conference of Christians and Jews, Washington, D.C., Nov. 10, 1949.

[21]Address to the American Society of Newspaper Editors, Washington, D.C., Apr. 9, 1950.

[22]Ibid.

[23]Ibid.

[24]Remarks, Grand Island, Nebr., May 8, 1950.

[25]Address, Pendleton, Ore., May 10, 1950.

[26]Personal letter to Dr. J.T. Salter, Univ. of Wisconsin, Madison, Mar. 17, 1952.

[27]White House Press and Radio Conference no. 311, Aug. 7, 1952.

[28]Rear platform remarks, Muskegon, Mich., Oct. 30, 1952.

[29]"President Checking Up on Newspaper Crowd Estimates," *Editor & Publisher,* 85 (Oct. 25, 1952), p. 8.

CHAPTER 4: BOUQUETS BEFORE BRICKBATS

[1]Personal letter to Jonathan Daniels, 1540 Caswell Street, Raleigh, N.C., Aug. 29, 1945.

[2]Personal letter to Russell Stewart, *Chicago Times,* Chicago, Ill., Nov. 27, 1945.

[3]White House Press and Radio Conference no. 36, Dec. 4, 1945.

[4]Personal letter to Bennet Roach, editor of the *Shelby News,* Shelbyville, Ky., May 13, 1946.

[5]"Truman Salutes Newspaper Week," *Editor & Publisher* 79 (Sept. 28, 1946), p. 9.

[6]Remarks in making the Wendell Willkie Awards for Journalism, National Press Club Auditorium, Washington, D.C., Feb. 28, 1947.

[7]Ibid.

[8]"Truman Hails Philadelphia Bulletin on Centenary," *Editor & Publisher,* 80 (Apr. 19, 1947), p. 36.

[9]"President Thanks Press for Kindness," *Editor & Publisher* (Aug. 9, 1947), p. 28.

[10]"Truman Greets Newspapers," *Editor & Publisher,* 80 (Oct. 4, 1947), p. 9.

[11]Remarks to Gridiron Club, Washington, D.C., May 11, 1947.

[12]Remarks, Kansas City, Mo., May 22, 1947.

[13]Rear platform remarks, Emporia, Kans., June 16, 1948.

[14]Address to Conference on Highway Safety, Washington, D.C., June 2, 1949.

[15]Personal letter to William Hillman, 1701 Massachusetts Ave., N.W., Washington, D.C., Jan. 9, 1951.

[16]Personal letter to R.P. Weatherford, Jr., mayor, Independence, Mo., Apr. 5, 1951.

[17]Personal letter to William T. Evjue, *Madison* (Wis.) *Capital Times,* June 6, 1951.

[18]Personal letter to Maple T. Harl, chairman, Federal Deposit Insurance Corp., Washington, D.C., Aug. 15, 1952.

[19]Tallulah Bankhead, *Tallulah: My Autobiography* (New York: Harper, 1952).

[20]Personal letter to Tallulah Bankhead, Hotel Elysee, 60 East 54th St., New York, N.Y., Aug. 4, 1952.

[21]Personal letter to Adlai E. Stevenson, governor of Illinois, Springfield, Sept. 10, 1952.

CHAPTER 5: SEEING DOUBLE

[1]This subject is developed in chapter 12.

[2]"Truman and Press," *Editor & Publisher*, 77 (June 2, 1945), p. 38.

[3]James E. Pollard, "Truman and the Press: Final Phase," *Journalism Quarterly,* 30 (Summer 1953), p. 286.

[4]Personal letter to Wayne Coy, chairman of the FCC, Washington, D.C., May 12, 1948.

[5]"Washington Outlook: Pleasant for Press, Maybe Not for Papers," *Editor & Publisher,* 81 (Nov. 13, 1948), p. 11.

[6]Personal letter to Claude C. Bowers, American embassy, Santiago, Chile, Dec. 1, 1948.

[7]White House Press and Radio Conference no. 200, Oct. 6, 1949.

[8]Ibid., no. 252, Jan. 18, 1952.

[9]Ibid.

[10]Remarks, St. Louis, Mo., Nov. 1, 1952.

[11]James E. Pollard, "Truman and the Press," *Journalism Quarterly,* 28 (Fall 1951), p. 462.

[12]Personal interview with the author, Kansas City, Mo., Sept. 3, 1953.

[13]Quoted in William Hillman, *Mr. President* (New York: Farrar, Straus and Young, 1952), p. 113. Reprinted by permission of Farrar, Straus and Girous, Inc. Excerpts from *Mr. President* by William Hillman, pictures by Alfred Wagg. Copyright ©1952 by William Hillman and Alfred Wagg.

[14]White House Press and Radio Conference no. 3, May 5, 1945.

[15]Ibid., no. 53, Mar. 8, 1946.

[16]"Shop Talk at Thirty," *Editor & Publisher*, 81 (Apr. 3, 1948), p. 68.

[17]Personal letter to Warren B. Francis, National Press Club, Washington, D.C., Sept. 3, 1949.

[18]Memorandum of the president, Jan. 23, 1948.

[19]White House Press and Radio Conference no. 208, Dec. 15, 1949.

[20] Ibid., no. 221, Mar. 30, 1950.

[21] Ibid.

[22] Ibid., no. 265, May 24, 1951.

[23] Jerry Greene, "Air Age at the White House," *Pegasus* (July 1951), p. 1.

[24] White House Press and Radio Conference no. 274, Aug. 9, 1951.

[25] Personal letter to Frank Bourgholtzer, Press Room, White House, Washington, D.C., May 23, 1952.

[26] Personal letter to William S. White, *New York Times* Washington Bureau, Albee Bldg., Washington, D.C., Dec. 31, 1952.

CHAPTER 6: WINDOW TO THE WHITE HOUSE

[1] Sidney Hyman, *The American President* (New York: Harper and Bros., 1954), p. 103.

[2] "Belair Contrasts FDR, Truman Conferences," *Editor & Publisher,* 79 (Mar. 16, 1946), p. 58.

[3] White House Press and Radio Conference no. 51, Mar. 4, 1946.

[4] Ibid., no. 52, Mar. 4, 1946.

[5] Ibid., no. 17, Aug. 8, 1945.

[6] Cyril Clemens, *The Man from Missouri* (Webster Groves, Mo.: International Mark Twain Society, 1945), p. 51.

[7] "Truman's First Press Conference," *Editor & Publisher,* 78 (Apr. 21, 1945), p. 9.

[8] James E. Pollard, "Truman and the Press," *Journalism Quarterly,* 28 (Fall 1951), p. 458.

[9] William D. Leahy, *I Was There* (New York: Whittlesey House, McGraw-Hill, 1950), p. 349.

[10] Personal letter to Martha and Mary Truman, Grandview, Mo., Apr. 13, 1945.

[11] Personal letter to Martha and Mary Truman, Grandview, Mo., Apr. 4, 1945.

[12] White House Press and Radio Conference no. 1, Apr. 17, 1945.

CHAPTER 7: THE NO-COMMENT COMMENT

[1] James E. Pollard, "Truman and the Press," *Journalism Quarterly,* 28 (Fall 1951), p. 458.

[2] White House Press and Radio Conference no. 61, Apr. 18, 1946.

[3] George E. Allen, *Presidents Who Have Known Me* (New York: Simon and Schuster, 1950), p. 167.

[4]Frank McNaughton and Walter Hehmeyer, *Harry Truman, President* (New York: McGraw-Hill, 1948), p. 107. Copyright 1948 by McGraw-Hill Book Co. Used by permission.

[5]Personal interview, Kansas City, Mo., Sept. 3, 1954.

[6]White House Press and Radio Conference no. 48, Feb. 15, 1946.

[7]Ibid., no. 247, Dec. 19, 1950.

[8]Ibid.

[9]Ibid., no. 256, Mar. 1, 1951.

[10]Ibid.

[11]Other typical expressions collected from the transcripts of the 324 press conferences include the following:
"All I know is what I read in the papers."
"You'd better wait and see how developments come out."
"The facts speak for themselves."
"You're the one who is supposed to have the answers."
"When I take the action, you will know all about it."
"I think I commented on that through Mr. Ross."

[12]White House Press and Radio Conference no. 298, Apr. 3, 1952.

[13]Ibid., no. 322, Dec. 31, 1952.

[14]Ibid., no. 287, Dec. 13, 1951.

[15]Memorandum to the president from OWMR, May 1, 1945.

[16]Memorandum to the president from the secretary of the treasury, Feb. 4, 1946.

[17]Memorandum to the president from Clinton P. Anderson, secretary of agriculture, Feb. 6, 1946.

[18]White House Press and Radio Conference no. 47, Feb. 7, 1946.

[19]Ibid.

[20]Memorandum to Charles Ross from Francis H. Russell, director, Office of Public Affairs, State Department, Washington, D.C., Feb. 27, 1950.

[21]Minutes of correspondents' committee meeting, Fish Room, White House, Washington, D.C., Apr. 17, 1950.

Chapter 8: Slips and Quips

[1]White House Press and Radio Conference no. 20, Aug. 23, 1945.

[2]Frank McNaughton and Walter Hehmeyer, *Harry Truman, President* (New York: McGraw-Hill, 1943), p. 108. Copyright 1943 by McGraw-Hill Book Co. Used by permission.

[3]White House Press and Radio Conference no. 38, Dec. 12, 1945.

[4]James E. Pollard, "Truman and the Press," *Journalism Quarterly*, 28 (Fall 1951), p. 459.

[5]White House Press and Radio Conference no. 80, Sept. 12, 1946.

⁶Ibid.

⁷Ibid., no. 82, Sept. 14, 1946.

⁸*Time,* Sept. 23, 1946, p. 22.

⁹White House Press and Radio Conference no. 246, Nov. 30, 1950.

¹⁰Ibid.

¹¹Addendum, White House Press and Radio Conference no. 246, Nov. 30, 1950.

¹²Note at the end of transcript of press conference no. 246 says: "extra copy for John Hersey, *New Yorker* magazine."

¹³White House Press and Radio Conference no. 312. Aug. 14, 1952.

¹⁴Ibid., no. 313, Aug. 21, 1952.

¹⁵Ibid., no. 320, Dec. 11, 1952.

¹⁶Ibid., no. 321, Dec. 18, 1952.

¹⁷Quoted in William Hillman, *Mr. President* (New York: Farrar, Straus and Young, 1952), p. 90. Reprinted by permission of Farrar, Straus and Girous, Inc. Excerpts from *Mr. President* by William Hillman, pictures by Alfred Wagg. Copyright ©1952 by William Hillman and Alfred Wagg.

CHAPTER 9: TEMPER TANTRUMS?

¹White House Press and Radio Conference no. 44, Jan. 19, 1946.

²Ibid., no. 61, Apr. 18, 1946.

³Ibid., no. 62, May 2, 1946.

⁴Ibid., no. 122, Oct. 9, 1947.

⁵Ibid., no. 134, Jan. 23, 1948.

⁶Ibid., no. 159, Dec. 2, 1948.

⁷Ibid., no. 215, Feb. 2, 1950.

⁸Ibid., no. 216, Feb. 9, 1950.

⁹Ibid., no. 122, Oct. 9, 1947.

¹⁰Ibid., no. 218, Feb. 23, 1950.

¹¹Meyer Berger, *The Story of the New York Times* (New York: Simon and Schuster, 1951), pp. 545-46. Copyright 1951 by Meyer Berger, renewed 1979 by Mae G. Berger. Used by permission.

¹²Personal letter to Mr. Orlando Blackburn, Texas City, Tex., Apr. 6, 1946.

¹³White House Press and Radio Conference no. 217, Feb. 15, 1950.

¹⁴James E. Pollard, "Truman and the Press: Final Phase," *Journalism Quarterly,* 30 (Summer 1953), p. 284.

¹⁵"Truman Scolds News Corps," *Editor & Publisher,* 83 (Feb. 18, 1950), p. 5; "Truman's Huff" (editorial), ibid., p. 30; "Shop Talk at Thirty," ibid. (Feb. 25, 1950), p. 60.

[16]White House Press and Radio Conference no. 261, Apr. 26, 1951.

[17]Ibid., no. 241, Sept. 28, 1950.

[18]Memorandum from the president to John L. Steele, Oct. 11, 1950.

[19]James E. Pollard, "Truman and the Press," *Journalism Quarterly*, 28 (Fall 1951), p. 465.

[20]White House Press and Radio Conference no. 246, Nov. 30, 1950.

[21]"Truman Slaps Reporters for Guesses, Lies," *Editor & Publisher*, 83 (Dec. 2, 1950), p. 8.

[22]White House Press and Radio Conference no. 249, Jan. 4, 1951.

[23]Ibid., no. 251, Jan. 13, 1951.

[24]Ibid., no. 287, Dec. 13, 1951.

[25]Ibid., no. 294, Feb. 14, 1952.

[26]Ibid., no. 300, Apr. 17, 1952.

[27]"Press and TV Have Field Day as HST Fumes," *Editor & Publisher*, 85 (Dec. 13, 1952), p. 8.

CHAPTER 10: SOFT ON SHUTTERBUGS

[1]Tris Coffin, *Missouri Compromise* (Boston: Little, Brown, 1947), p. 29.

[2]"Truman Is Photogs' 'Best Friend,'" *Editor & Publisher,* 78 (Oct. 20, 1945), p. 68.

[3]"Lensmen Find Truman Very Lively Subject," *Editor & Publisher*, 81 (Dec. 25, 1948), p. 36.

[4]Address, Fire Prevention Conference, Washington, D.C., May 6, 1947.

[5]White House Press and Radio Conference no. 298, Apr. 3, 1952.

[6]Remarks, Rose Garden of the White House, Sept. 22, 1952.

[7]Remarks, Ogden, Utah, Sept. 21, 1948.

[8]Rear platform remarks, Montgomery, W. Va., Oct. 1, 1948.

[9]Personal letter to H.A. Chipman, Battle Creek, Mich., Nov. 19, 1949.

[10]Personal letter to Maury Maverick, 1000 Transit Tower, San Antonio, Tex., July 9, 1952.

[11]Remarks, White House Photographers Assn. 1951 Award Ceremonies, Washington, D.C., Feb. 24, 1951.

[12]Quoted by Pollard, "Truman and the Press," *Journalism Quarterly*, 28 (Fall 1951), p. 461.

CHAPTER 11: A FIGHT FOR FACTS

[1]Personal letter to Supreme Court Judge James M. Douglas, Jefferson City, Mo., Feb. 25, 1946.

[2]Charles M. Knapp, "Editorial Influence Dies from Anonymity," *Editor & Publisher*, 85 (Oct. 11, 1952), p. 65.

[3]Ernest Havemann, "The Master Politician," *Life* (Oct. 24, 1949), p. 96.

[4]Lambert A. Wilmer, *Our Press Gang* (Philadelphia, Penn.: Lloyd, 1859).

[5]Personal letter to W.L. Hemingway, 721 Locust St., St. Louis, Mo.: Dec. 23, 1946.

[6]Memorandum to the secretary of the treasury, May 7, 1947.

[7]Rear platform remarks, Dodge City, Kans., June 16, 1948.

[8]Rear platform remarks, Albany, Ore., June 11, 1948.

[9]Rear platform remarks, Fresno, Calif., Sept. 23, 1948.

[10]Personal letter to DeLesseps S. Morrison, mayor of New Orleans, La., Dec. 16, 1948.

[11]Remarks, Shoshone, Idaho, May 10, 1950.

[12]Remarks, American Dental Association Trustees, Rose Garden of the White House, Sept. 16, 1951.

[13]White House Press and Radio Conference no. 315, Sept. 11, 1952.

[14]Address, Spokane, Wash., Oct. 1, 1952.

[15]Telegram, Secretary Byrnes to President Truman, Mar. 5, 1946.

[16]Telegram, Press Secretary Ross to Assistant Press Secretary Ayers, Mar. 4, 1946.

[17]White House Press and Radio Conference no. 53, Mar. 8, 1946.

[18]Byrnes stayed on, though, until February 10, 1947, making Brown's prognostication premature but nevertheless correct.

[19]Personal letter to Henry A. Wallace, Department of Commerce, Washington, D.C., June 7, 1946.

[20]Personal letter to Bryce B. Smith, 1012 Baltimore Ave., Kansas City, Mo., Jan. 12, 1948.

[21]Personal letter to Joseph C. O'Mahoney, U.S. Senate, Washington, D.C., Mar. 13, 1948.

[22]White House Press and Radio Conference no. 142, Apr. 15, 1948.

[23]Personal letter to John T. Barker, Wardman Park Hotel, Washington, D.C., Dec. 13, 1943.

[24]White House Press and Radio Conference no. 206, Nov. 17, 1949.

[25]Personal letter to Clarence Cannon, U.S. House of Representatives, Washington, D.C., Oct. 21, 1950.

[26]Cf. bibliography.

[27]Personal letter to Mrs. Franklin D. Roosevelt, Park Sheraton Hotel, New York, N.Y., Apr. 12, 1951.

[28]Personal letter to Sherman Minton, Associate Justice of the Supreme Court, Washington, D.C., June 20, 1951.

[29] John Hersey, "Profiles: Mr. President," *New Yorker*, April 7 through May 5, 1951.

[30] Personal letter to George Biddle, Commission of Fine Arts, Office of the Secretary, Interior Department Bldg., Washington, D.C., June 23, 1951.

[31] Address, Washington, D.C., Sept. 11, 1951.

[32] Personal letter to Merrill C. Meigs, vice-president, Hearst Corporation, Chicago, Ill., Feb. 7, 1952.

[33] Ibid.

[34] Personal letter to Fred J. Bowman, 3940 Frontier Ave., Chicago, Ill., Dec. 15, 1951.

[35] Personal letter to Edward D. McKim, 300 Marbach Bldg., Omaha, Nebr., Feb. 7, 1952.

[36] Personal letter to Carl A. Hatch, judge, U.S. District Court, Albuquerque, N.M., Feb. 12, 1952.

[37] White House Press and Radio Conference no. 313, Aug. 21, 1952.

[38] Personal letter to Eddie Meisburger, 601 Davidson Bldg., Kansas City, Mo., Sept. 24, 1952.

[39] White House Press and Radio Conference no. 236, Aug. 24, 1950.

[40] Ibid.

[41] Ibid., no. 246, Nov. 30, 1950.

[42] Ibid., no. 257, Mar. 15, 1951.

[43] Ibid., no. 274, Aug. 9, 1951.

[44] Ibid., no. 292, Jan. 31, 1952.

[45] Ibid., no. 319, Dec. 4, 1952.

[46] Quoted by John Hersey, "Profile: Mr. President—I. Quite a Head of Steam," *New Yorker* (Apr. 7, 1951), p. 46.

[47] Personal letter to Harry C. Jobes, 4983 Ward Pkwy., Kansas City, Mo., Feb. 7, 1949.

[48] Personal letter to Jonathan Daniels, *Raleigh* (N.C.) *News and Observer*, Oct. 31, 1946.

[49] Personal letter to Hubert H. Humphrey, U.S. Senate, Washington, D.C., July 8, 1952.

[50] Personal letter to Claude G. Bowers, American ambassador to Chile, Santiago, Dec. 1, 1948.

[51] Personal letter to Thomas L. Stokes, National Press Bldg., Washington, D.C., Nov. 17, 1950.

[52] Personal letter to Louis Johnston, Clarksburg, W. Va., Jan. 5, 1952.

CHAPTER 12: WHOSE RESPONSIBILITY?

[1] Personal interview with the author, Kansas City, Mo., Sept. 3, 1954.

[2]White House Press and Radio Conference no. 134, Jan. 22, 1948.

[3]Ibid., no. 141, Apr. 8, 1948.

[4]Ibid., no. 152, Aug. 5, 1948.

[5]"Need for Secrecy Seen in Atomic Information," *Editor & Publisher*, 81 (Apr. 24, 1948), p. 22.

[6]White House Press and Radio Conference no. 171, Mar. 3, 1949.

[7]"Press Reaction to AEC Conference Is Mixed," *Editor & Publisher,* 82 (Dec. 3, 1949), p. 15.

[8]White House Press and Radio Conference no. 190, July 21, 1949.

[9]Ibid.

[10]Personal interview with the author, Kansas City, Mo., Sept. 2, 1954.

[11]Personal letter to Harold L. Ickes, 3624 Prospect Ave., N.W., Washington 7, D.C., Feb. 1, 1950.

[12]James E. Pollard, "Truman and the Press: Final Phase," *Journalism Quarterly,* 30 (Summer 1953), p. 275.

[13]"Need for Publicity," *Editor and Publisher*, 83 (Mar. 25, 1950), p. 34; *Time,* one of Truman's bitterest critics on charges of censorship, completely ignored the order in its weekly section, "The Press."

[14]White House Press and Radio Conference no. 215, Feb. 2, 1950.

[15]Memorandum of the president, Dec. 5, 1950.

[16]Ibid.

[17]Personal interview with the author, Kansas City, Mo., Aug. 20, 1954.

[18]Memorandum to the secretary of defense, Sept. 24, 1951.

[19]White House press release, Sept. 25, 1951.

[20]White House Press and Radio Conference no. 280, Sept. 27, 1951.

[21]*Editor & Publisher* alone carried no less than seventy-six articles and editorials on this subject during the six months following issuance of the order.

[22]White House Press and Radio Conference no. 281, Oct. 4, 1951.

[23]Quoted by James E. Pollard, "President Truman and the Press," *Journalism Quarterly*, 28 (Fall 1951), p. 275-76.

[24]*Editor & Publisher,* 84 (Sept. 29, 1951), p. 38.

[25]"The Presidency: Embarrassing Half Hour," *Time* (Oct. 15, 1951), pp. 24-25.

[26]Senator Blair Moody, as a member of the Senate Committee on Government Operations, was an outspoken foe of the security order. The investigation was ineffective. Cf. "Senators Get Plan to Nullify 'Security' Gag," *Editor & Publisher*, 84 (Dec. 8, 1951), p. 8.

[27]Personal letter to Arthur Krock, *New York Times* bureau, Washington, D.C., Oct. 7, 1951. According to William Hillman, *Mr. President* (New York: Farrar, Straus and Young, 1952), p. 47 (who does not identify the

correspondent as Krock), this letter was never mailed. Reprinted by permission of Farrar, Straus and Girous, Inc. Excerpts from *Mr. President* by William Hillman, pictures by Alfred Wagg. Copyright ©1952 by William Hillman and Alfred Wagg.

[28] White House Press and Radio Conference no. 287, Dec. 13, 1951.

[29] Ibid.

[30] "Washington: C-for-Censorship Day Arrives—And Protests Pile Up," *Editor & Publisher,* 84 (Oct. 10, 1951), p. 8; "What Goes On" (editorial), *Editor & Publisher*, 85 (Feb. 23, 1952), p. 34.

[31] *New York Times* (Sept. 19, 1951), p. 10.

[32] Ibid.

[33] Personal interview with the author, Kansas City, Mo., Sept. 23, 1954.

[34] Ibid.

CHAPTER 13: OF SPECIAL INTEREST

[1] William P. Helm, *Harry Truman: A Political Biography* (New York: Duell, Sloan and Pearce, 1947). Examples that illustrate this well-known political attitude of Truman occur *passim* in this work and also in the president's speeches, 1945-1953.

[2] Quoted by William Hillman, *Mr. President* (New York: Farrar, Straus and Young, 1952), p. 140. The special session referred to is the famous "Turnip Day" session ordered by Truman in his nomination acceptance speech, Philadelphia, Penn., July 15, 1948. Reprinted by permission of Farrar, Straus and Girous, Inc. Excerpts from *Mr. President* by William Hillman, pictures by Alfred Wagg. Copyright ©1952 by William Hillman and Alfred Wagg.

[3] Rear platform remarks, Hillsboro, Tex., Sept. 27, 1948.

[4] Rear platform remarks, McLester, Okla., Sept. 28, 1948.

[5] Address, Louisville, Ky., Sept. 30, 1948.

[6] To members of the Association of Radio News Analysts in 1945, after H.V. Kaltenborn had explained that the society was analogous to the ASNE, Truman suggested: "You are not so well controlled by the sponsors as they are." (White House Press and Radio Conference no. 13, June 16, 1945)

[7] Rear platform remarks, Geneve, N.Y., Oct. 8, 1948.

[8] Address, St. Louis, Mo., Oct. 30, 1948.

[9] Rear platform remarks, Terre Haute, Ind., Oct. 30, 1948.

[10] Quoted by Hillman, *Mr. President*, p. 149, who adds, ". . . not delivered 'because of shortage of radio time.'" Reprinted by permission of Farrar, Straus and Girous, Inc. Excerpts from *Mr. President* by William

Hillman, pictures by Alfred Wagg. Copyright ©1952 by William Hillman and Alfred Wagg.

[11] Address, Jefferson-Jackson Day dinner, Washington, D.C., Feb. 24, 1949.

[12] White House Press and Radio Conference no. 171, Mar. 3, 1949.

[13] Personal letter to Max Lowenthal, 467 Central Park West, New York 25, N.Y., Apr. 2, 1950.

[14] Message to National Rural Electric Cooperative Association Convention, Chicago, Ill., Mar. 13, 1952 (read for the president by Secretary of the Interior Chapman).

[15] Ibid.

[16] Remarks, Electric Consumers Conference, Washington, D.C., May 26, 1952.

[17] Draft of letter to Philip L. Graham, publisher, *Washington Post*, Dec. 12, 1952 (not sent).

[18] Personal letter to Mrs. Albert D. Lasker, 29 Beekman Place, New York, N.Y., Dec. 14, 1945.

[19] Remarks to the Advertising Council, Washington, D.C., Sept. 18, 1946.

[20] Remarks to the Advertising Council, Washington, D.C., Feb. 9, 1949.

[21] Personal letter to Frank W. Abrams, 30 Rockefeller Plaza, New York, N.Y., July 31, 1950.

[22] Personal letter to Governor Chester Bowles, Hartford, Conn., June 23, 1950.

[23] Note written by President Truman, Oct. 11, 1952.

[24] Personal letter to Frank Hodges, St. Luke's Hospital, Kansas City, Mo., May 15, 1952.

CHAPTER 14: MASS MEDIA MOTIVES

[1] Personal letter to Wayne Morse, Eugene, Ore., Aug. 27, 1945.

[2] Personal letter to Henry A. Bundschu, U.S. Court House, Kansas City, Mo., Aug. 25, 1945.

[3] Personal letter to Jonathan Daniels, 1540 Caswell St., Raleigh, N.C., Aug. 29, 1945.

[4] Personal letter to Edward D. McKim, Mutual Benefit Health and Accident Assn., Omaha, Nebr., Nov. 9, 1945.

[5] Personal letter to Francis Biddle, APO 124 A, c/o Postmaster, New York City, N.Y., Feb. 2, 1946.

[6] Personal letter to Vernon E. Moore, Filipino Rehabilitation Commission, Washington, D.C., Feb. 9, 1946.

[7] Remarks of the president to the Advertising Council, Old State Department Bldg., Washington, D.C., Feb. 9, 1949.

[8]Personal letter to Shannon C. Douglass, Dwight Bldg., Kansas City, Mo., Feb. 16, 1949.

[9]Personal letter to Eddie Meisburger, 601 Davidson Bldg., Kansas City, Mo., Sept. 14, 1950.

[10]Personal letter to Clarence W. Beatty, Jr., special assistant to the U.S. attorney, Chicago, Ill., Sept. 22, 1950.

[11]W.H. Lawrence, "Truman—Portrait of a Stubborn Man," *New York Times* magazine, Apr. 22, 1951, p. 8.

[12]White House Press and Radio Conference no. 287, Dec. 13, 1951.

[13]Personal letter to Carl A. Hatch, Judge, U.S. District Court, Albuquerque, N.M., Jan. 12, 1952.

[14]Personal letter to Buford C. Tynes, Huntington, W. Va., Aug. 18, 1950.

[15]"The Road Back to America," *Washington Post*, May 22, 1950, p. 16.

[16]Personal letter to Philip L. Graham, president and publisher, *Washington Post*, Washington, D.C., June 13, 1950.

[17]Personal letter to William Benton, U.S. Senate, Washington, D.C., Aug. 17, 1951.

[18]Memorandum to the president, Apr. 19, 1952.

[19]Personal interview with the author, Kansas City, Mo., Aug. 20, 1954.

[20]Personal letter to J.W. Fulbright, U.S. Senate, Washington, D.C., Mar. 12, 1947.

[21]Personal letter to J.M. Arvey, Democratic National Committeeman of Illinois, 1 North LaSalle St., Chicago 2, Ill. Oct. 30, 1951.

[22]Reference is to White House Press and Radio Conference no. 289 of Jan. 10, 1952, in which the president discussed frankly with correspondents the prospects of Eisenhower as a nominee on either the Democratic or Republican ticket.

[23]Personal letter to General of the Army Dwight D. Eisenhower, Paris, France, Jan. 15, 1952.

[24]Personal letter to General of the Army Dwight D. Eisenhower, Paris, France, Jan. 31, 1952.

[25]Personal letter to John J. Nangle, 418 Olive St., St. Louis, Mo., June 2, 1952.

[26]Personal letter to William Benton, U.S. Senate, Washington, D.C., Aug. 12, 1952.

[27]Quoted by Hillman, *Mr. President* (New York: Farrar, Straus and Young, 1952), p. 118. Reprinted by permission of Farrar, Straus and Girous, Inc. Excerpts from *Mr. President* by William Hillman, pictures by Alfred Wagg. Copyright ©1952 by William Hillman and Alfred Wagg.

[28]"Truman Tag 'Worst Papers' Draws Fire," *Editor & Publisher,* 81 (June 12, 1948), p. 13.

[29]Personal letter to Robert G. Simmons, chief justice of the Supreme Court of Nebraska, Lincoln, Nov. 24, 1948.

[30]Personal interview with the author, Kansas City, Mo., July 17, 1954.

[31]Quotes by Hillman, *Mr. President*, p. 177. Reprinted by permission of Farrar, Straus and Girous, Inc. Excerpts from *Mr. President* by William Hillman, pictures by Alfred Wagg. Copyright ©1952 by William Hillman and Alfred Wagg.

[32]"Editor Hears Pleas for Press Aid in Foreign Affairs," *Editor & Publisher*, 83 (Apr. 29, 1950), p. 18.

[33]Personal letter to John Davis Lodge, U.S. House of Representatives, Washington, D.C., Aug. 13, 1948.

[34]Memorandum from the president to Elmer Davis, May 26, 1950.

[35]White House Press and Radio Conference no. 242, Oct. 19, 1950.

[36]Memorandum from the president to Charles E. Wilson, director of the Office of Defense Mobilization, Apr. 11, 1951.

[37]White House Press and Radio Conference no. 205, Nov. 10, 1949.

[38]Ibid., no. 247, Dec. 19, 1950.

[39]Personal interview with the author, Kansas City, Mo., Aug. 12, 1954.

[40]John Hersey, "Profiles: Mr. President: II—Ten O'clock Meeting," *New Yorker* (April 14, 1951), pp. 54-55.

[41]"Shop Talk at Thirty," *Editor & Publisher,* 83 (June 18, 1949), p. 60.

[42]Personal letter to David H. Morgan, Eureka, Kans., July 3, 1952.

[43]Address, National Convention of Americans for Democratic Action, Washington, D.C., May 17, 1952.

[44]Ibid.

CHAPTER 15: THE POLITICS OF PUBLICITY

[1]Thomas L. Stokes, "Harry Truman, Politician Extraordinary," *New York Times* magazine (May 7, 1950), p. 13.

[2]Ellis Whitfield, "The Mind of Harry Truman," *Why, The Magazine of Popular Psychology* (May 1951), p. 9.

[3]"68% of Dailies Back Dewey; Truman Endorsed by 16%," *Editor & Publisher*, 81 (Sept. 11, 1948), p. 5.

[4]James E. Pollard, "Truman and the Press," *Journalism Quarterly*, 28 (Fall 1951), p. 463.

[5]Ibid., p. 462. Cf. earlier comments, ch. 9.

[6]Personal interview with the author, Kansas City, Mo., Aug. 25, 1954.

[7]White House Press and Radio Conference no. 300, Apr. 17, 1952.

8 Ibid., no. 179, Apr. 22, 1949.

9 Remarks to delegates to the CIO-PAC rally, Rose Garden of the White House, Aug. 15, 1952.

10 Address, Democratic National Convention, Chicago, Ill., July 26, 1952.

11 Address by Adlai E. Stevenson, Democratic nominee for president, Portland, Ore., Sept. 8, 1952.

12 "Truman Seconds Stevenson, Sneers at Press Opinion," *Editor & Publisher,* 85 (Sept. 13, 1952), p. 7.

13 Personal letter to Adlai E. Stevenson, governor of Illinois, Springfield, Sept. 10, 1952.

14 Source of the statistics is not revealed.

15 White House Press and Radio Conference no. 315, Sept. 11, 1952.

16 Frank Luther Mott, "Has the Press Lost Its Political Punch?" *Rotarian,* 81 (Oct. 1952), p. 14.

17 Ibid., p. 14.

18 Ibid., p. 52.

19 Ibid.

20 Robert U. Brown, "Shop Talk at Thirty," *Editor & Publisher*, 85 (Oct. 4, 1951), p. 64.

21 Address, Boston, Mass., Oct. 17, 1952.

22 Address, St. Paul, Minn., Oct. 28, 1952.

23 Ibid.

24 Address, Chicago, Ill., Oct. 29, 1952.

25 Address, St. Louis, Mo., Nov. 1, 1952.

26 Ibid.

27 White House Press and Radio Conference no. 287, Dec. 13, 1951.

28 Personal letter to Robert M. White II, *Mexico* (Mo.) *Ledger,* Oct. 6, 1949.

29 Personal letter to Joe L. Evans, U.S. House of Representatives, Washington, D.C., Apr. 8, 1952.

30 Personal letter to Russell Stewart, general manager, *Chicago Times,* Nov. 27, 1945.

31 Jonathan Daniels, *The Man of Independence* (New York: Lippincott, 1950).

32 Personal letter to Jonathan Daniels, *Raleigh* (N.C.) *News and Observer,* Jan. 2, 1946.

33 Personal letter to Frank H. Lee, editor of the *Joplin* (Mo.) *Southwestern,* Dec. 9, 1947.

34 Remarks to supporters in Great Falls, Mont., May 12, 1950.

35 Personal letter to James M. Cox, *Dayton* (Ohio) *News League,* July 9, 1951.

36 White House Press and Radio Conference no. 292, Jan. 31, 1952.

[37]Address to Democratic party leaders in Scranton, Penn., Oct. 22, 1952.

[38]Personal letter to Maple T. Harl, Chairman, FDIC, Washington, D.C., Mar. 8, 1947.

[39]Personal letter to T.H. Van Sant, Fulton, Mo., Apr. 16, 1947.

[40]Personal letter to Joseph B. Keenan, Woodward Bldg., Washington, D.C., Feb. 24, 1952.

[41]Personal letter to Maple T. Harl, chairman, Federal Deposit Insurance Corp., Washington, D.C., Feb. 2, 1949.

[42]Ibid., Aug. 30, 1950.

[43]Ibid., Sept. 15, 1950.

[44]Ibid., Jan. 16, 1951.

[45]Ibid., Apr. 26, 1951.

[46]Ibid., July 17, 1951.

[47]Ibid., Oct. 31, 1951.

[48]Ibid., Sept. 12, 1952.

[49]Ibid., Aug. 13, 1952.

[50]Cf. chapter 10.

[51]White House Press and Radio Conference no. 322, Dec. 31, 1952.

[50]Cf. chapter 10.

[51]White House Press and Radio Conference no. 322, Dec. 31, 1952.

CHAPTER 16: A MATTER OF OPINION

[1]Cf. chapter 1.

[2]Harold D. Smith, personal diary (photostatic copy in Truman Collection, Kansas City, Mo.), entry of Sept. 13, 1945.

[3]"Truman Appearance Convention Highspot," *Editor & Publisher*, 80 (Apr. 26, 1947), p. 10.

[4]White House Press and Radio Conference no. 124, Oct. 17, 1947.

[5]Personal letter to Dr. Frank P. Graham, president of the University of North Carolina, Chapel Hill, Dec. 18, 1948.

[6]Personal letter to Frank W. Rucker, president and general manager of the *Independence* (Mo.) *Examiner,* Sept. 5, 1950.

[7]Personal letter to F.R. von Windegger, president of the Plaza Bank of St. Louis, Mo., Apr. 9, 1948.

[8]Quoted by William Hillman, *Mr. President* (New York: Farrar, Straus and Young, 1952), p. 149. Reprinted by permission of Farrar, Straus and Girous, Inc. Excerpts from *Mr. President* by William Hillman, pictures by Alfred Wagg. Copyright ©1952 by William Hillman and Alfred Wagg.

[9]Personal letter to Max Lowenthal, New Milford, Conn., Jan. 27, 1951.

[10]Ibid., Feb. 15, 1951.

[11]Quoted by Hillman, *Mr. President,* p. 232. Reprinted by permission of Farrar, Straus and Girous, Inc. Excerpts from *Mr. President* by William Hillman, pictures by Alfred Wagg. Copyright ©1952 by William Hillman and Alfred Wagg.

[12]Personal letter to Henry Gillen, *Boston* (Mass.) *Post,* Dec. 13, 1948.

[13]Personal letter to Arthur Krock, *New York Times* Bureau, Albee Bldg., Washington, D.C., Oct. 10, 1949.

[14]Personal letter to Roy W. Howard, 230 Park Ave., New York, N.Y., July 26, 1950.

[15]Personal letter to Estes Kefauver, U.S. Senate, Washington, D.C., Sept. 21, 1950.

[16]Letter from Estes Kefauver to the president, Sept. 26, 1950.

[17]Personal letter to Estes Kefauver, U.S. Senate, Washington, D.C., Sept. 28, 1950.

[18]Personal letter to John T. O'Rourke, editor, *Washington* (D.C.) *Daily News,* Nov. 28, 1952.

[19]Personal letter to the Reverend Edward H. Pruden, First Baptist Church, Washington, D.C., Sept. 9, 1950.

[20]Personal letter to John D. Clark, Council of Economic Advisers, Washington, D.C., July 5, 1952.

[21]Personal letter to John L. Sullivan, 1200 18th St., Washington, D.C., Oct. 15, 1951.

[22]Richard H. Rovere and Arthur M. Schlesinger, Jr., *The General and the President* (New York: Farrar, Straus and Young, 1951).

[23]Personal letter to Dr. Arthur M. Schlesinger, Jr., c/o Farrar, Straus and Young, New York, N.Y., Nov. 5, 1951.

[24]Personal letter to Mr. Robert M. White II, Mexico, Mo., Oct. 6, 1949.

[25]Personal interview with the author, Independence, Mo., Aug. 13, 1954.

[26]Memorandum to Attorney General J. Howard McGrath, Feb. 24, 1951.

[27]Personal letter to Clark M. Clifford, 1523 L. St., N.W., Washington, D.C., Apr. 27, 1951.

[28]Personal letter to Edwin C. Johnson, U.S. Senate, Washington, D.C., Oct. 14, 1949.

[29]William P. Helm, *Harry Truman: A Political Biography* (New York: Duell, Sloan and Pearce, 1947).

[30]Informal remarks, William Jewell College, Liberty, Mo., May 20, 1946.

[31]Personal letter to Major General Ralph E. Truman, 5106 Garfield Ave., Kansas City, Mo., Mar. 13, 1948.

[32]Cf. chapter 15.

[33]Personal letter to Claude G. Bowers, American ambassador to Chile, Santiago, Dec. 1, 1948.

³⁴Ibid.

³⁵Personal letter to Carter T. Barron, National Capital Sesquicentennial Commission, 1400 Pennsylvania Ave., Washington, D.C., Aug. 5, 1950.

³⁶Cf. chapter 17.

³⁷Helm, *Truman,* p. 20.

³⁸Personal letter to Jacob Billikopf, 805 Bankers Security Bldg., Philadelphia, Penn., May 24, 1949.

³⁹Personal letter to Jack Naulty, 1413-15 McGee St., Kansas City, Mo., Nov. 24, 1945.

⁴⁰Personal letter to John Franklin Carter, Dominion Hill, Lovettsville, Va., Aug. 12, 1948.

⁴¹Personal letter to Carl W. McCasland, 1046 West 42nd St., Los Angeles, Calif., Dec. 29, 1950.

⁴²Quoted in Hillman, *Mr. President*, p. 133. Reprinted by permission of Farrar, Straus and Girous, Inc. Excerpts from *Mr. President* by William Hillman, pictures by Alfred Wagg. Copyright ©1952 by William Hillman and Alfred Wagg.

⁴³White House Press and Radio Conference no. 54, Mar. 14, 1946.

⁴⁴Personal letter to Nelle Noland, 216 North Delaware St., Independence, Mo., Mar. 19, 1946.

⁴⁵Rear platform remarks, Sacramento, Calif., June 12, 1948.

⁴⁶Personal letter to Theo J. Quinn, postmaster, Saint Joseph, Mo., Aug. 8, 1946.

⁴⁷Personal letter to Claud G. Bowers, American ambassador to Chile, Santiago, Dec. 1, 1948.

⁴⁸Personal letter to Silliman Evans, president and publisher, Tennessean Newspapers, Inc., Nashville, Tenn., Dec. 2, 1952.

⁴⁹"Truman S.O.B. Crack Brightens Banquet Beat," *Editor & Publisher*, 82 (Feb. 26, 1949), p. 10.

CHAPTER 17: MORE BARK THAN BITE

¹Jonathan Daniels, *The Man of Independence* (Philadelphia, Penn.: Lippincott, 1950), p. 289.

²Ibid., p. 350.

³Cf. William Hillman, *Mr. President* (New York: Farrar, Straus, and Young, 1952), p. 81. Reprinted by permission of Farrar, Straus and Girous, Inc. Excerpts from *Mr. President* by William Hillman, pictures by Alfred Wagg. Copyright ©1952 by William Hillman and Alfred Wagg.

⁴Ibid., p. 106. Reprinted by permission of Farrar, Straus and Girous, Inc. Excerpts from *Mr. President* by William Hillman, pictures by Alfred Wagg. Copyright ©1952 by William Hillman and Alfred Wagg.

⁵Personal letter to Ed Harris, *St. Louis Post-Dispatch* Washington Bureau, 1422 F. Street, N.W., Washington, D.C., Oct. 11, 1951.

⁶White House Press and Radio Conference no. 257, Mar. 15, 1951.

⁷Personal letter to Joseph C. Hutcheson, Jr., U.S. Circuit Judge, Houston, Tex., Nov. 15, 1945.

⁸Quoted by Hillman, *Mr. President*, p. 130. Reprinted by permission of Farrar, Straus and Girous, Inc. Excerpts from *Mr. President* by William Hillman, pictures by Alfred Wagg. Copyright ©1952 by William Hillman and Alfred Wagg.

⁹Personal letter to Morris Higley, Childress Index, Childress, Tex., Apr. 19, 1947.

¹⁰Albert Z. Carr, *Truman, Stalin and Peace* (Garden City, N.Y.: Doubleday, 1950), p. 117.

¹¹White House Press and Radio Conference no. 222, Apr. 13, 1950.

¹²Personal letter to Max Lowenthal, New Milford, Conn., Feb. 15, 1951.

¹³Personal letter to Maple T. Harl, chairman, FDIC, Washington, D.C., Feb. 13, 1952.

¹⁴*The Philadelphia Aurora,* Mar. 6, 1979.

¹⁵Memorandum to Bedell Smith, Central Intelligence Agency, Washington, D.C., July 21, 1952.

¹⁶This subject is discussed particularly in chapters 12 and 14.

¹⁷John Hersey, "Profiles: Mr. President. I. Quite a Head of Steam," *New Yorker* (April 7, 1951), p. 46.

¹⁸Personal letter to Mary and Martha Truman, Grandview, Mo., Apr. 29, 1945.

¹⁹Personal letter to Joseph J. McGee, Fidelity Bldg., Kansas City, Mo., Nov. 22, 1950.

²⁰Personal letter to Duke Shoop, 610 Albee Bldg., Washington, D.C., Dec. 29, 1947.

²¹"Music Critics Inured to Threats of Abuse," *Editor & Publisher*, 83 (Dec. 16, 1950), p. 55; "Hume Note Filed With 'Objects of Violence,'" ibid., 84 (Mar. 3, 1951), p. 6.

²²"The Presidency," *Time* (Dec. 18, 1950), pp. 16-17.

²³Ibid.

²⁴Ibid.

²⁵Ibid.

²⁶Ellis Whitfield, "The Mind of Harry Truman," *Why, The Magazine of Popular Psychology* (May 1951), pp. 4–9.

²⁷Quoted by Hillman, *Mr. President,* p. 36.

²⁸Personal letter to G. Walter Gates, 819 1411 4th Avenue Bldg., Seattle, Wash., Dec. 13, 1950.

[29] Personal letter to Edward Arnold, 9538 Brighton Way, Beverly Hills, Calif., Jan. 19, 1951.

[30] Personal letter to the Reverend J.H. Allison, Smyrna Methodist Church, Smyrna, Ga., Oct. 24, 1952.

[31] "Swedish Press Attacks Bodyguards as 'Gorillas' for Alleged Molestations," *New York Times* (Aug. 20, 1952), p. 12.

[32] Personal letter to Leonard Lyons, *New York Post*, Aug. 27, 1952.

[33] Truman Diary, entry of Aug. 21, 1952.

[34] Hersey, "Profiles," p. 46.

[35] White House Press and Radio Conference no. 259, Apr. 5, 1951.

[36] Personal letter to David M. Noyes, 10527 Wilshire Blvd., Beverly Hills, Calif., July 27, 1950.

[37] James A. Pollard, "Truman and the Press: Final Phase," *Journalism Quarterly*, 30 (Summer, 1953), p. 280.

[38] White House Press and Radio Conference no. 300, Apr. 17, 1952.

[39] "'Seizure' of the Press," *Editor & Publisher*, 85 (Apr. 26, 1952), p. 108.

[40] White House Press and Radio Conference no. 301, Apr. 24, 1952

[41] Personal letter to Harold Moody, principal of Wheeler High School, Wheeler, Ind., May 21, 1952, in answer to question submitted by the school children to the president.

[42] Personal letter to Claude G. Bowers, American ambassador to Chile, Santiago, Dec. 1, 1948.

[43] Personal letter to Governor Forrest Smith, Jefferson City, Mo., Mar. 6, 1950.

[44] Robert S. Allen and William V. Shannon, *The Truman Merry-Go-Round* (New York: Vanguard Press, 1950), p. 18.

[45] Personal letter to Governor Chester Bowles, Hartford, Conn., June 23, 1950.

[46] Personal letter to Daniel J. Mahoney, *Miami* (Fla.) *Daily News,* Nov. 10, 1949.

[47] Personal letter to Arthur Krock, Washington Bureau of the *New York Times*, Washington, D.C., Oct. 10, 1949.

[48] Personal interview with the author, Independence, Mo., July 14, 1954.

[49] James E. Pollard, "Truman and the Press," *Journalism Quarterly*, 28 (Fall 1951), p. 467.

[50] Ibid.

[51] Henry Steele Commager, "A Few Kind Words for Harry Truman," *Look* (Sept. 12, 1951), pp. 60-66.

[52] Cyril Clemens, *The Man from Missouri: A Biography of Harry S Truman* Webster Groves, Mo.: International Mark Twain Society, 1945), p. 121.

[53]William P. Helm, *Harry Truman: A Political Biography* (New York: Duell, Sloan and Pearce, 1947), pp. 78-79.

CHAPTER 18: PLUSES AND MINUSES: A RECAP

[1]Personal letter to Roy A. Roberts, *Kansas City* (Mo.) *Star,* Jan. 9, 1952.

APPENDIX

[1]Personal letter to David H. Morgan, Eureka, Kans., Feb. 21, 1952.

INDEX